GARDENS OF ART

The Sculpture Park at the Frederik Meijer Gardens

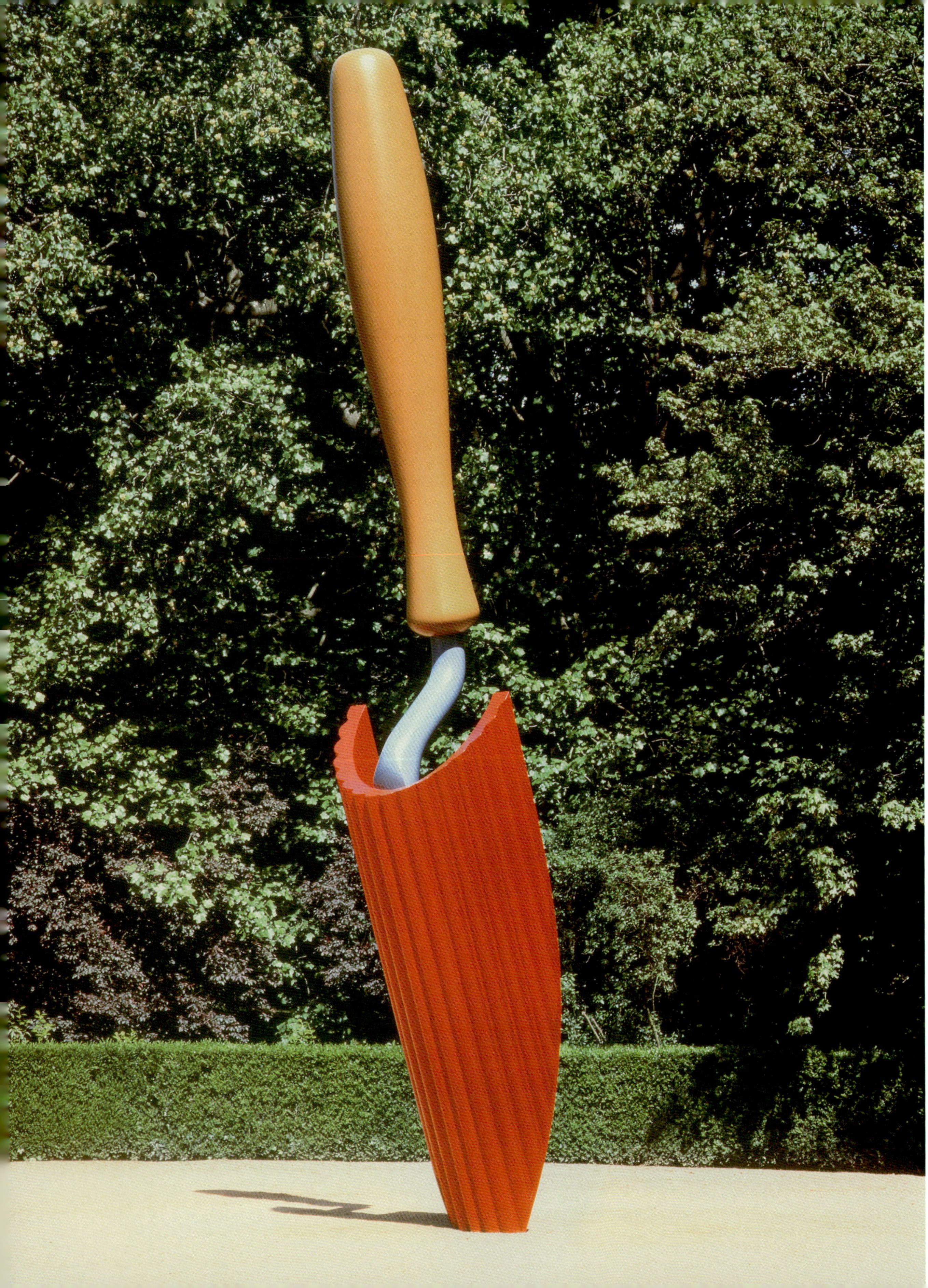

GARDENS OF ART

The Sculpture Park at the Frederik Meijer Gardens

— Joseph Antenucci Becherer —

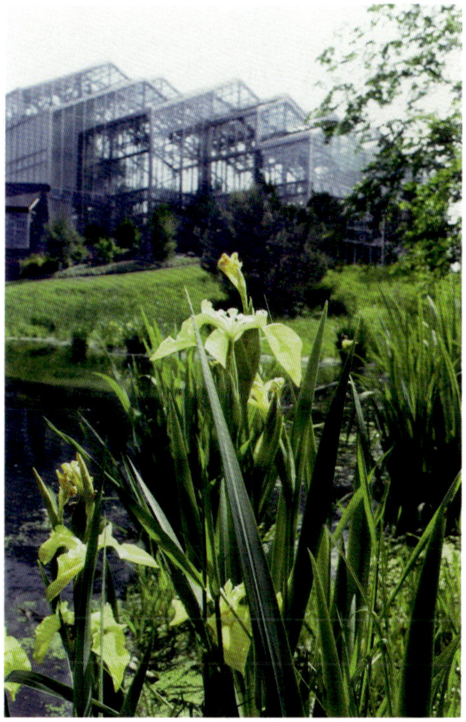

Frederik Meijer Gardens and Sculpture Park
Grand Rapids, Michigan

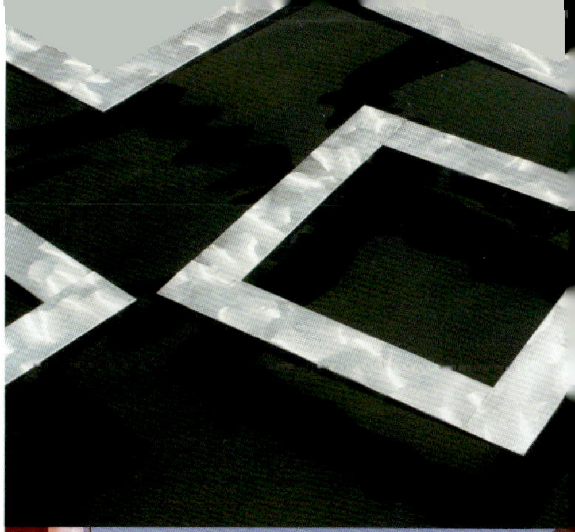
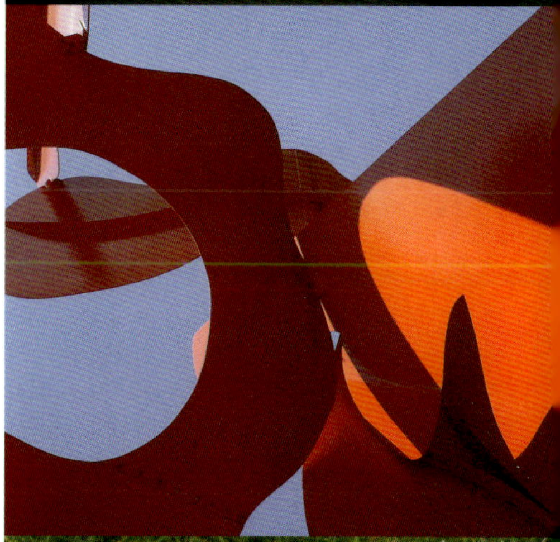
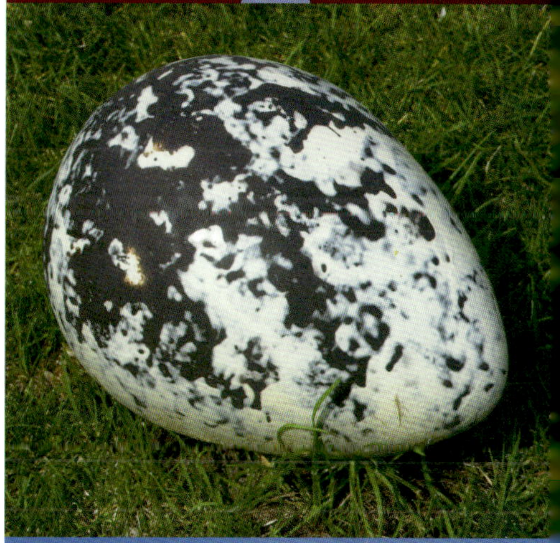
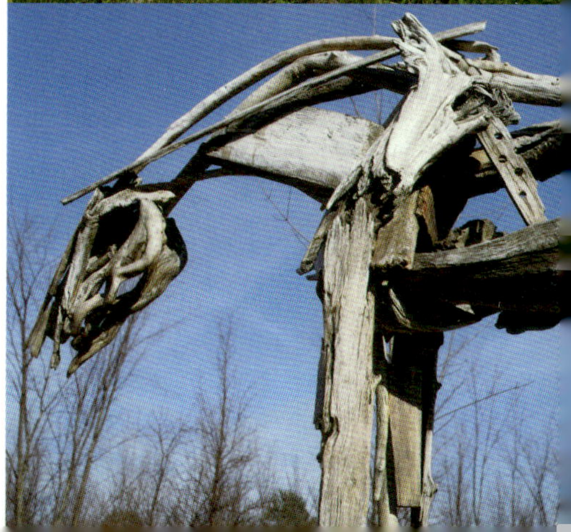

This book has been published on the occasion of the dedication of the Sculpture Park at the Frederik Meijer Gardens on May 16, 2002.

Joseph Antenucci Becherer is Curator of Sculpture, Frederik Meijer Gardens and Sculpture Park, and Lena Meijer Professor in the History of Art, Aquinas College, Grand Rapids, Michigan.

First published in the United States of America in 2002 by

Frederik Meijer Gardens and
Sculpture Park
1000 East Beltline NE
Grand Rapids, Michigan 49525

in part through the generosity of the Meijer Foundation.

Distributed by Wayne State University Press.

Library of Congress Control Number:
2002090755
ISBN: 0-9712034-1-5 (cloth)
ISBN: 0-9712034-2-3 (paper)

Photography and copyright credits can be found on page 117.

Project director and editor: E. Jane Connell

Copyedited by Jennifer Harris

Designed by Susan E. Kelly

Principal photography by Chuck Heiney

Produced by Marquand Books, Inc., Seattle
www.marquand.com

Color separations by iocolor, Seattle

Printed and bound by CS Graphics Pte., Ltd., Singapore

CONTENTS

Preface
6

Gardens of Art: The Sculpture Program at the Frederik Meijer Gardens
10

— HIGHLIGHTS OF THE SCULPTURE COLLECTION —

Magdalena Abakanowicz
Figure on a Trunk
20

Nina Akamu
The American Horse
25

Deborah Butterfield
Cabin Creek
29

Jim Dine
The Thunder
33

Mark di Suvero
Scarlatti
37

Antony Gormley
One and Other
41

Keith Haring
Julia
45

Barbara Hepworth
Summer Dance
49

Richard Hunt
Column of the Free Spirit
53

Dietrich Klinge
Grosser Trofroo
57

Alexander Liberman
Aria
60

Jacques Lipchitz
Hagar
65

Aristide Maillol
Torso of Summer
69

Igor Mitoraj
Light of the Moon
73

Henry Moore
Working Model for Divided Oval: Butterfly
76

Henry Moore
Bronze Form
81

Manuel Neri
Odalisque IV
85

Louise Nevelson
Atmosphere and Environment XI
89

Claes Oldenburg and Coosje van Bruggen
Plantoir
92

Carolyn Ottmers
Full Circle
96

Arnaldo Pomodoro
Disk in the Form of a Desert Rose
101

George Rickey
Four Open Squares Horizontal Gyratory—Tapered
104

Auguste Rodin
Eve
109

Bill Woodrow
Listening to History
113

PREFACE

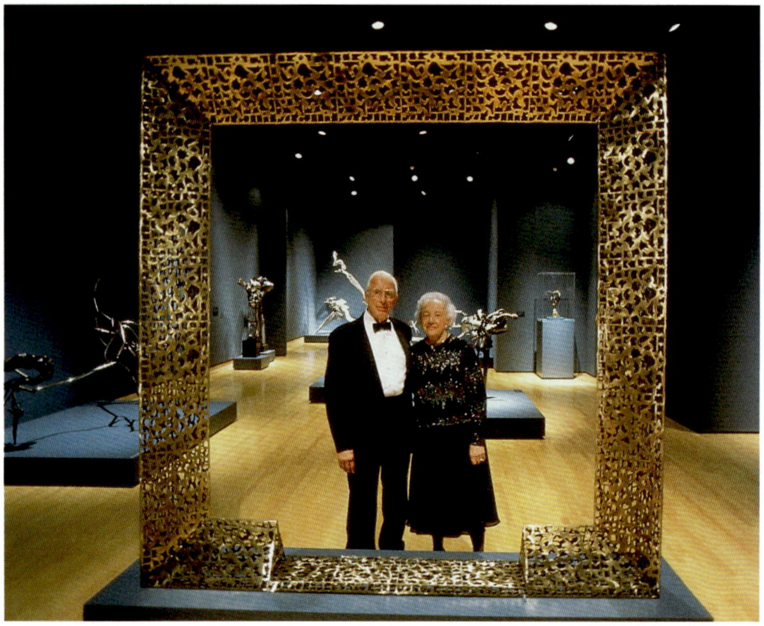

Fred and Lena Meijer in the sculpture galleries for the opening of *Richard Hunt: American Visionary*, September 2000

IT IS WITH proud excitement that we welcome you to the Sculpture Park at the Frederik Meijer Gardens. A dream born years before the original April 20, 1995, opening of the Frederik Meijer Gardens has come to a much anticipated fruition. We celebrate as a greater community the United States' newest sculpture park through this beautiful publication.

Public sculpture has been part of the cultural fabric of metropolitan Grand Rapids, Michigan, for decades. Perhaps best known is Alexander Calder's monumental *La Grande Vitesse* of 1969. Other notable works that are integral to the aesthetic identity of the city include Joseph Kinnebrew's *Grand Rapids River Sculpture and Fish Ladder* of 1965, Mark di Suvero's *Motu Viget* of 1977, and Maya Lin's *Ecliptic* of 2001. Today, the Sculpture Park, introducing twenty-four recently acquired works of art to the public, makes a significant new contribution to Grand Rapids' sculptural offerings. The equally important entities of park and gardens unite the visual art of humankind and the visual art of nature. Art expressed in three dimensions and dramatically displayed within a landscape that benefits from the change of seasons provides visitors with a multitude of reasons to return and experience the sculpture in an ever-changing context throughout the year.

The Gardens offers expanding opportunities for visitors to explore nature and art in the same setting. Imaginative interdisciplinary educational programs developed around both the botanical and sculpture collections bring a better understanding of this rich setting to children, students, and adults, who learn alongside one another. With more than 120 sculptures exhibited in and among the indoor and outdoor botanical gardens, the Frederik Meijer Gardens and Sculpture Park has made tremendous strides toward fulfilling its mission "to promote the enjoyment, understanding, and appreciation of gardens, sculpture, the natural environment, and the arts."

The distinguished marriage of culture and horticulture at the Frederik Meijer Gardens is probably most apparent in the Sculpture Park. Our vision of the park surpasses that of a mere sprinkling of objects across more than thirty acres of land. Evident are the many influences artists have had on one another, as well as the influences that nature, the setting, natural materials, principles, and phenomena have had on the sculptors represented.

The outdoor sculpture installation opened in the spring of 2002. It is the first of seven major thematic areas within a master plan for the 125-acre Frederik Meijer Gardens and Sculpture Park. Leading the way in our overall development, the park will ultimately comprise over seventy sites for the out-of-doors display of a significant portion of our permanent collection. Joining the park over a progressive schedule within the next ten years will be the addition of the Cultural Arts Center, an outdoor performance area complete with a 1,000-person amphitheater; Michigan's Landscape Heritage, a view of the region's natural history; AdventureScapes, one of the nation's largest interactive children's gardens; America's Backyard, an array of home idea gardens focusing on a residential scale of gardening; Gardens of the World, a culturally rich and design-diverse presentation of international gardens; and Gardens of Innovation, a glimpse into the future through engaging and enlightening demonstration plantings. Incorporated into the master plan since its inception is our determination that all areas of future development will include sculpture to complement the focus of each garden and its attendant landscape.

No single seed was planted from which the Sculpture Park sprouted, grew, and matured; instead, many dedicated individuals, visionary leaders, creative artisans and designers, and the generosity of an entire community have all come together to create a presentation bright with promise. Of the myriad contributors of time, talent, and resources, we want to thank first and foremost Fred and Lena Meijer. Their genuine devotion and commitment to "growing" the Frederik Meijer Gardens and Sculpture Park have become an inspiration to countless individuals. The Meijers' greatest pleasure comes from seeing others enjoy the Gardens. Fred's original sculpture

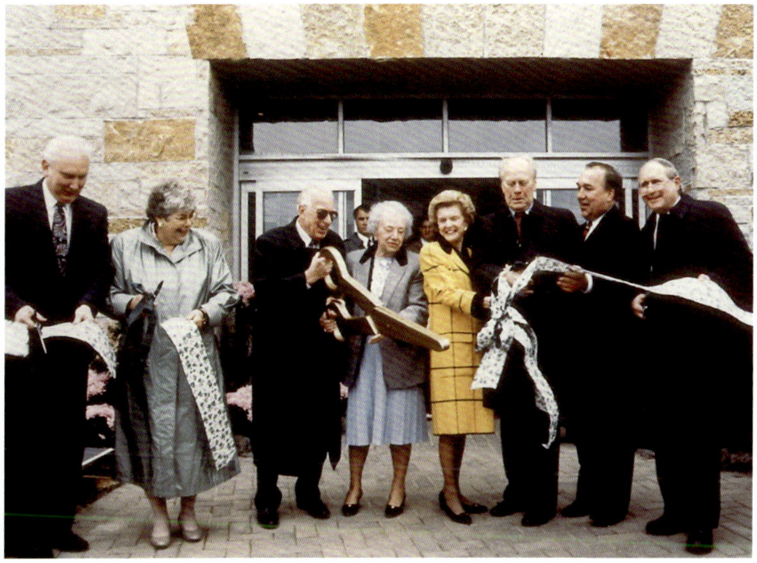

Ribbon cutting for the Frederik Meijer Gardens, April 20, 1995, with (left to right) Reverend Jim Carlson, Marsha Bouwkamp, Fred and Lena Meijer, Mrs. Betty Ford and former President Gerald Ford, Governor John Engler, and Senator Carl Levin

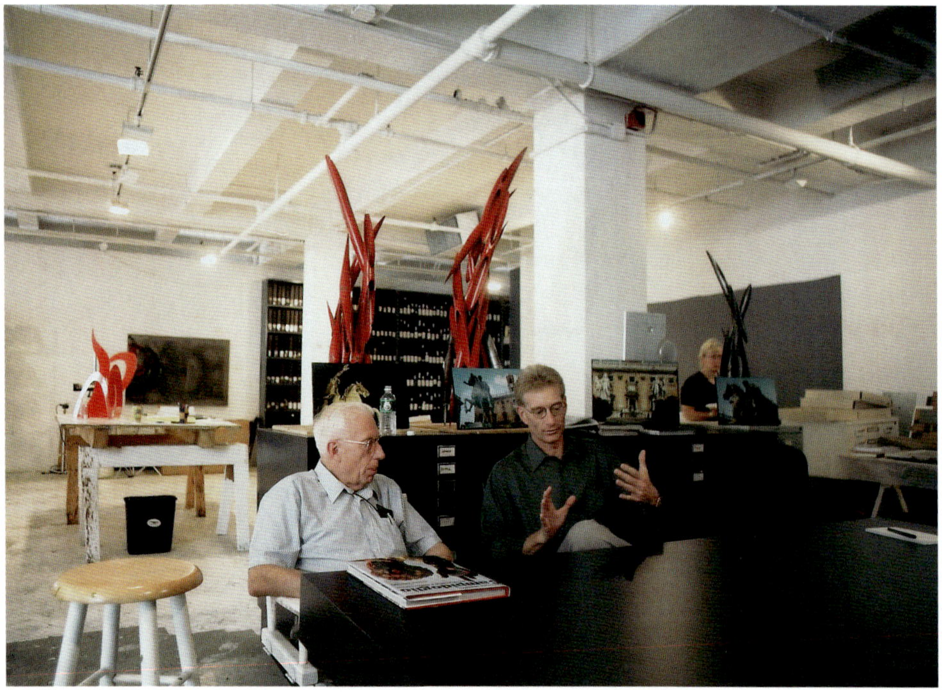

Fred Meijer and son Hank in Alexander Liberman's New York studio, Paintworks, October 1999

collection, a gift to the Gardens, has grown rapidly to a new level of prestige and educational value. Numerous persons have provided excellent guidance and advice regarding the collection and have effectively defined and directed its accelerated growth.

The sculpture advisory committee continues to be instrumental in shaping the sculpture collection. With appreciation, we acknowledge the dedicated service of committee co-chairs Henry Matthews and Lynn Vinkemulder and committee members Bernard Bowhuis, Jill Donabauer, Chip Emery, Jean Enright, Larry ten Harmsel, Don Hunt, Starr Meijer, William Padnos, Mat Peabody, Eleanor Scheifele, and Rob VerHeulen. Our sculpture department staff benefits from the visionary and creative leadership of Joseph Antenucci Becherer, curator of sculpture at the Gardens.

Joe Becherer and I had the privilege of serving on the committee responsible for the planning and design of the Meijer Sculpture Park along with design team members Paul Byrd, Darwin Feuerstein, Larry Finneran, Rebecca Finneran, Linda Thompson, Ian Warnock, and Steve Windemuller. The sculpture department staff contributed greatly to the development of the site design as coordinated by the design team. Sculpture department staff members include Caleb Brennan, Heidi Holst Leestma, Ben Pederson, Marlene Vanderhill, and Laurene Warren.

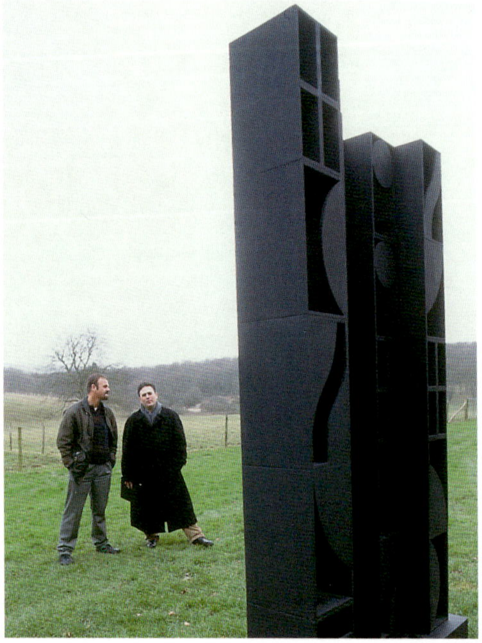

Executive Director Brent Dennis and Curator of Sculpture Joseph Becherer discuss Louise Nevelson's *Atmosphere and Environment XI,* March 2001

As a landscape architect, I have an appreciation for the power of place. One of the distinct qualities of the Sculpture Park is the wonderful fit of each work of art into the landscape. Whenever possible, sculptors have been involved with structuring the setting, placement, and orientation of their sculptures. The Sculpture Park has benefited from the site visits and design input of the following sculptors, whose work is represented in the park's debut: Nina Akamu, Crosby Coughlin on behalf of Alexander Liberman, Mark di Suvero, Richard Hunt, Claes Oldenburg and Coosje van Bruggen, Carolyn Ottmers, and Arnaldo Pomodoro. The shaping of the land forms, the enhancement of each site with appropriate landscaping, the control and refinement of sight lines and viewing distances, and the alignment of walkways have all been orchestrated with artistic considerations to establish a progressive experience for visitors to the park. We are thankful for the creative participation of these artists.

While the origins of the Frederik Meijer Gardens are based on a vision to develop a botanical garden and sculpture park with its own distinctive signature, the ultimate assemblage of world-class sculpture has taken the vision of the Gardens to an entirely new level. This book is dedicated to the modern and contemporary sculptors for whom this Sculpture Park is home to a part of their artistic legacy, and to the many Gardens visitors—past, present, and future—who find inspiration and enjoyment within the Sculpture Park.

In closing, our heartfelt thanks are due to the collaborative efforts of those who helped make this wonderful publication possible. We gratefully acknowledge everyone at Marquand Books, especially Ed Marquand, Marie Weiler, Susan Kelly, and Laura Hulscher, for their special attention to detail, style, and beauty; our author, Joseph Antenucci Becherer, for his commitment to excellence; our photographer, Chuck Heiney, for capturing the true essence of sculpture; and our talented project director, Jane Connell, for her gentle yet effective manner of keeping everyone focused, on schedule, and mindful of the ultimate goal: to create a book designed for our eye, yet catering to our desire to honor a special place for sculpture, nature, and people—*Gardens of Art: The Sculpture Park at the Frederik Meijer Gardens.*

R. Brent Dennis
Executive Director, Frederik Meijer Gardens and Sculpture Park

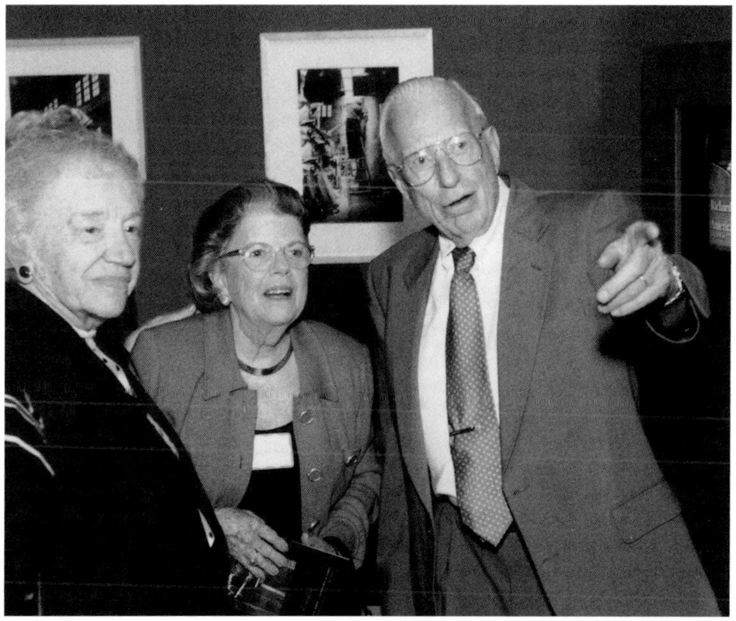

Sculpture Society member Mary Ann Keeler (center) with Lena and Fred Meijer, at the opening of *Richard Hunt: American Visionary*, September 2000

People deserve a place that inspires them, challenges them, and offers opportunities to consider the beauty and mysteries of the human experience.

FREDERIK MEIJER

IN ITS DEVOTION to horticulture and sculpture, the Frederik Meijer Gardens and Sculpture Park is a multifaceted institution of abundant offerings. It is dedicated equally and fully to the beauty and wonder of both nature and the visual arts. Opportunities to seek and understand the connections and distinctions between nature and art are but one of the stimulating experiences that this rich setting provides. With its interdisciplinary resources, welcoming diverse audiences of all ages and interests, a visit to the Gardens is without parallel.

Now in its seventh year, the breadth and depth of the institution's development is astounding to even the most casual of visitors. The more than thirty-acre Sculpture Park, dedicated on May 16, 2002, and celebrated in this publication, is a prominent part of the 125-acre indoor and outdoor botanical gardens. Nearly 400,000 adults, children, and students enjoy the conservatories and art galleries, woodlands and wetlands, nature and sculpture trails, and educational facilities and library on an annual basis. The design and beauty of the gardens—the result of the efforts of a great many experts and volunteers—have been lovingly admired and critically acclaimed since their inception. The articulation and implementation of a formal plan for sculpture is more recent, and is linked to the vision of Michigan retailer and philanthropist Frederik Meijer. It has been his goal to build, in his own words, "a world-class sculpture collection."

Fred Meijer was born and raised on a farm in the community of Greenville, Michigan, northeast of Grand Rapids. It was here that his family opened its first grocery store, whose reputation for quality evolved

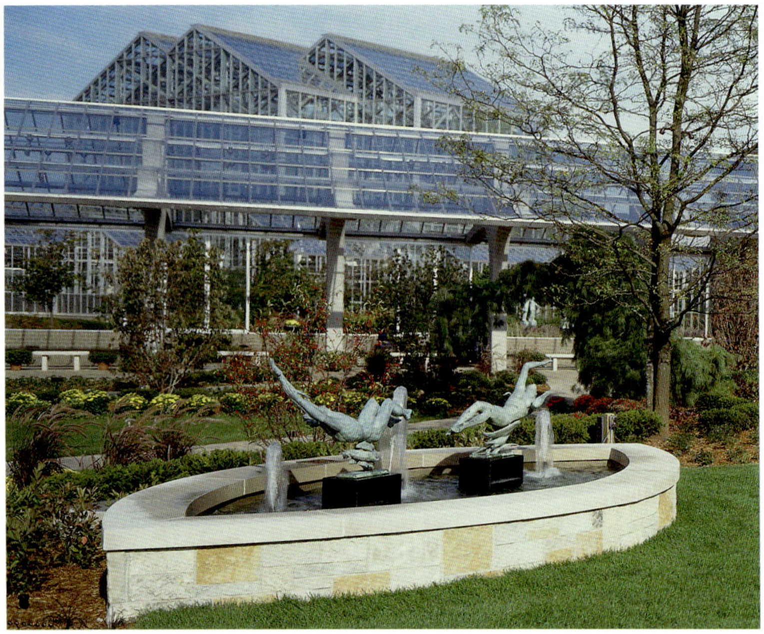

Marshall Fredericks, *Day and Night,* 1991, near the entrance to the Gardens' main building

into combined grocery-retail markets that bear the Meijer name in five Midwestern states. Although Meijer and his wife, Lena, moved to Grand Rapids in 1951, the couple has maintained close ties to Greenville. The town hosts a popular Danish Festival that proved pivotal to our story. In 1983, the Detroit sculptor Marshall Fredericks (1908–1998) was asked to create a work for public display based on the classic Danish children's tale, "The Ugly Duckling," by Hans Christian Andersen. The Meijers sponsored the project, which sparked Fred Meijer's interest in sculpture. Bronzes by Marshall Fredericks became the main focus of the early collection that, without a permanent home, was first held in storage and exhibited only on special occasions.

In 1990, Meijer was approached by the West Michigan Horticultural Society to become the lead donor for a new botanical garden to be located in Grand Rapids. He recognized an opportunity to combine his wife's love of gardens and flowers with his own desire to build a significant sculpture collection. In his initial gift, Meijer donated seventy acres of land, operational and foundation support, and more than sixty sculptures from his extensive collection.

When the Frederik Meijer Gardens opened to the public on April 20, 1995, thirty-three bronzes by Marshall Fredericks were installed on the grounds. The public immediately embraced these works, several of which quickly emerged as icons for the institution. Today, more than a third of these sculptures welcome visitors around the main entrance to the building complex, and the remainder are located throughout the interior spaces and conservatories and along the nature trails. In addition to works by Fredericks, Meijer collected a variety of sculpture that appealed to him on a personal level. Frequently, such objects were connected to his family life or reflected aspects of local and regional history. *Pine Stumps,* by Michigan artist Tom Hillis (1933–1998), is a case in point: it was created from molds made from actual stumps of pine trees that grow on the farm where Lena Meijer was raised. The work recalls the extensive pine forests that once filled Michigan and that farmers traditionally "stumped" to farm their land, using the stumps to build fences. This convergence of personal and regional history, granted longevity in bronze, remains dear to the Meijers. While there are many visitors to the Gardens who relish such layers of meaning, equal numbers appreciate the formal and compositional elements

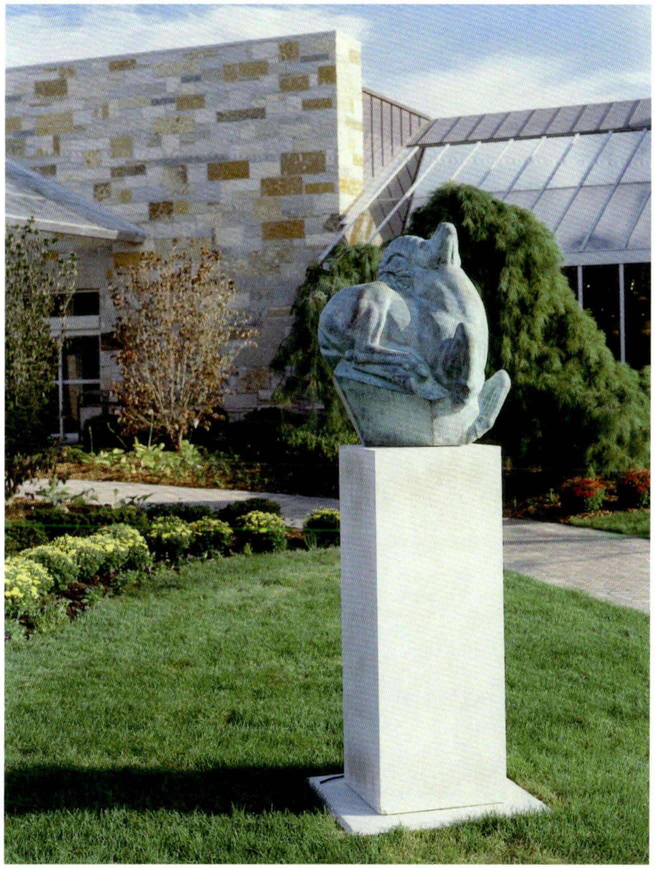

Marshall Fredericks, *Siberian Ram,* 1995, in the Ram's Garden

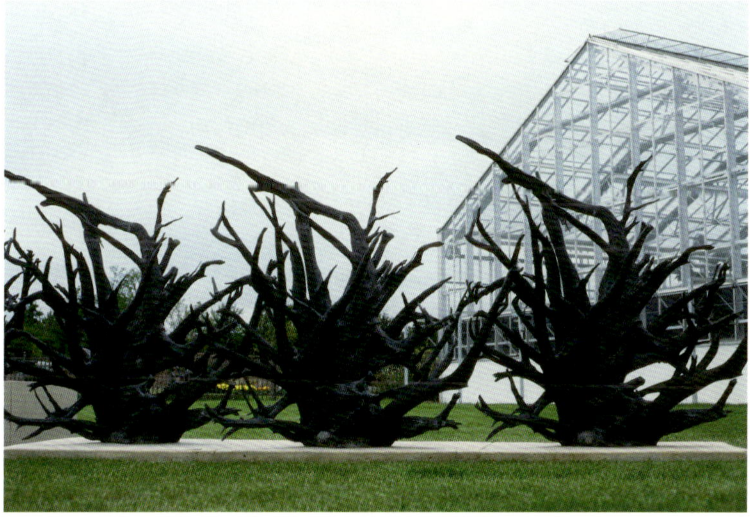

Tom Hillis, *Pine Stumps,* 1997

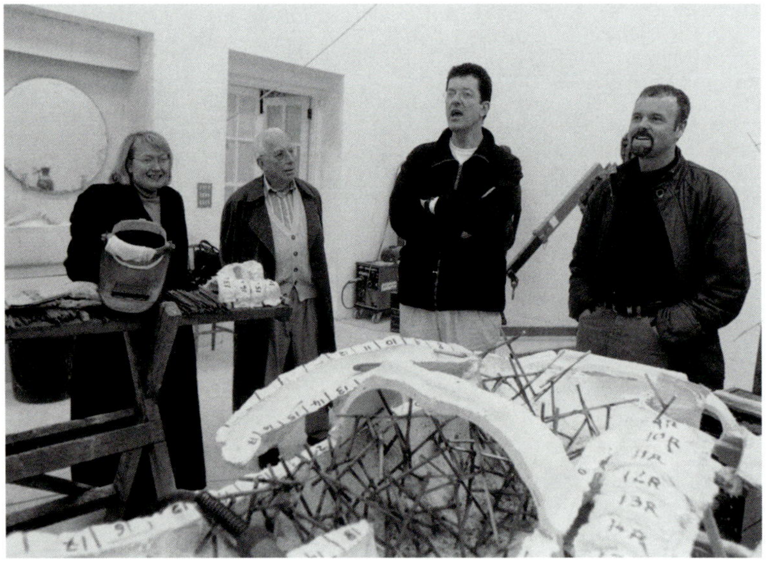

Sculpture advisory committee co-chair Lynn Vinkemulder, Fred Meijer, Antony Gormley, and Executive Director Brent Dennis, in Gormley's London studio

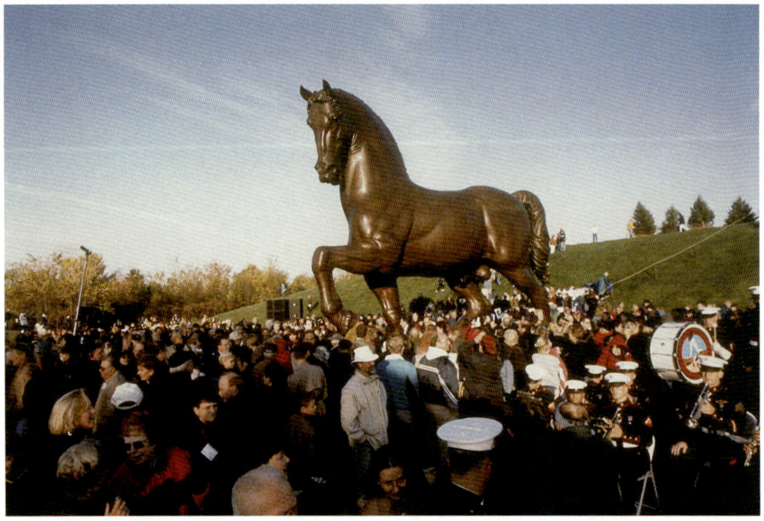

Unveiling of *The American Horse,* by Nina Akamu, October 7, 1999

of the sculpture, and still others might reflect on its potential Surrealist associations.

To further Meijer's wish to build a significant sculpture collection, the board of the newly opened Gardens appointed a sculpture advisory committee comprising visual arts professionals, collectors, academics, and Meijer Foundation counsel. The acquisition, focus, and installation of a permanent collection, as well as the formulation of policies and procedures, were primary considerations. The committee approved the addition of a sculpture conservator to the staff, was active in expanding the scope of sculpture-related initiatives including several temporary exhibitions, and administered the first Meijer Sculpture Competition in 1997–1998. As a result of their dedicated efforts, the profile of the institution's sculpture component greatly increased and the foundation was laid for an astounding series of developments over the course of the next six years.

In 1997, planning began for Phase II of the Gardens' expansion—a 65,000-square-foot addition that would more than double the interior space. In addition to new offices, classrooms, and visitor service centers, the plan included sculpture acclimation studios and storage and three new state-of-the-art sculpture galleries, totaling more than 4,500 square feet of exhibition space. A public campaign commenced in the spring of 1998. In the late summer of that year, the Gardens received a generous gift from Meijer, Inc., of fifty-five additional acres of land contiguous with the northwestern end of the existing property. A new boulevard entrance was constructed, and more than thirty acres were reserved for a sculpture park.

Considering the momentum of the previous two years, 1999 was destined to be a significant milestone in the annals of the Gardens. Groundbreaking for Phase II began and a sculpture trail was mapped out to create a footprint for the future sculpture park. A full-time curator was also added to the staff. Over the course of the summer, three sculptures were acquired and dedicated: Alexander Liberman's *Aria,* Deborah Butterfield's *Cabin Creek,* and, as a result of the first Meijer Sculpture Competition, Carolyn Ottmers' *Full Circle.* These additions to the permanent collection signaled a new era for contemporary objects at the Gardens and suggested the institution's potential for the display and interpretation of outdoor sculpture. Finally, Nina Akamu's monumental *The American Horse,* a work created in homage to Leonardo da Vinci, was unveiled to an audience of 3,500 on October 7, 1999, garnering national and international attention. The installation of these four sculptures out of doors established the compelling dual emphasis on horticulture and sculpture that has become the cornerstone of the institution's identity and mission.

From the fall of 1999 through the spring of 2000, the staff and sculpture advisory committee closely examined the content and potential growth of the permanent collection, and with it, the need to more narrowly define the scope of the exhibition program. It was decided that all concerns related to collections and exhibitions would be coordinated as functions of the sculpture program. A mission to focus on "works by established and emerging sculptors from the modern tradition to the present" was written, with the objective of acquiring sculpture from the late nineteenth century to the present. Considering the divergent trends of the existing collection, representational objects based on themes from nature were grouped as the Garden Trails and Conservatory Collection, whereas works of a more challenging aesthetic became the Sculpture Park and Gallery Collection. The exhibition program, planned with great sensitivity toward the important endeavors of other area arts organizations, would concentrate on "sculptural traditions of all periods for the purposes of education, appreciation, and enjoyment." Under this rubric, exhibitions could examine works of art from historical and non-Western cultures beyond the focus of the permanent collections and offer visitors an opportunity to explore two-dimensional objects and works in other media created by artists recognized primarily as sculptors.

As the framework for the sculpture program took shape, several significant acquisitions were pursued. First, *Figure on a Trunk* by Magdalena Abakanowicz was acquired from an exhibition of her recent work at New York's Metropolitan Museum of Art. The challenging imagery and subject matter of the life-size bronze helped introduce the public to the more diverse spectrum of contemporary sculpture. Soon thereafter came acquisitions of works by masters including Aristide Maillol, Jacques Lipchitz, and Henry Moore who were critical to the development of currents in twentieth-century sculpture. In equal measure, objects were sought by artists ranging from Arnaldo Pomodoro and George Rickey to Keith Haring who are diverse exponents of contemporary trends. In addition, the Gardens' first commission was given to Richard Hunt for a monumental bronze to be sited on the sculpture trail and dedicated when the Phase II building addition was completed.

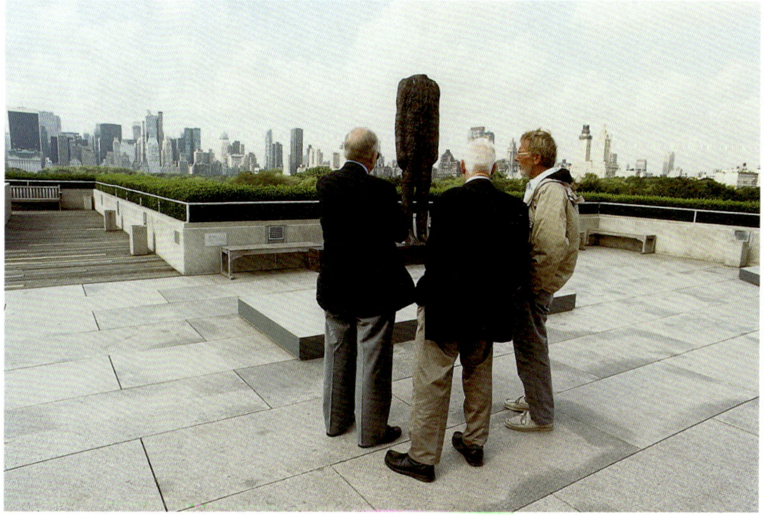

Earl Holton and Fred Meijer with sculpture advisory committee member Larry ten Harmsel, examining Magdalena Abakanowicz's *Figure on a Trunk*, on exhibition at the Metropolitan Museum of Art, New York, October 1999

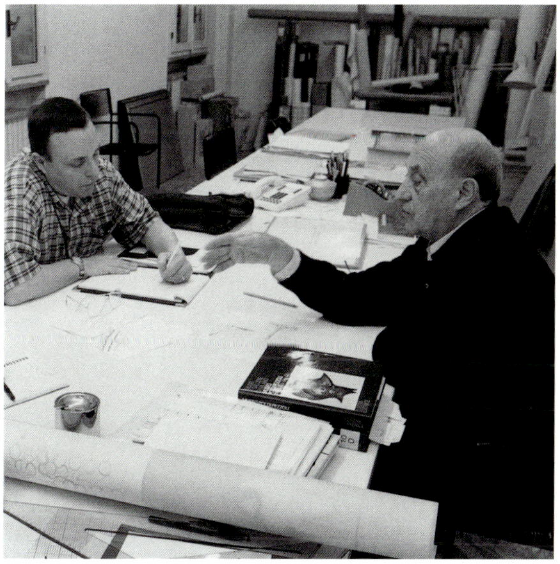

Sculpture advisory committee member and counsel to the Meijer Foundation Robert VerHeulen with sculptor Arnaldo Pomodoro, in Pomodoro's Milan studio, March 2000

Throughout the research and acquisition process, the staff and advisory committee remained mindful of important considerations unique to the Gardens. First, there was a desire to build an important representative collection of modern and contemporary works that did not duplicate existing sculpture collections in the region. The Hunt commission, *Column of the Free Spirit,* and the selection of the Rickey water piece, *Four Open Squares Horizontal Gyratory—Tapered,* an atypical example of the master's work, offered such opportunities. The second consideration was to explore sculptural connections to the botanical component of the Gardens. Acquisitions including Maillol's *Torso of Summer,* Moore's *Working Model for Divided Oval: Butterfly,* and Pomodoro's *Disk in the Form of a Desert Rose,* each with decided but varied references to the natural world, helped establish such a bridge. Finally, there was great interest in collecting works by emerging artists or those largely unknown to American audiences. This incentive was undertaken in 2000 and 2001 through the acquisition of Antony Gormley's *One and Other,* Bill Woodrow's *Listening to History,* and Dietrich Klinge's *Grosser Trefree.*

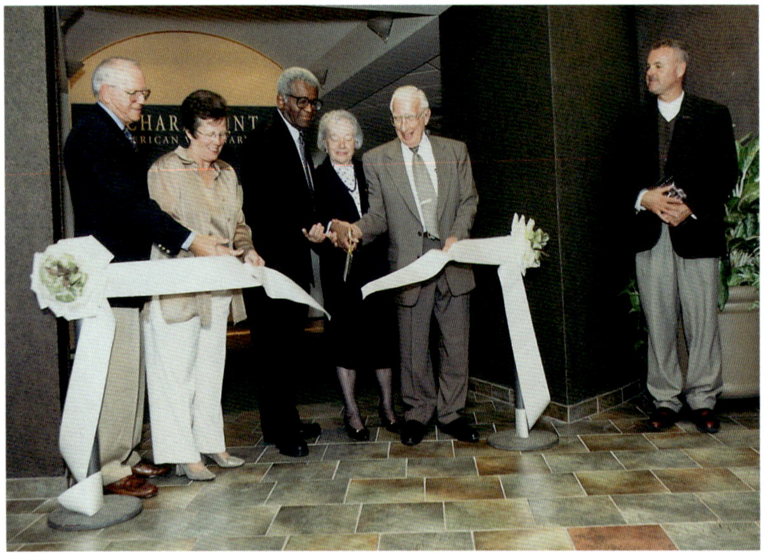

Ribbon cutting for the dedication of the sculpture galleries, part of the Phase II expansion, with (left to right) Earl and Donnalee Holton, Richard Hunt, Lena and Fred Meijer, and Executive Director Brent Dennis, September 2000

In September 2000, the Phase II expansion was opened to the public. Two significant exhibitions premiered in the new sculpture galleries. *Richard Hunt: American Visionary* inaugurated the Holton and Balk Galleries, and *Imaging the Divine: Religious and Spiritual Themes of Marshall Fredericks* debuted in the Michigan National Gallery. The Hunt exhibition, timed to coincide with the unveiling of *Column of the Free Spirit,* introduced many to the work of this highly regarded abstract sculptor, while the Fredericks exhibition shed new light on an artist familiar to the Gardens' audiences. The concept that art exhibitions are a vital counterpart to the botanical displays was firmly embraced, and an exhibition schedule calling for temporary installations rotating on a quarterly basis was adopted. To coordinate these and future shows, an assistant curator for exhibitions and a curator of arts education were added to the staff. To attend to the growing permanent collection, the original conservator's position was redefined as assistant curator for collections and conservator, and a curatorial assistant's position was added to the roster. Even as the staff and public were acquainting themselves with the new facilities, Fred Meijer—always ready to forge ahead—encouraged the continued development of the collection and asked the staff and sculpture advisory committee for recommendations on the permanent display of the works.

Foremost among the acquisitions of this period was *Eve* by Auguste Rodin, a master universally regarded as the father of modern sculpture. Enthusiasm for this early bronze was so great that a public unveiling and temporary installation of the sculpture were implemented in the winter of 2000. Concurrently, planning began for Phase III, the primary goal of which was the formal development of a sculpture park on land surrounding the sculpture trail. The setting of more than thirty acres was designed to complement the siting of the twenty-four works highlighted in this publication and to provide the infrastructure for the anticipated future growth of the collection. A waterfall, two waterways with ponds, and other distinctive landscaping of the terrain exemplify the special features that showcase the sculpture. Beyond the completion of the Sculpture Park, Phase III also offered support for additional tram and boardwalk paths to form a contiguous loop around the exterior gardens, as well as the construction of a 1,000-person outdoor amphitheater, utility corridors, and three outdoor restroom and comfort stations. As with the sculpture acquisitions, significant funding for the project was provided by the Meijer Foundation. Additionally, the Arthur and Elizabeth Snell Sculpture Center opened to the public in the fall of 2001. An orientation and discovery space, the Snell Sculpture Center provides a substantial educational and interpretive component for all works of sculpture in the permanent collection, with a critical emphasis placed on those works featured in the Sculpture Park.

The sculpture described and illustrated herein was unveiled in its new outdoor setting in the spring of 2002. The installation achieves the mission of the Frederik Meijer Gardens and Sculpture Park and is a major addition to the cultural landscape of Michigan and the Great Lakes region. The benevolence and attention that Fred and Lena Meijer have invested in the institution is exemplary, even exceptional. Fred Meijer was in his early sixties when he was first inspired by sculpture. That interest evolved into a passion that continues nearly two decades later as he has developed relationships with sculptors and curators and visited many public and private sculpture gardens in the United States and abroad. Fred Meijer is disarmingly outspoken on many aspects of life and art. He is at once youthful and inquisitive in his exploration of uncharted territory, and, in

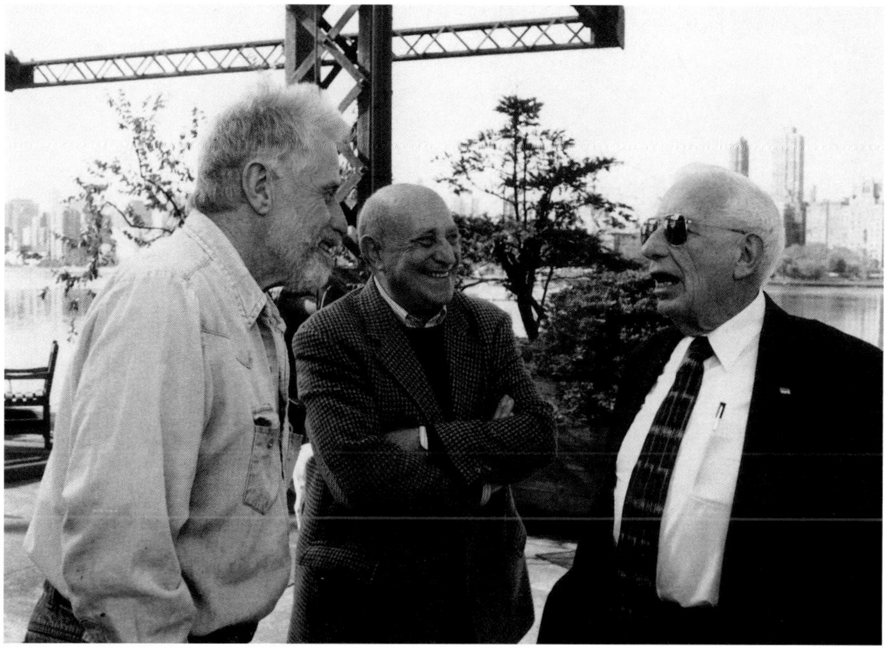

Fred Meijer with sculptors Mark di Suvero and Arnaldo Pomodoro, at di Suvero's New York studio, November 2000

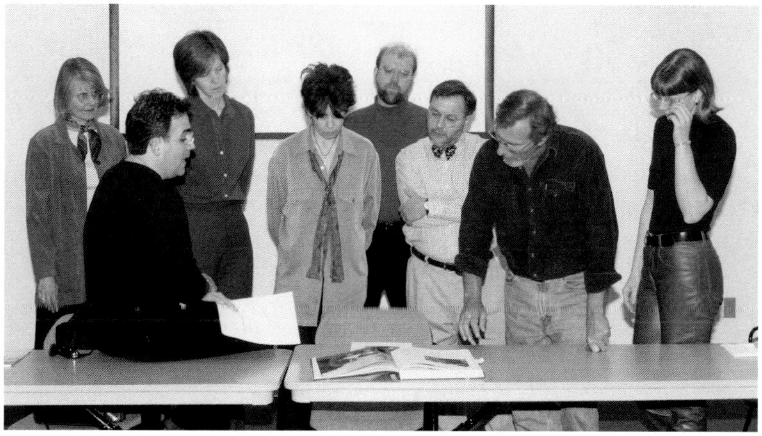

Sculpture advisory committee members (left to right) Marlene Vanderhill, Joseph Becherer, Heidi Holst Leestma, Eleanor Scheifele, Caleb Brennan, sculpture advisory committee co-chair Henry Matthews, Larry ten Harmsel, and Laurene Warren, examining plans for the Sculpture Park, February 2001

Installation of Alexander Liberman's *Aria,* June 1999

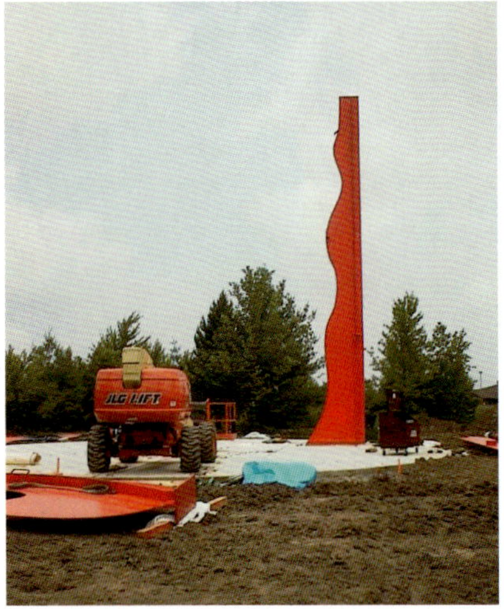

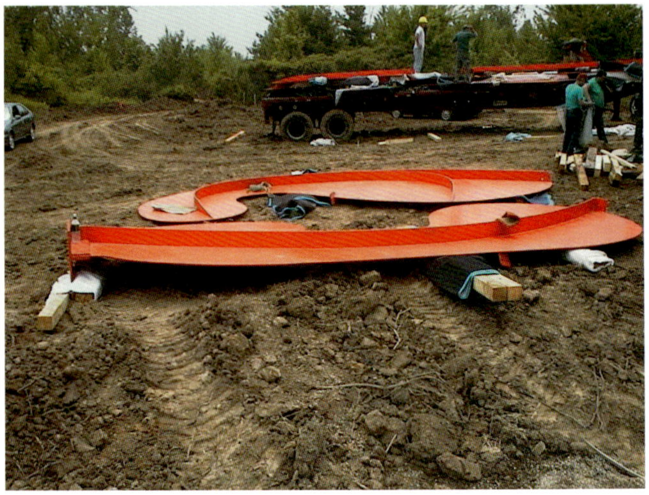

the wisdom of age, confident and philosophical, with a salt-of-the-earth charm. He built a thriving business around serving ordinary and extraordinary people. His philanthropic interests are based on the same purpose. It is noteworthy, and entirely true to form, that his first exposure to three-dimensional objects was the result of the Meijers' generous support of a sculpture project for the benefit of the public at large. It is equally consistent that he would favor sculpture, particularly bronze, for its durability through the generations.

Fred and Lena Meijer would like people from all walks of life to share in the rewards of their combined love of sculpture and horticulture. Whether a visitor is interested in the botanical world, gravitates toward sculpture and the visual arts, or simply seeks a meaningful respite, a debt of gratitude is ultimately owed to the insightful patronage of the Meijers. Reflecting on his desire to create an important sculpture collection and park to be enjoyed by the public, Fred Meijer has said, "There must be more to life than work. People deserve a place that inspires them, challenges them, and offers opportunities to consider the beauty and mysteries of the human experience." This poignant message informs ongoing aspects of the sculpture program and prompts wondrous discussions and decisions about the future of the Frederik Meijer Gardens and Sculpture Park.

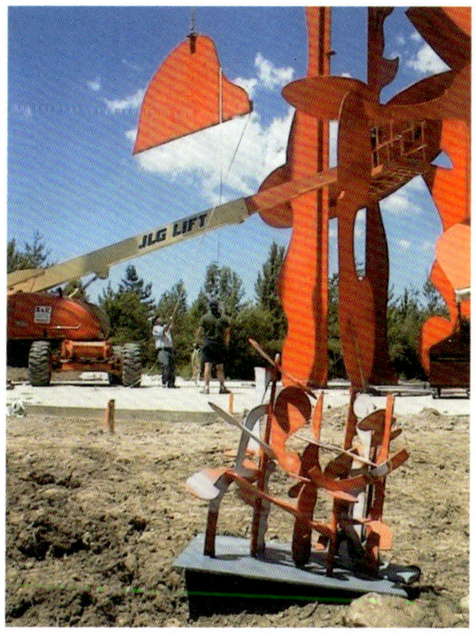

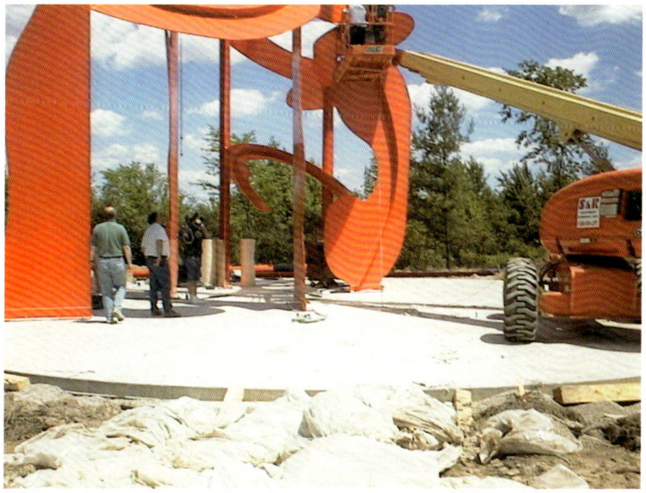

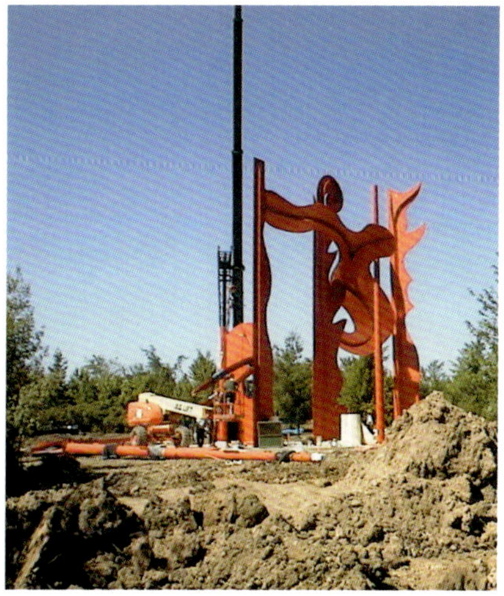

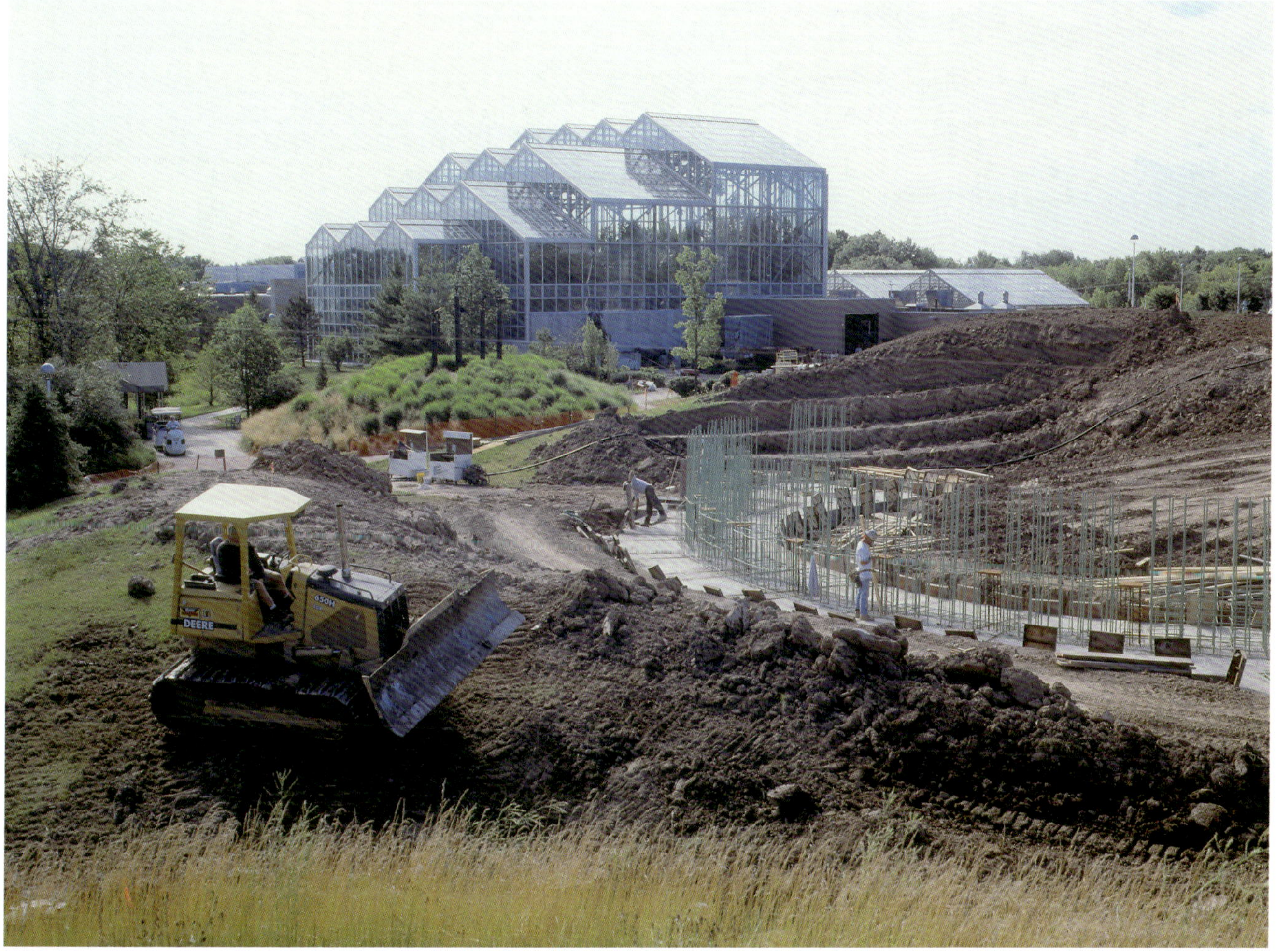

Work on the Sculpture Park, summer 2001

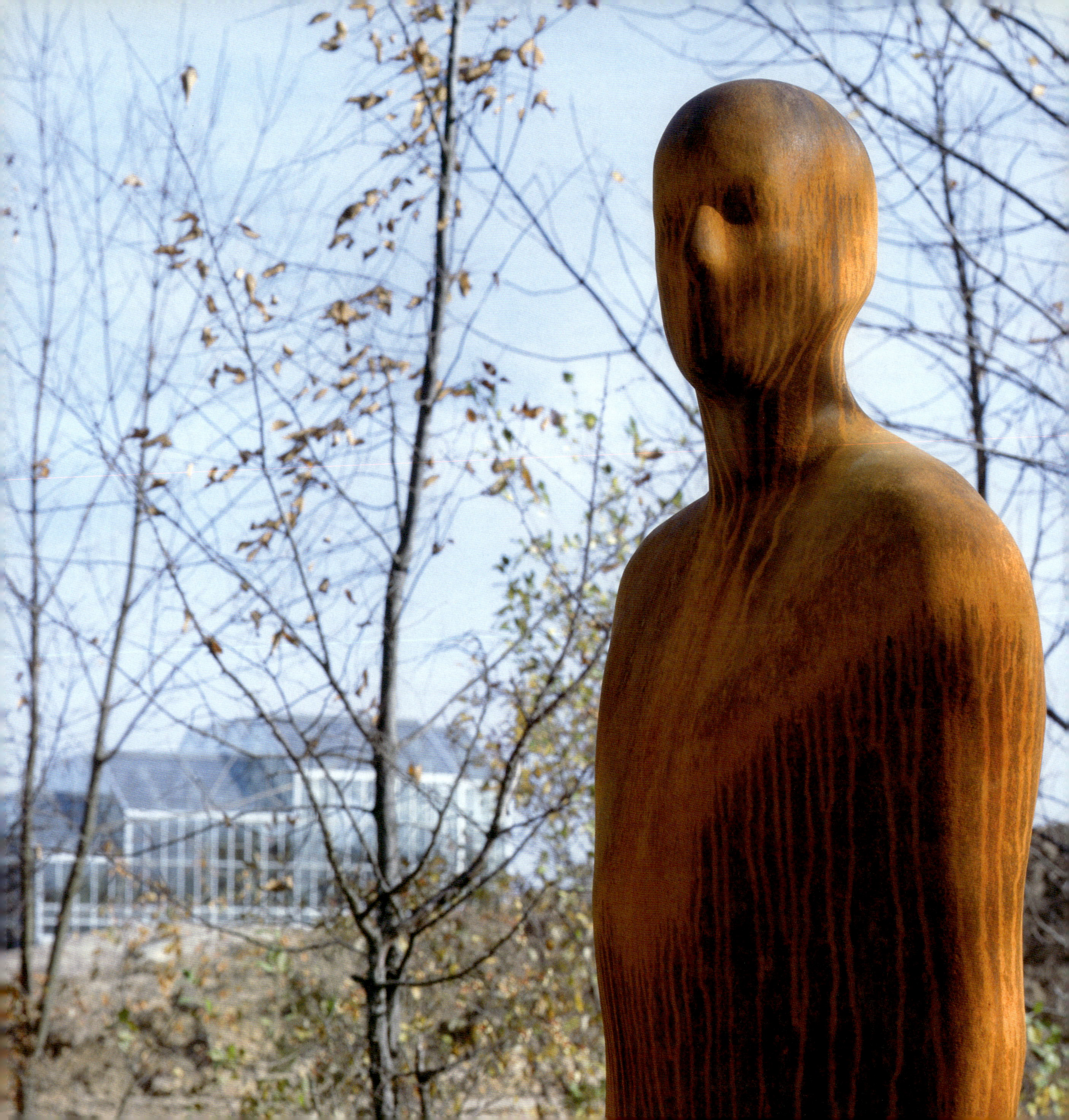

HIGHLIGHTS OF THE SCULPTURE COLLECTION

Polish, born 1930

MAGDALENA ABAKANOWICZ :: FIGURE ON A TRUNK (FIGURA SU TRONCO)

1998
Bronze, unique, h. 96 inches (243.8 cm)
Gift of the Meijer Foundation, 2000.04

MAGDALENA ABAKANOWICZ has emerged as one of the most profound and influential of contemporary sculptors, but her origins are relatively removed from the mainstream of the art world. Her life and work are informed by the tumultuous historical context of her native Poland over the course of the last century, and together they contribute to a unique reflection on critical developments within the history of sculpture. Born into a wealthy and intellectual family in rural Poland, Abakanowicz was emotionally distanced from her parents and favored the out-of-doors over formal education. She spent much of her childhood pursuing interests that would inform her career: art and the natural world. Her family lost everything during World War II, and in postwar Poland, it became necessary for her to deny the family's privileged origins in order to receive a university education.

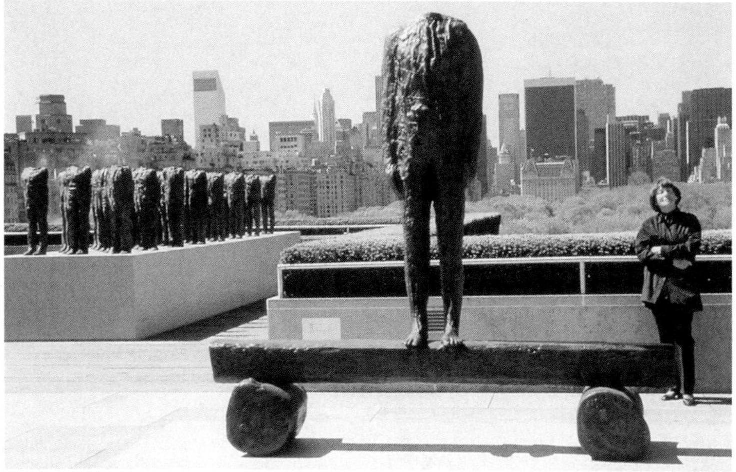

Magdalena Abakanowicz with *Figure on a Trunk,* Metropolitan Museum of Art, New York, roof installation, 1999

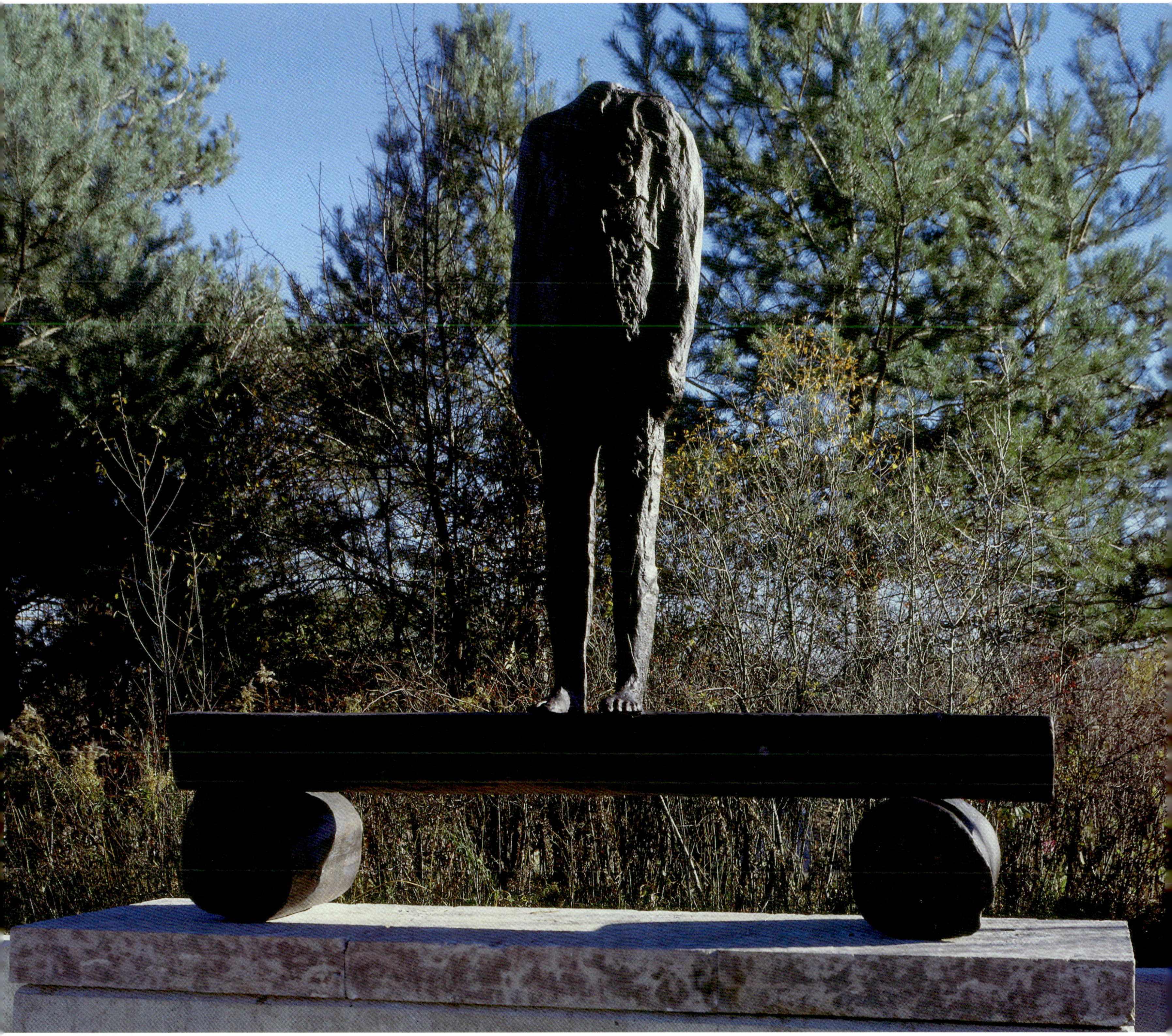

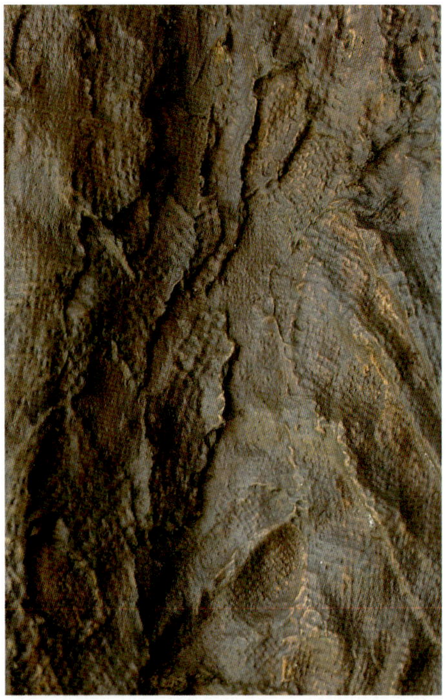

Abakanowicz completed degrees at the College of Fine Arts, Sopot, in 1949, and the Academy of Fine Arts, Warsaw, in 1955. At the beginning of her career, she was interested in drawing, painting, and sculpture, but in the 1960s, she focused on textiles, in the broadest definition of the term. Cloth, burlap, and weaving materials were accessible to her in sparse Communist conditions, and she employed them in her experiments. She first produced large-scale weavings in 1961, and in the following year, her work began to gain international recognition. Against the traditional concept that tapestries were to be flat forms with relatively smooth surfaces, Abakanowicz approached her subjects as three-dimensional reliefs with an array of distinguished textures. Her revolutionary work contributed greatly to the recognition of fiber art as an artistic pursuit that was viable within the rubric of modern sculpture.

In the 1970s, the artist started to experiment with materials like burlap stiffened with resin. The structural solidity of this medium encouraged greater exploration of sculptural forms. During this period, Abakanowicz began to concentrate on the human figure; the torso, the head, and bodies without heads in particular captured her attention. Anonymous and androgynous, these highly tactile forms suggested both tragedy and wisdom, asserting the profound mysteries of life sobered by human suffering. They were exhibited individually or in groups and could easily be seen as reflections on the human condition. Within the parameters of the artist's lifetime alone, these figurative objects bore witness to a cavalcade of atrocities, from the Nazi and Communist regimes to the Cold War era and its demise.

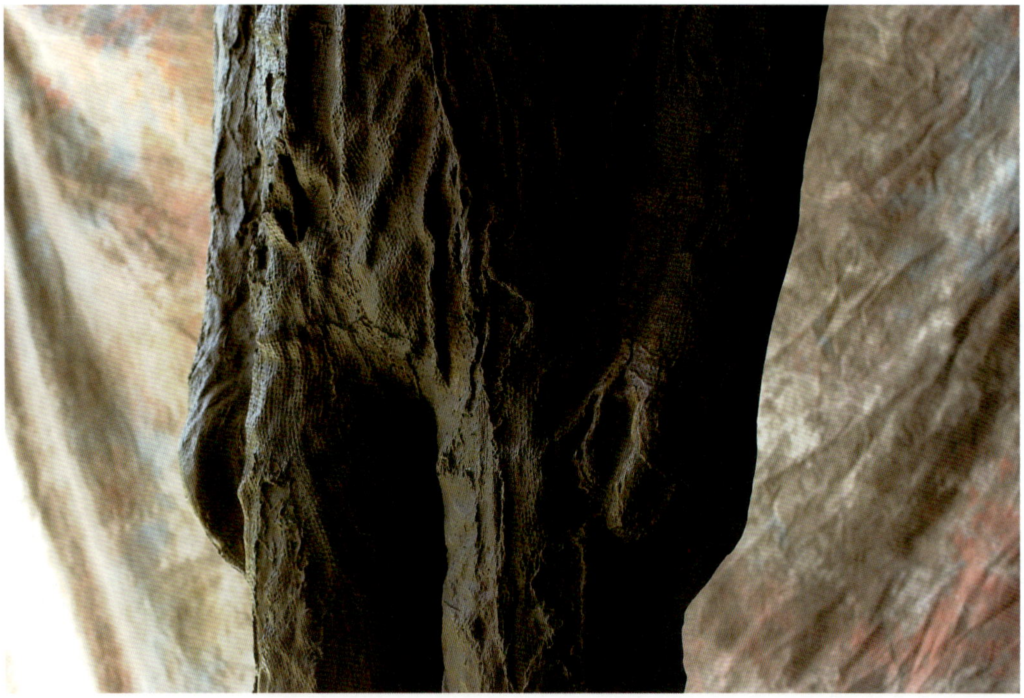

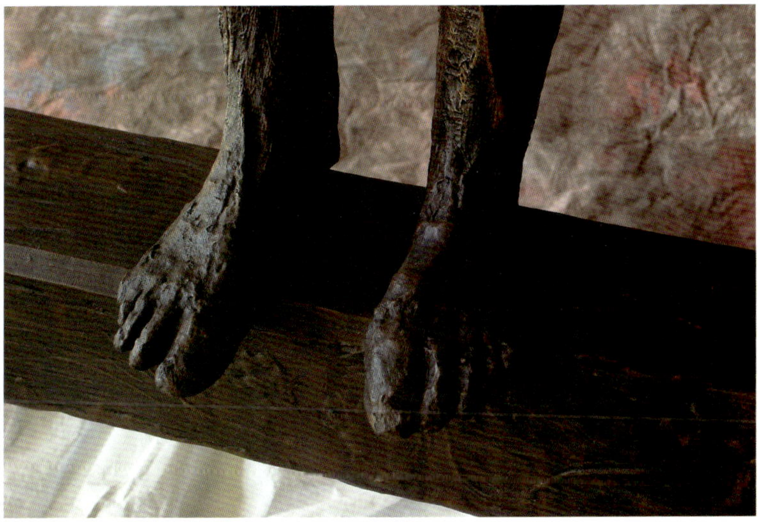

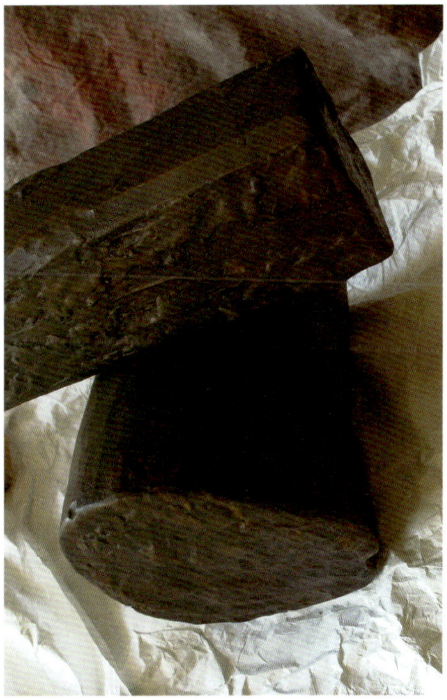

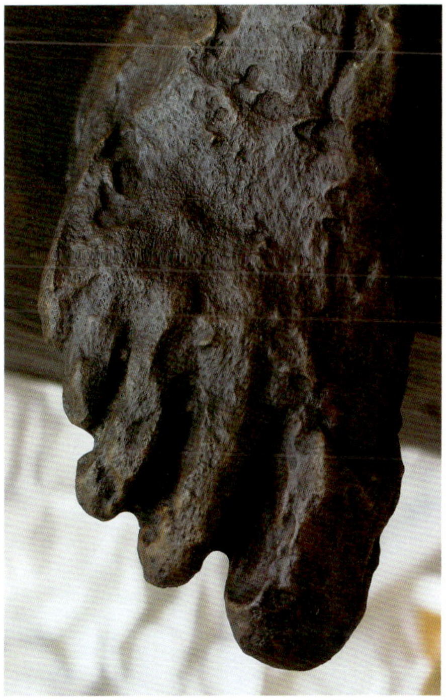

Abakanowicz commenced work in bronze in the 1980s, while continuing with fiber materials. In works like *Figure on a Trunk,* irregular surfaces are legible even at a distance, revealing the path of the artist's career through textiles. The permanence of bronze is juxtaposed against the illusion of fibrous fragility. The sculpture portrays a figure standing barefoot on a lengthy beam. This horizontal element traverses two slabs of a tree trunk, further elevating the figure. The overall composition is carefully balanced within a strongly implied triangular framework. The central form is life size and decidedly frontal. Its stiff pose encourages the stillness anticipated at any memorial monument. With neither a head nor any indication of gender, the viewer is asked to confront humanity rather than a specific human being. The elevation and erect posture of the figure, unlike Abakanowicz's sculptures in which the form is placed directly on the ground, suggest vindication or, at a minimum, a momentary recognition of pride and self worth. Although notions of endured tragedy and loss may be inherent in much of the artist's work, her very choice of bronze as the medium promises longevity and durability—qualities that have been appreciated through the ages.

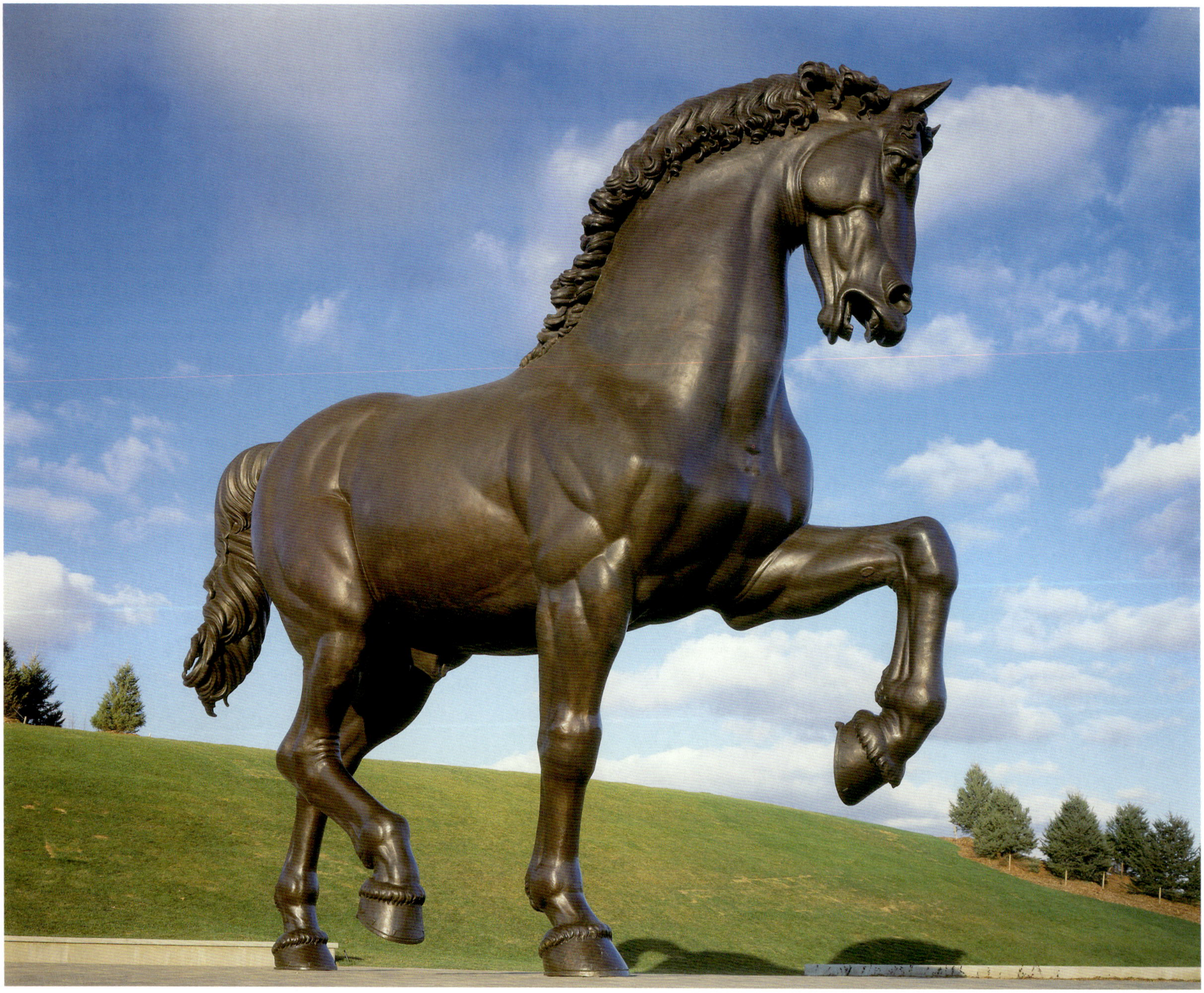

American, born 1955

NINA AKAMU :: THE AMERICAN HORSE

1998

Bronze, 2/2 (second in an edition of two), h. 24 feet (731.5 cm)

Gift of the Meijer Foundation, 1999.06

FOLLOWING THE centuries-old tradition of artists specializing in fine animal sculpture, Nina Akamu is widely recognized as one of its most important contemporary exponents. Akamu was born in Midwest City, Oklahoma, of both Japanese and Chinese ancestry. Because of her father's position in the U.S. Air Force, the family traveled extensively and lived in numerous countries. As a result, Akamu was introduced to a wide array of artistic and cultural traditions, as well as a variety of natural environments. At an early age, she developed a deep interest in and fondness for animals; in addition, she found herself gravitating toward drawing and other forms of visual expression. These inclinations would eventually converge as her vocation. She went on to earn a bachelor of fine arts degree from the Maryland College of Art, where she studied drawing, anatomy, and painting. During this period, Akamu credits her study with noted academic painter and sculptor Joseph Sheppard as critical to her development as an artist.

In 1979, Akamu moved to Florence, Italy, to nurture her interest in sculpture while studying the masters and monuments of the Italian Renaissance. She was inspired by the depth and breadth of the sculpture and drawings held by the city's numerous museums.

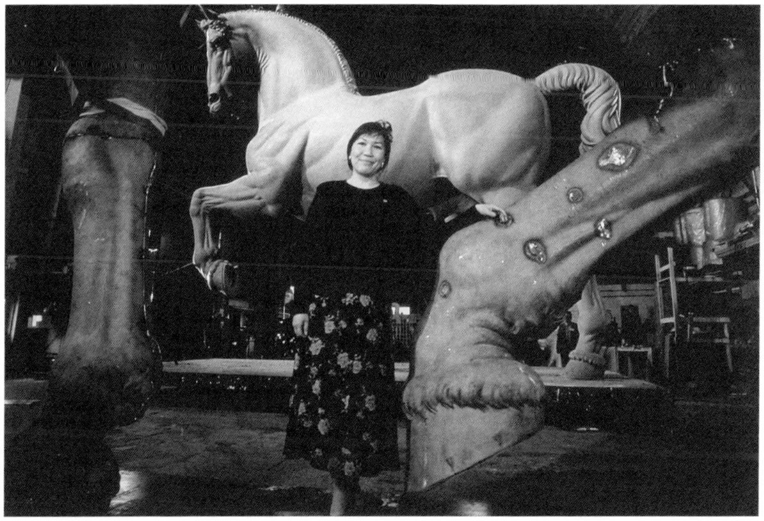

Nina Akamu at Tallix Foundry, Beacon, New York, 1999

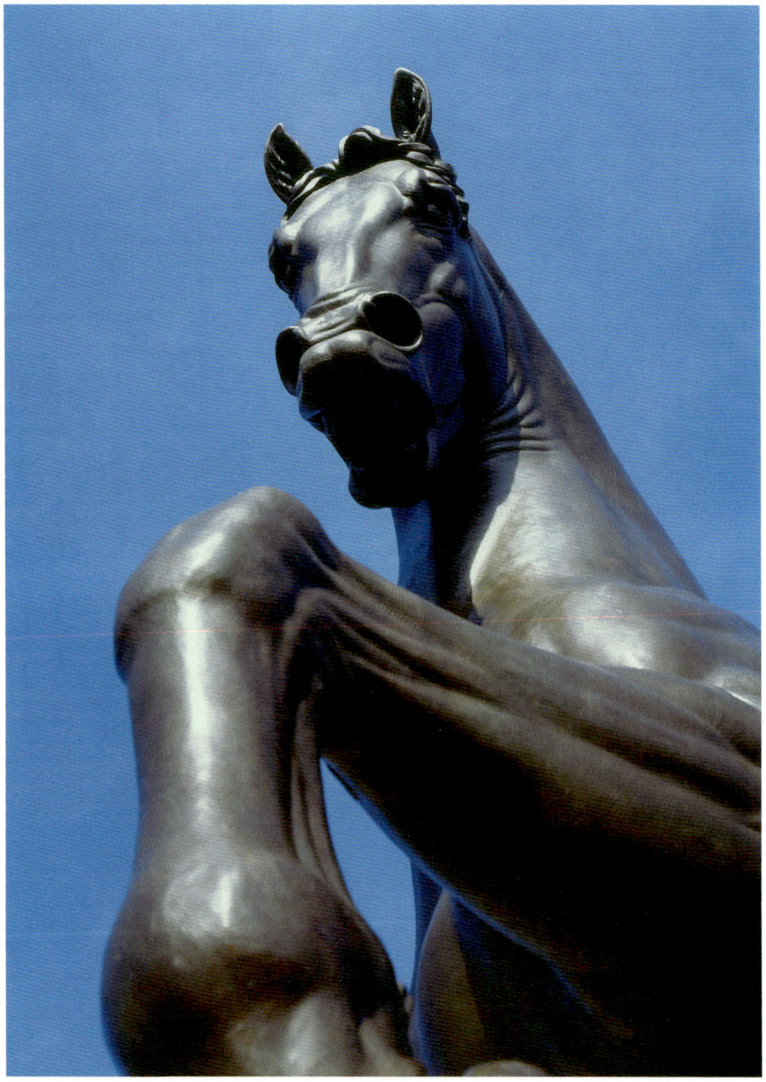

After five years in Florence, she moved to Pietrasanta, Italy, world-renowned for its stone-carving studios and bronze foundries. Akamu remained for seven years, mastering both marble carving and bronze casting. The processes required for working in bronze would prove critical to her artistic success. At Pietrasanta, she produced many of her earliest sculptures, which not only speak of the aesthetic sensibilities distilled from works of historical sculptors such as Donatello and Verrocchio, but also are marked by the fine craftsmanship gained through her proficiency with contemporary sculpture techniques.

Akamu is among the most celebrated contemporary American sculptors working in a time-honored, representational mode. Undoubtedly, she is best known for her massive bronze equine monuments that pay homage to the Renaissance master Leonardo da Vinci. Two identical twenty-four-foot bronze horses were dedicated in the autumn of 1999—*Leonardo da Vinci's Horse* in Milan, Italy, as a gift of the American people, and *The American Horse* at the Frederik Meijer Gardens. The genesis of the idea for a monumental bronze horse began in 1977, when Pennsylvania pilot and art collector Charles Dent read an article in *National Geographic* magazine about a sculpture Leonardo had designed in Milan during the 1480s. Leonardo created a scale model in clay, but it was destroyed in 1499 by invading French troops before the intended bronze version could be cast. This tragic loss became one of the great mysteries in the history of Western art and, nearly five centuries later, inspired Dent and a team of dedicated, amateur assistants to re-create Leonardo's vision. By the time of Dent's death in 1994, an eight-foot model had been made, but it was flawed by anatomical and proportional errors. Because of her reputation as an animal sculptor, Akamu was hired in 1996 to try to remedy these flaws. By 1997, when it was determined that the problems could not be corrected, Akamu was commissioned to fashion an original equine sculpture honoring Leonardo da Vinci.

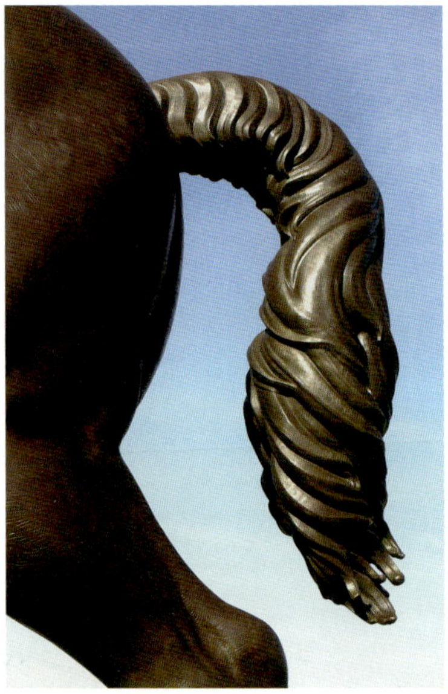

In addition to her classical academic training and familiarity with Renaissance bronzes and drawings, Akamu brought to the project an understanding of and sensitivity to horses. In the absence of any models or definitive studies for Leonardo's original design, she examined his other drawings and the surviving animal and equestrian monuments that the Renaissance master would have known and found inspirational. Akamu first made an eight-foot clay model, which was then translated into twenty-four-foot scale. Both the eight- and twenty-four-foot models were then cast in bronze. Sand and lost-wax casting methods were employed for the two twenty-four-foot works—*The American Horse* and *Leonardo da Vinci's Horse.* More than fifty individual pieces were cast for each sculpture and assembled around stainless steel armatures. Akamu carefully selected a deep brown patina reminiscent of the finish that was popular in the fifteenth and sixteenth centuries. As contemporary monumental sculptures conceived in the Renaissance tradition, the Frederik Meijer Gardens' horse and its Milanese twin pay tribute to one of the world's best-loved masters through the creative efforts of an emerging American talent.

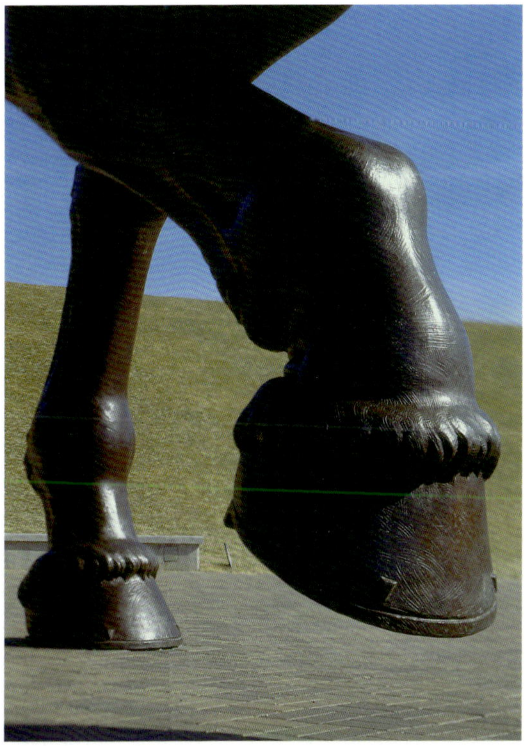

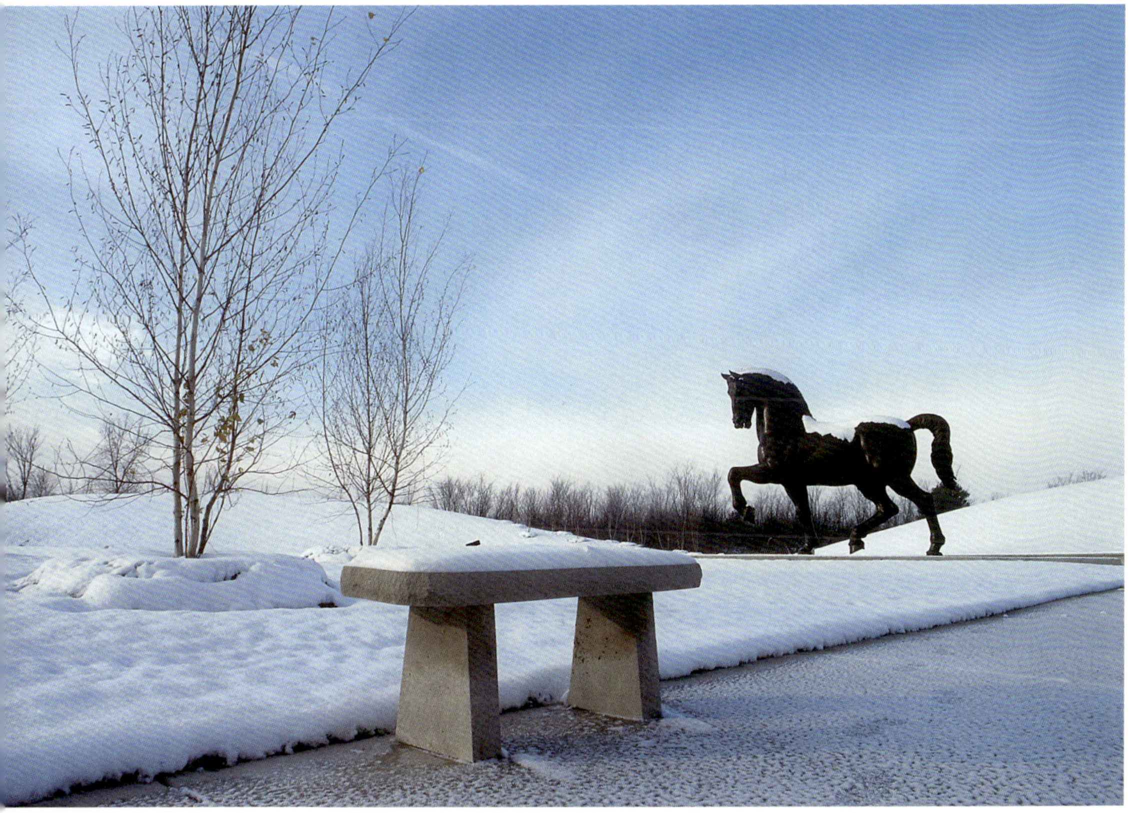

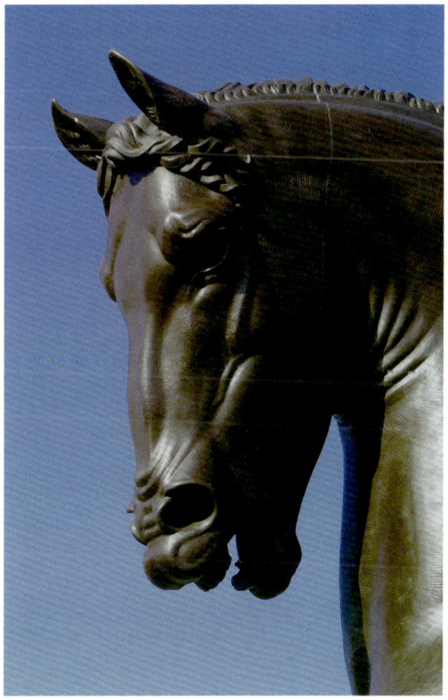

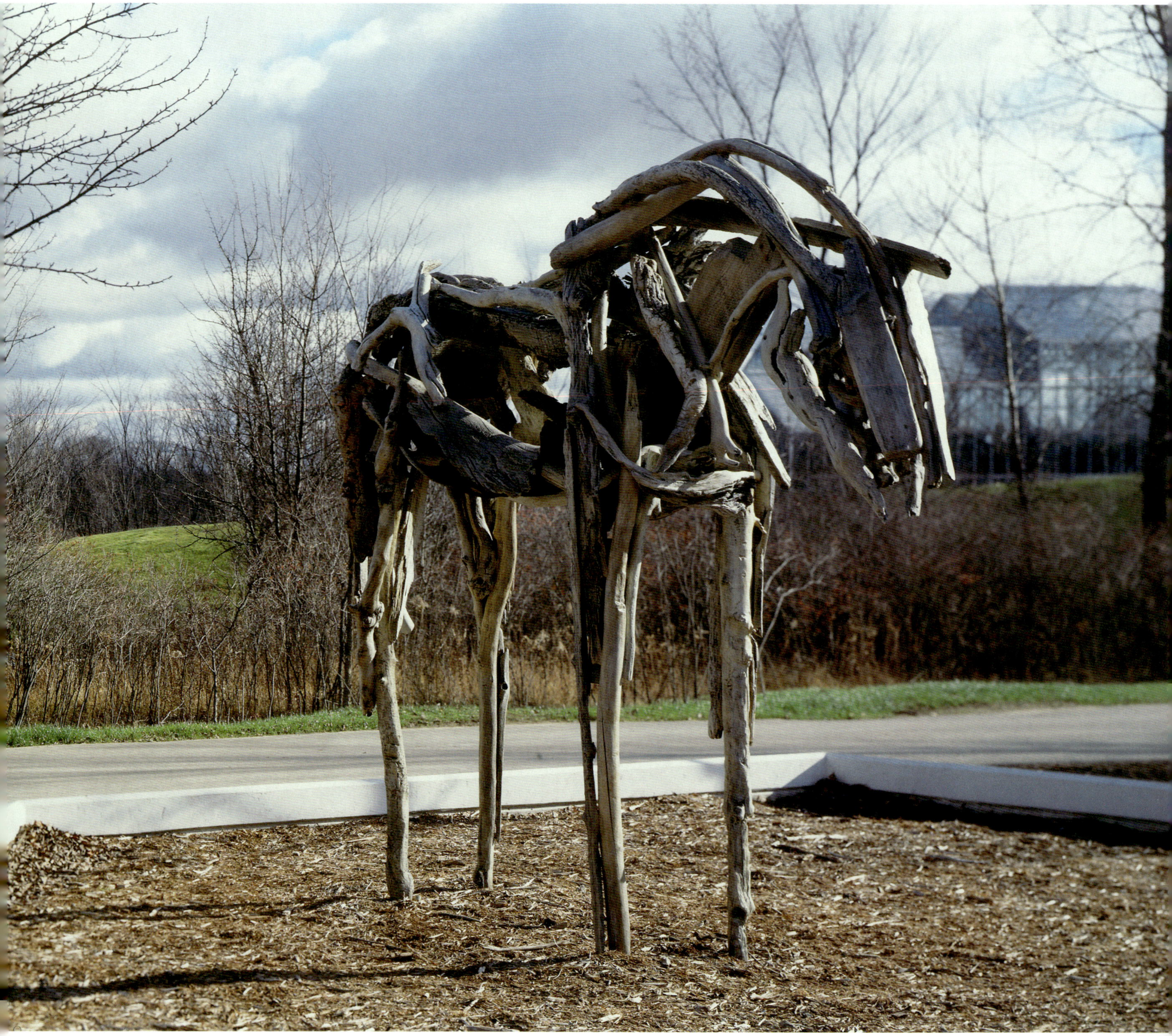

DEBORAH BUTTERFIELD :: CABIN CREEK

1999

Bronze, unique, h. 88 inches (223.5 cm)

Gift of the Meijer Foundation, 1999.02

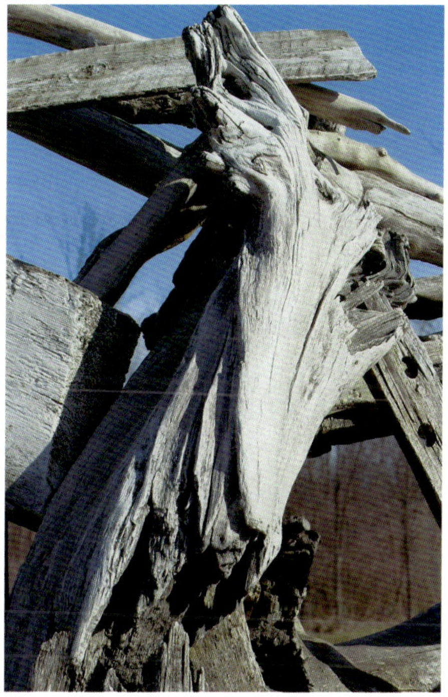

FROM PREHISTORY through the early years of the twentieth century, the horse has been a critical force in many cultures and, by extension, a potent subject in the history of art. Industrial and technological advances, however, eroded the eminent role the horse once played in Western civilization, and led painters and sculptors to pursue subjects more reflective of the currents of contemporary life. Perhaps the most profound exception to this notion is the American sculptor Deborah Butterfield. For nearly three decades, she has explored the theme of the horse through a variety of found materials and reestablished the animal as a poignant, referential icon.

That Butterfield developed a career centered on equine imagery is not surprising. Her passion for horses dates to her childhood in San Diego, where she was born in 1949. Upon entering the University of California, San Diego, she found herself torn between studying veterinary medicine and art. It was art—specifically the field of ceramics—that she chose. In 1970, Butterfield transferred to the University of California, Davis, where she earned a bachelor of fine arts degree in 1972 and a master of fine arts degree in 1973. She then taught at the University of Wisconsin, Madison, from 1974 through 1977. Later in 1977, she served as a lecturer at Montana State University, Bozeman. She established a studio in that city and continues her association with the university there.

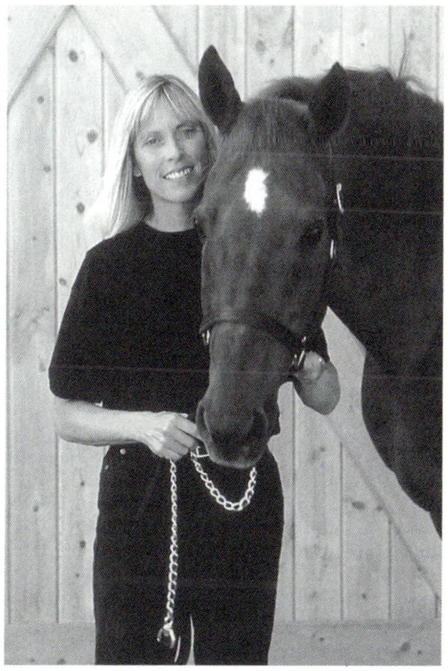

Deborah Butterfield and Rex, 1991

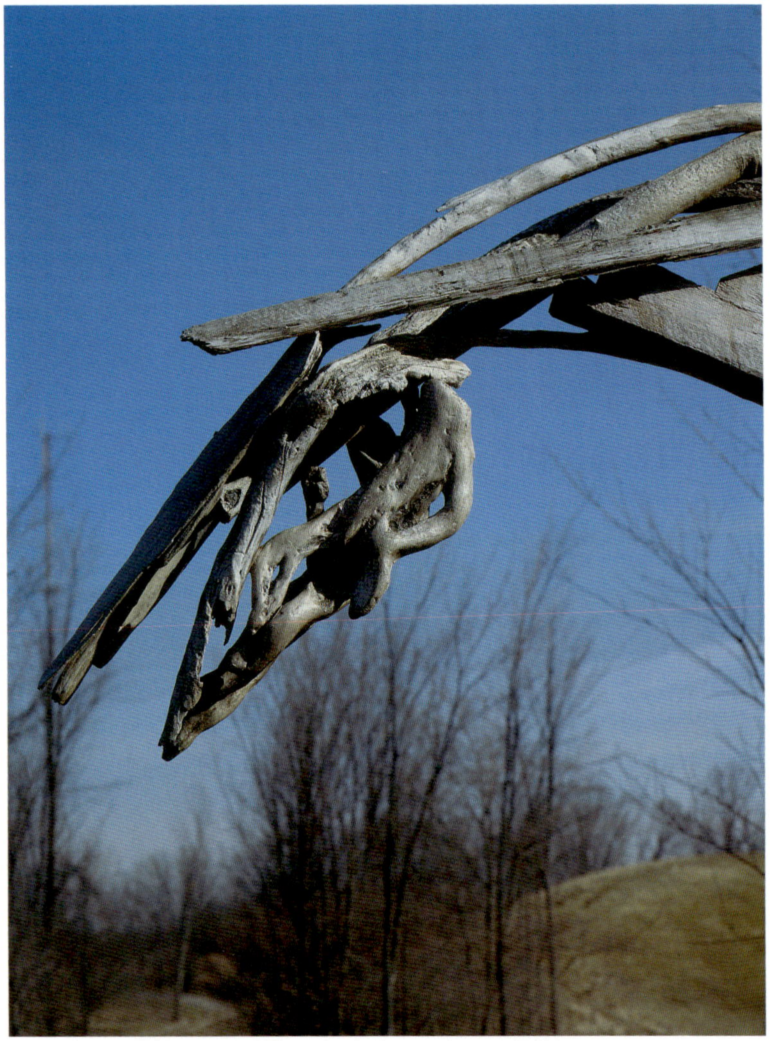

During her stay at the University of California, Davis, Butterfield purchased her first horse, and in 1973, she created her first equine sculpture. Since that time, the artist's direction has been singular. She readily admits two important considerations regarding her work: first, she has been primarily drawn to the history of non-Western art, and second, she has devoted much of her attention to the mare, instead of the stallions and warhorses frequently encountered in art since antiquity. Her decision to focus on the female may have held political overtones early on. But the artist's real desire was to create works that emphasize the horse's pastoral existence, rather than commemorate its service to warriors and conquerors of the past.

Unlike traditional historical monuments, Butterfield has employed a wide variety of found objects in her sculpture. Many of the earliest examples were constructed of mud and sticks, but her repertoire quickly expanded to include discarded wood, metal, steel, glass, and wire. Whether they are objects from nature or industrial castaways, these materials are rarely transformed beyond recognition. Instead, they enhance our understanding of the form as that of a horse in communion with or in contrast to the physical presence and original function of the objects employed. Both medium and pose will vary from one sculpture to the next, but the highly tactile quality of the work remains constant. Considering the diversity of materials used, Butterfield is uncannily successful in capturing the kinesthetic essence of the horse. The artist's sensitivity goes beyond her instinctive comprehension of the animal's bodily form and movement. An inner life, even a personality, is gradually revealed in her equine subjects.

Like each of Butterfield's sculptures, *Cabin Creek* is a unique work of art. The name comes from the location in Montana where the artist gathered many of the elements used to create the sculpture. Numerous branches, twigs, and boards were examined, selected, and assembled to establish the horse's essential form and stance. Once Butterfield was satisfied with the overall composition and individuality of her subject, she had each piece individually cast in bronze, carefully reassembled, and patinated to evoke the palette of the original objects. Nuances of color associated with weathering wood were painstakingly replicated, as were eloquent details such as rusty nails emerging from slabs of board. As a result, the

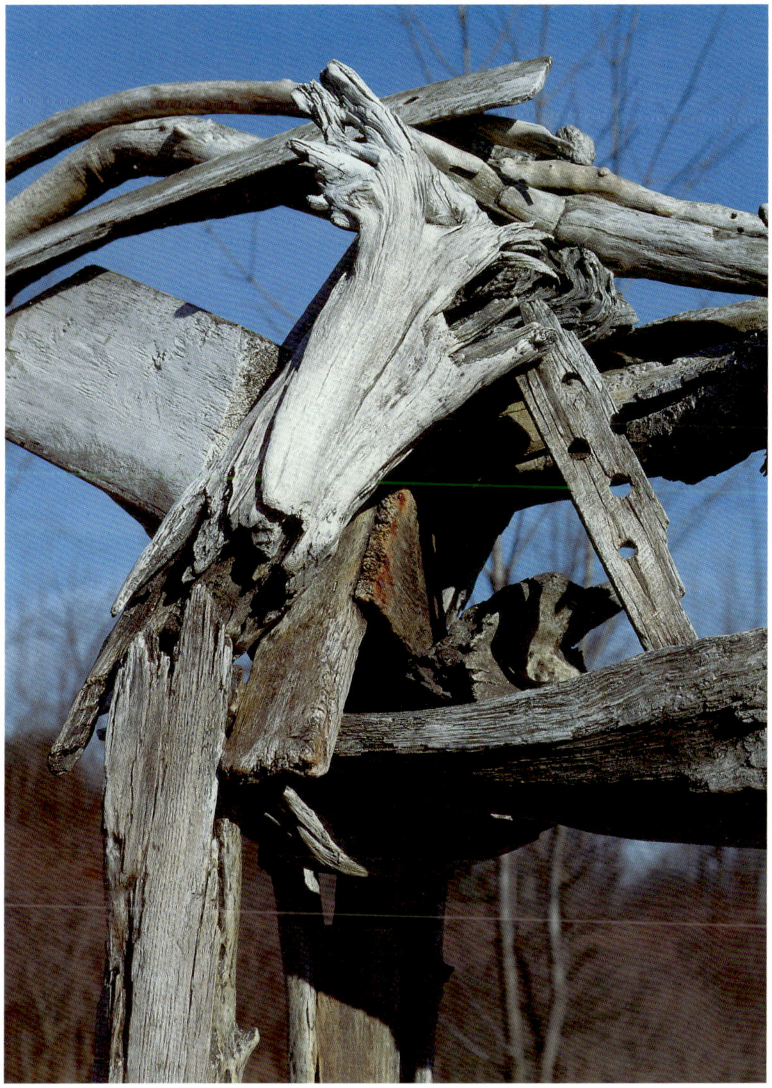

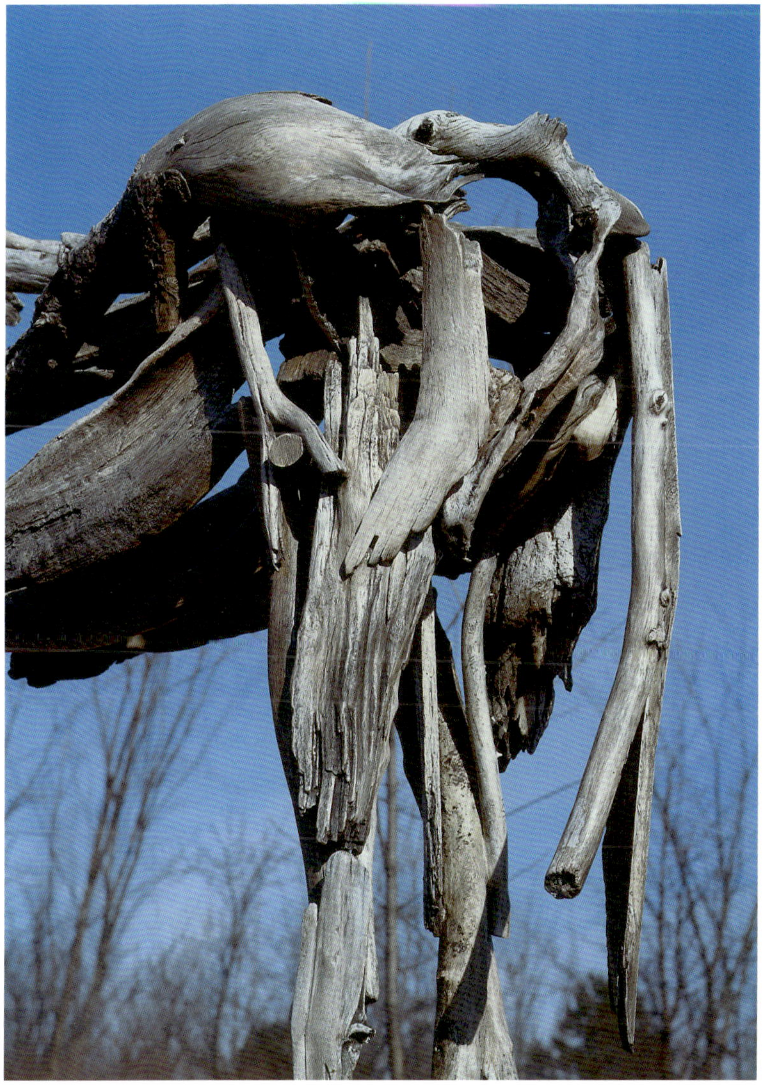

artist masterfully juxtaposes the identity and fragility of the original materials and their transformation into the durable medium of bronze. Likewise, she contrasts the form and function of her subject, specific to the notions and vocabulary of contemporary art, with the venerable traditions of bronze equine and equestrian imagery. Even the most casual viewers will be compelled to consider a broad array of issues of reality and creativity as they admire the work, but ultimately it is the very spirit of the horse that Butterfield honors.

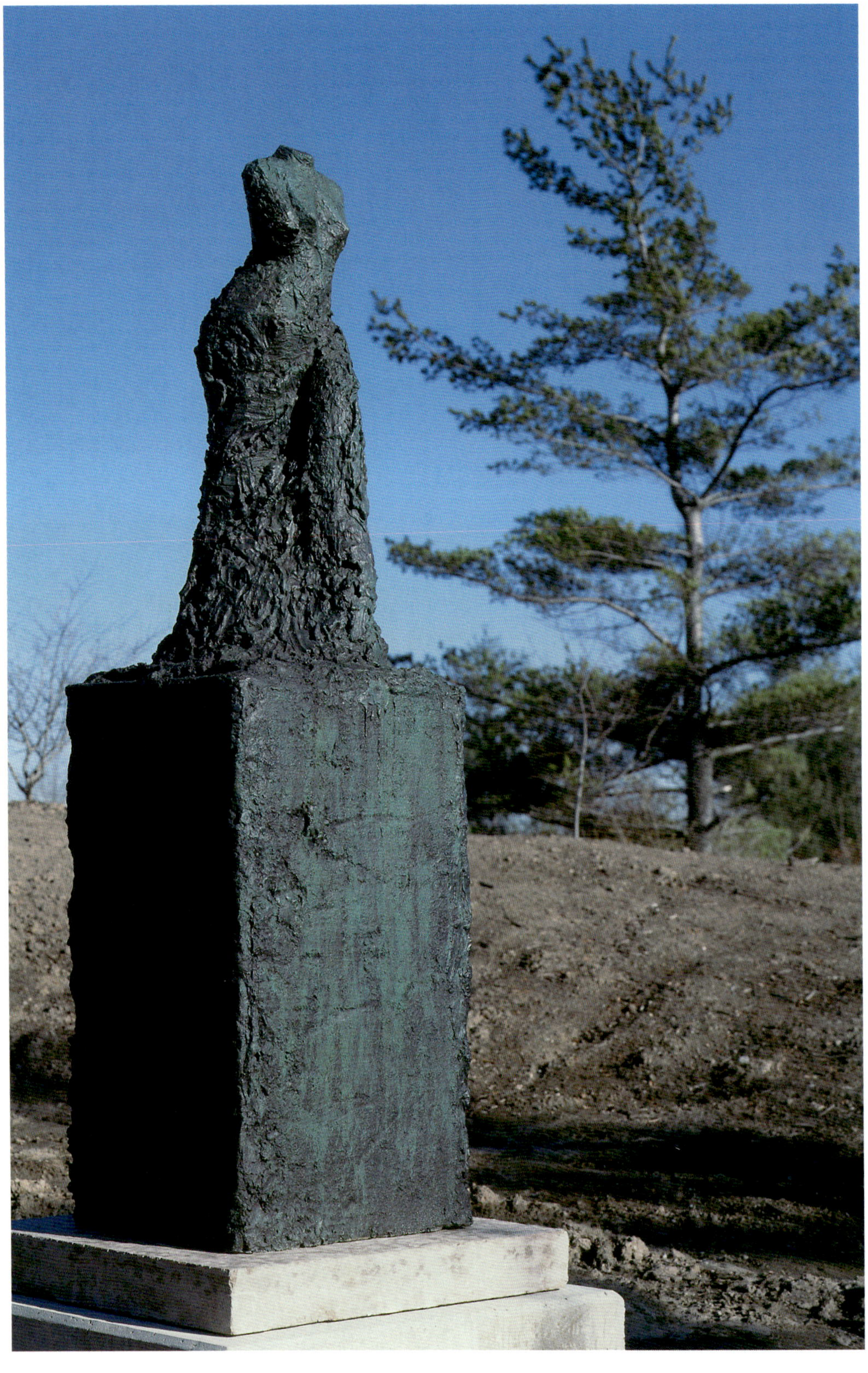

JIM DINE :: THE THUNDER

1991–1995

Bronze, 1/6 (first in an edition of six), h. 9 feet, 6 inches (289.5 cm)

Gift of the Meijer Foundation, 2001.04

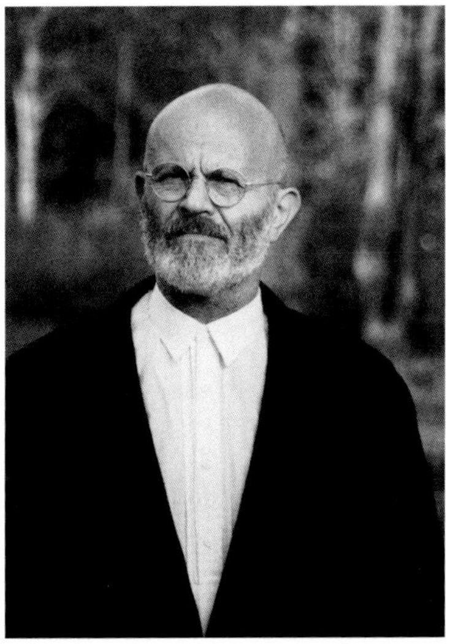

Portrait of Jim Dine, Connecticut, spring 1993

JIM DINE is one of the most significant figures to emerge on the U.S. art scene during the second half of the twentieth century. Born in Cincinnati, he attended adult evening classes at the Cincinnati Art Academy while still in high school. He then studied at the University of Cincinnati, the Boston Museum School, and Ohio University, from which he received a bachelor of fine arts degree in 1957. In that same year, he married fellow student Nancy Minto, and in 1959, the couple moved to New York. Shortly thereafter, Dine joined Claes Oldenburg and Marc Ratliff in founding the celebrated Judson Gallery—a pivotal center for the city's experimental art scene. It was here that Dine presented his first Happening, or performance art piece, *The Smiling Workman.* In addition, the young artist joined Oldenburg, Red Grooms, Allan Kaprow, Lucas Samaras, and George Segal at the Reuben Gallery. Dine began painting on a full-time basis in 1961, through the support of the Martha Jackson Gallery. He also participated in his first European exhibition, the critically acclaimed *Modern American Painting* in London, through which the artist established a strong reputation for innovation and aesthetic merit.

Throughout the 1960s, Dine's reputation grew rapidly. He was intimately associated with the New York School—a loose collection of young, talented artists who were in the very midst of redefining contemporary American art. Along with Oldenburg, Jasper Johns, Robert Rauschenberg, and Andy Warhol, Dine was tangentially identified with the phenomenon of Pop Art. In unique and often highly personal ways, each of these artists called upon a variety of objects from everyday life or popular culture as sources of inspiration. For Dine, tools and clothing frequently served as

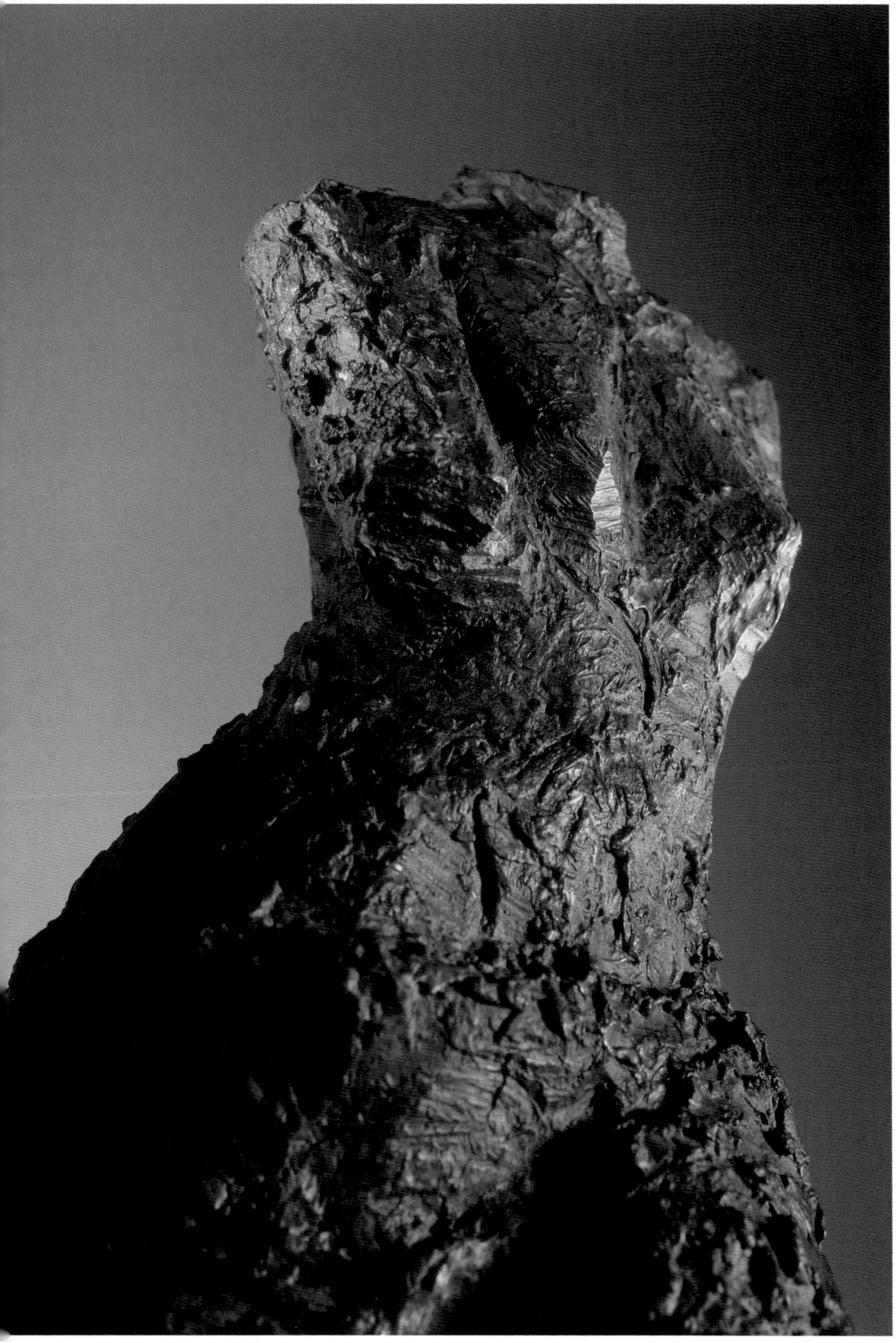

unmistakable icons within his repertoire. Addressing a limited number of subjects time and again enabled him to explore many stylistic and aesthetic issues in different media, from drawing and painting to prints and sculpture. It is immediately apparent when surveying works from this period that formal issues of line, color, and texture, advanced by the application, and often manipulation, of materials, were critical pursuits for the artist. By the late 1970s, Dine's work was widely collected by American and European museums and galleries and was the subject of numerous important one-person and group exhibitions.

The Thunder is a monumental bronze sculpture of a large female form rising from an upright, rectangular plinth. The seminude figure derives from an ancient Hellenistic sculpture, the *Venus de Milo* (also known as the *Aphrodite of Melos*), which has been revered as both an icon of Western beauty and a standard of figurative sculpture for centuries. Dine first approached this subject in 1982, following several years of concentrated study of the human figure from life. His transition from this overtly academic practice to one of focused commentary on a staple within the history of art was seamless. Furthermore, his use of the *Venus de Milo* as the thematic basis for a new group of works paralleled his earlier Pop Art–related imagery; the ancient sculpture had long since penetrated popular culture through postcards, inexpensive plastic copies, and other reproductions. Although *The Thunder* cannot be considered Pop Art, Dine's interests associated with this art movement—the concern for the plebeian, the challenge to canons of Western art, and the opportunity to explore and exploit a variety of media—remain intact.

Dine's Venus theme has taken form in painting, prints, and sculpture over the course of the last two decades. The sculptures have been realized in various materials, most frequently wood and bronze. In these works, figure and plinth are inseparable, as if the form has emerged from the block but is held fast to it. This inextricable bond negates any reference to the notion of placing an independent object on a pedestal in traditional fashion. In scale, the Venus-inspired sculptures range from doll-size to the colossal height of the versions encountered on Sixth Avenue in midtown Manhattan. *The Thunder,* though notably smaller, bears a striking relationship to the Manhattan works in its tumultuous texture and dense gray-green patina. The rugged surface suggests the turbulence of a stormy, summer night, while the dark patina bears the hue of ominous skies or agitated seas. The brooding surface and patina and the powerful integration of figure and base both enhance *The Thunder*'s monumentality and heighten the illusion that this female form was born of the natural phenomenon for which it is named.

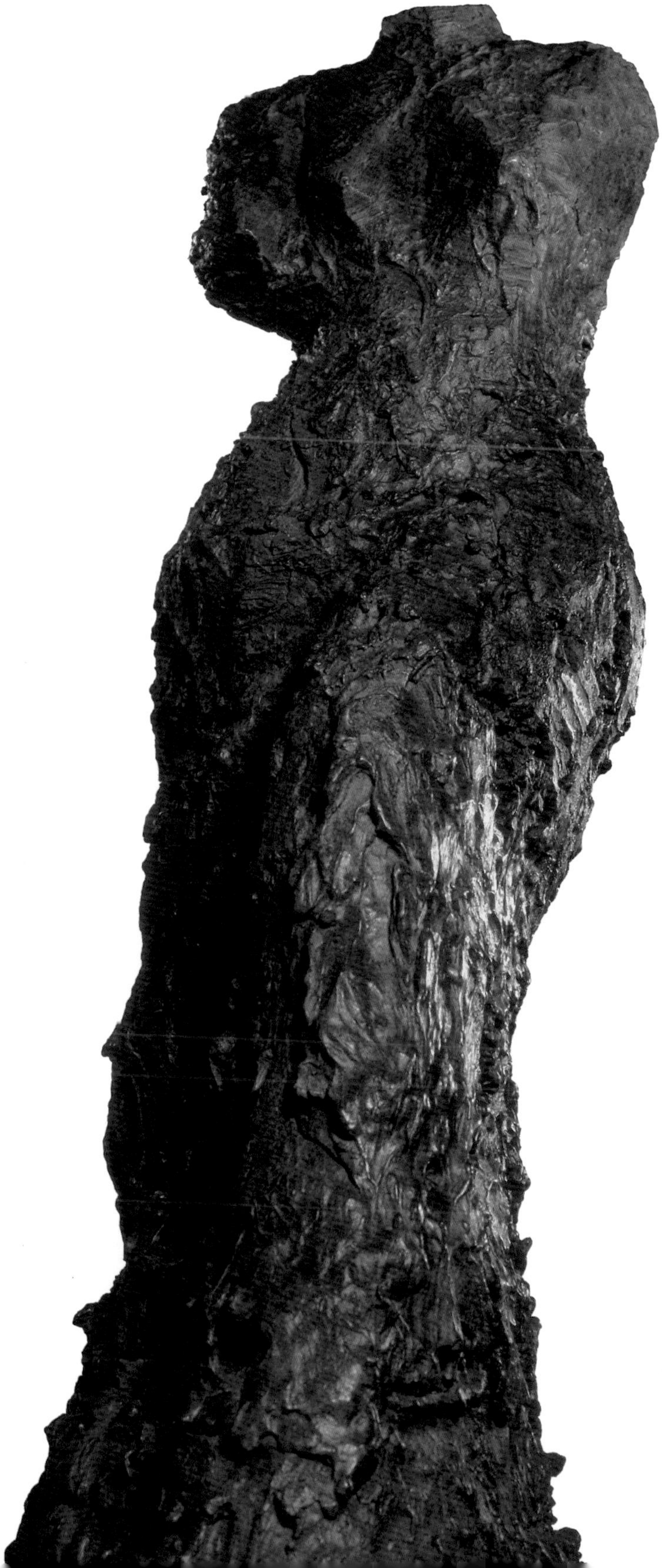

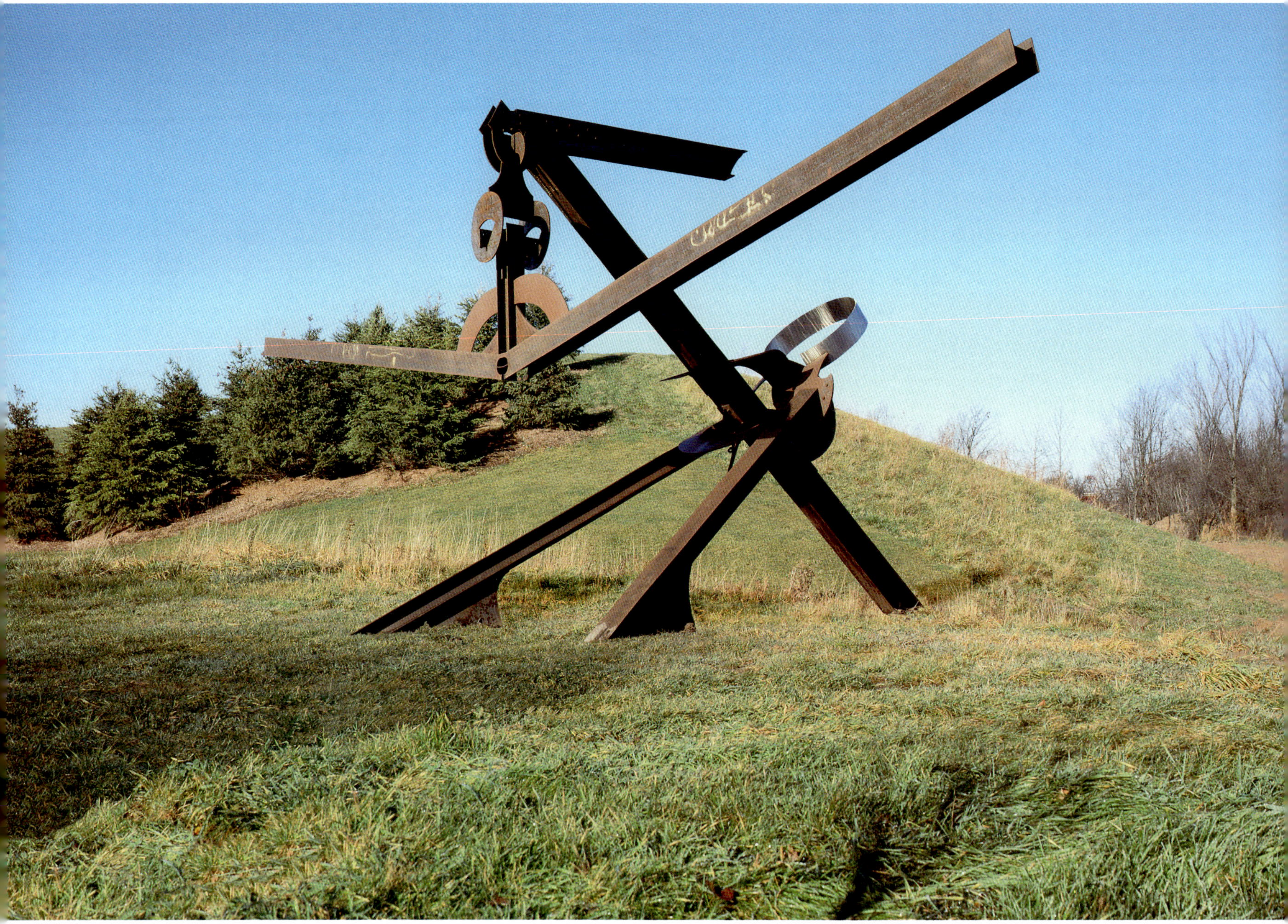

American, born 1933

MARK DI SUVERO :: SCARLATTI

1994–2000

Weathering (corten) and stainless steel, h. 25 feet, 4 inches (772.2 cm)

Gift of the Meijer Foundation, 2001.14

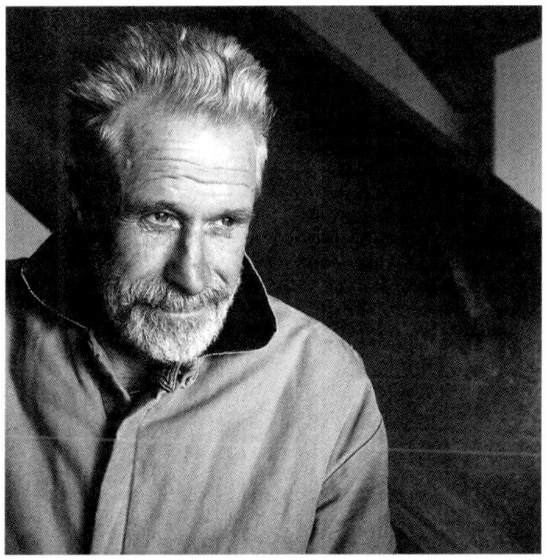

Mark di Suvero, 2001

FROM A POIGNANT intersection of several critical currents within the panorama of twentieth-century art, Mark di Suvero has emerged at the very forefront of contemporary American sculpture. Constructivism, Assemblage, and Kinetic Art, combined with unfailing instincts for composition and space, have enabled di Suvero to work on a heroic scale. Born Marco Polo di Suvero to Italian expatriates living in Shanghai, he grew up in San Francisco, where the family immigrated in 1941. The diary of his youth reads like a novella worthy of his namesake: travels by bicycle, motorcycle, and boat; work as housepainter and boatbuilder; personal discovery of philosophy, painting, and sculpture. He entered San Francisco City College to study fine arts and philosophy, then moved to the University of California, Santa Barbara, and finally, to the University of California, Berkeley, where he studied sculpture with Robert Thomas and Stephen Novak, respectively. In 1958, di Suvero moved to New York and was exposed to the work of the Abstract Expressionists and the related sculptures of David Smith. In the following year, di Suvero began to assemble discarded wood from destroyed buildings in open, spatial compositions. In 1960, he was crushed in an elevator accident and underwent painful rehabilitation. Still, he continued to work from his wheelchair and even began to use an electric arc welder. Initial acclaim dates from this period, with the critical success of his first one-person show.

The mid-1960s were decisive for di Suvero. His first open-air sculptures and initial site-specific commissions occurred at this time, and he added cranes, cherry-picker lifts, and torch welding to his construction

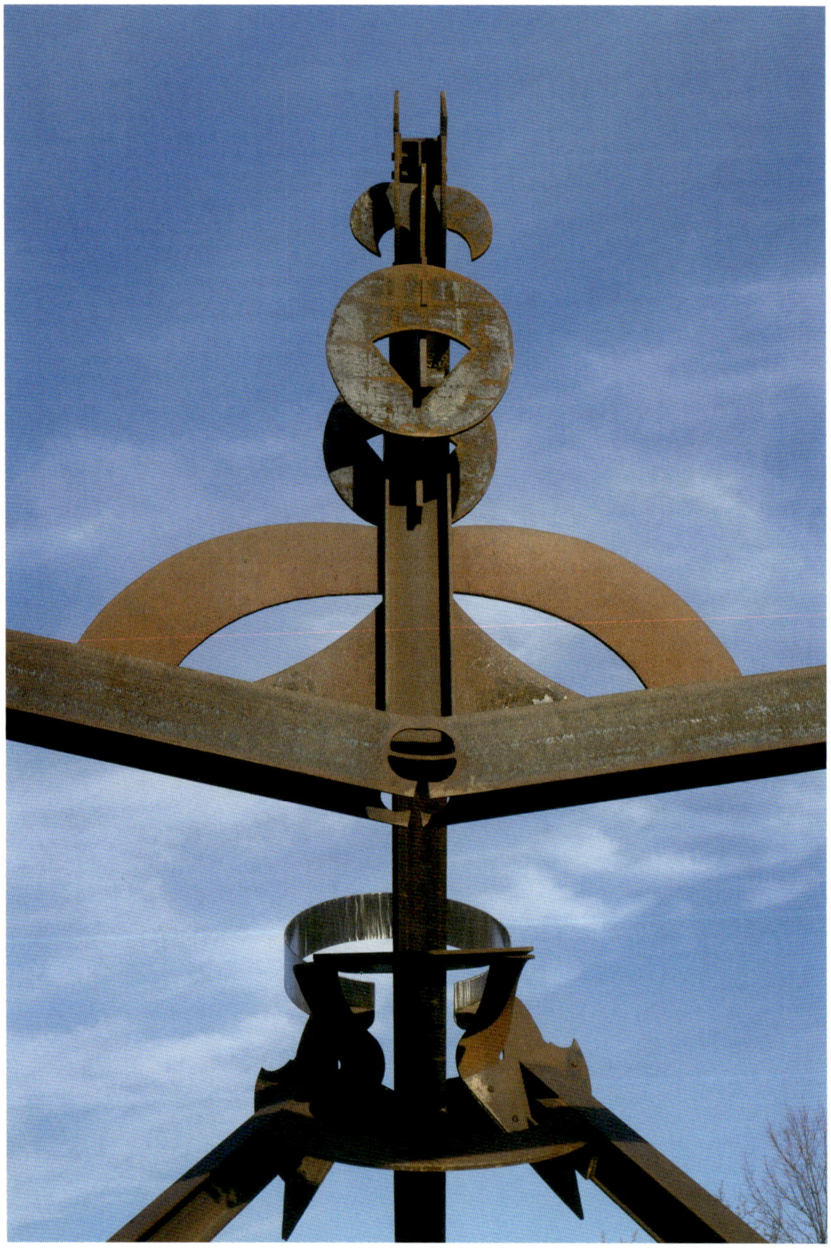

repertoire. Furthermore, he began to use industrial materials in his work. Scrap metal, I beams, steel cables, and wooden railroad ties were employed, but in keeping with the aesthetics of Abstract Expressionism, they were rarely transformed beyond recognition. Even when surfaces are painted or boldly manipulated, the raw energy of original materials remains intact and serves as a poignant witness to the milieu in which the sculpture was created. As heir to the Constructivist and Assemblage artists of the early twentieth century, di Suvero fashioned works in which the gestural and compositional elements are arguably as significant as any narrative, philosophical, or symbolic meaning. His sculptures are rarely static. Movement may be implied, but it is frequently actual. Kinetic elements suspended from cables or carefully engineered among interlocking parts are notable, as is the novel role of the viewer who, owing to the scale of a given work, becomes a participant in a dramatic swaying colossus. As early as the mid-1970s, di Suvero's reputation as a major force in contemporary sculpture was confirmed by a retrospective at the Whitney Museum of American Art in New York, and by his participation in the Venice Biennale. He was also honored as the first living artist to be afforded an exhibition at the famed Tuileries Garden adjacent to the Louvre in Paris. He continues to work fervently on a dramatic scale for institutions and sites across the globe.

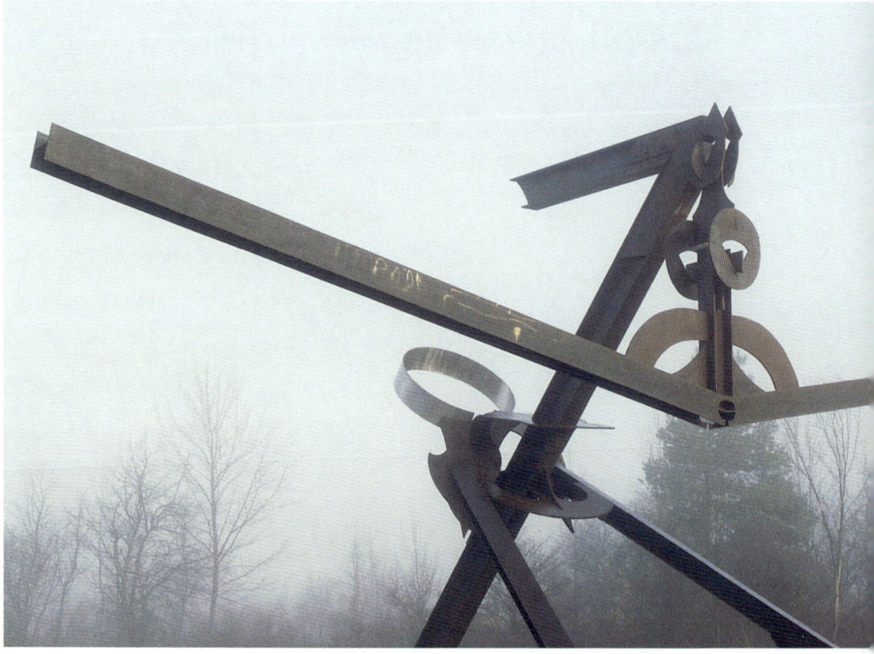

Scarlatti is a majestic steel work initiated in 1994 and completed in 2000. It is named for Domenico Scarlatti, the eighteenth-century Italian composer whose music di Suvero greatly admires. The sculpture's driving vertical force is a single central beam that surges upward at a dramatic angle. Near midpoint, two shorter beams converge, forming a momentous tripod that lays claim to the surrounding ground space. The architectonic sobriety of the tripod configuration is enlivened by a cluster of roughly circular elements surmounted by an open stainless steel ring. The shimmer of light across the silvery, metallic finish of stainless steel is in distinguished contrast with the more somber hues of the weathering (corten) steel elements. The central beam continues above this tense, lively intersection and climaxes with an abbreviated horizontal beam and a small circular element seen in profile. As a result of the relationship among all of the parts, di Suvero has established a masterful visual essay about balance, order, and space. The composition is not yet complete, however. Two I beams are connected as an elongated "V" and suspended beneath the tip of the central beam in two interlocking slips. Engineered to gently rock from side to side or to sway to and fro, the balletic gestures of these giant forms activate the entire sculpture. Di Suvero has rendered motion, time, and space as forces that are inextricable from the physical constructs of the work, and has likewise infused the whole with a three-dimensional tempo as spirited as a Scarlatti sonata.

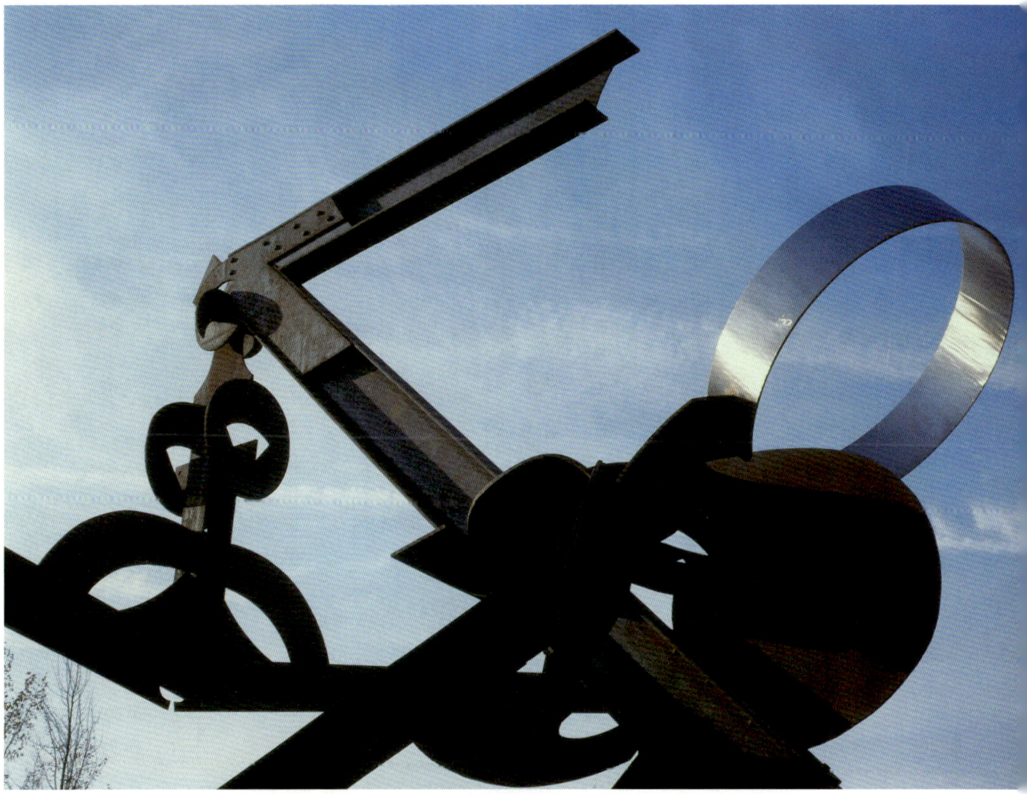

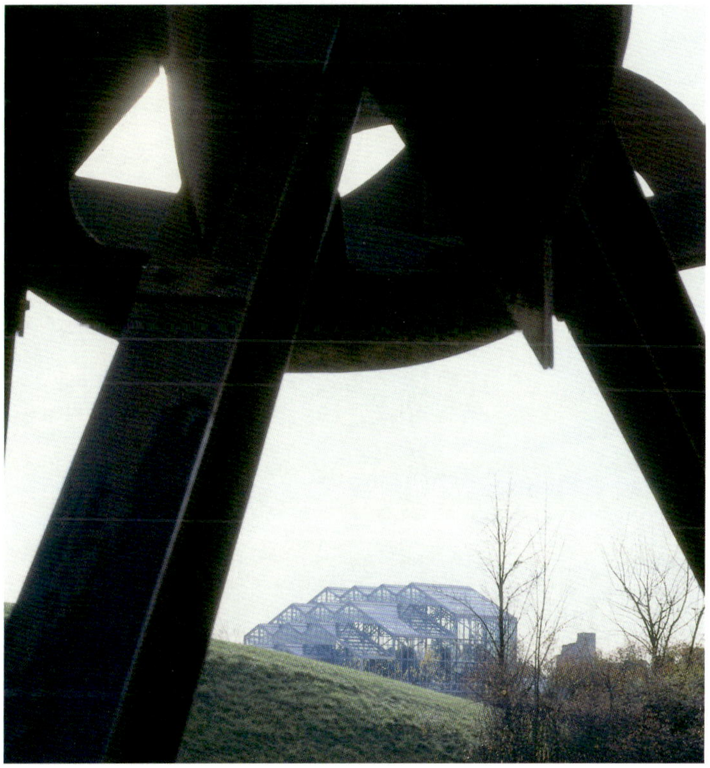

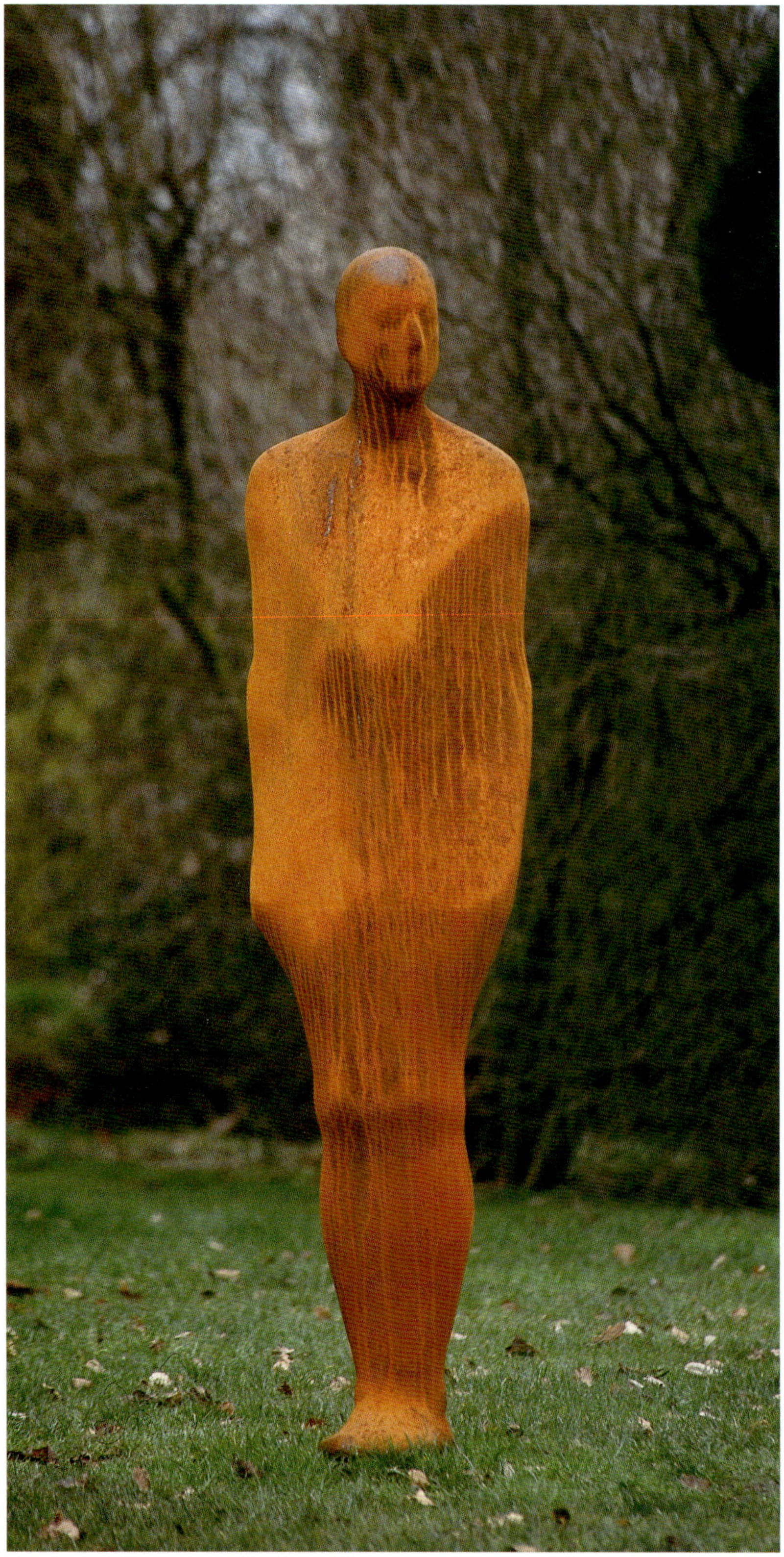

ANTONY GORMLEY :: ONE AND OTHER

2000

Iron, A/P (artist's proof for an edition of five), h. 73 inches (185.4 cm)

Gift of the Meijer Foundation, 2001.11

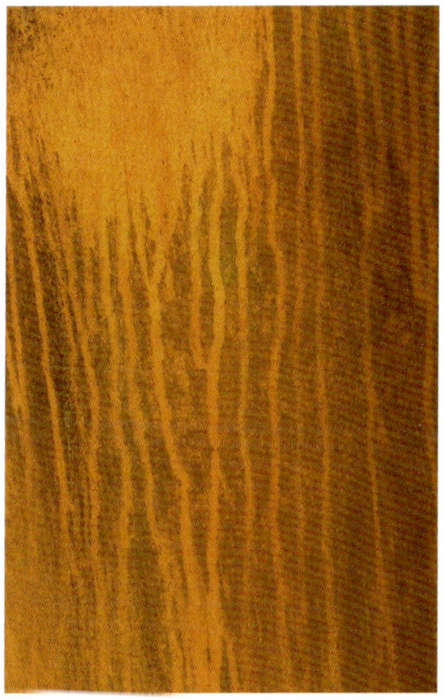

ANTONY GORMLEY is among a group of contemporary British sculptors, including Anish Kapoor and Bill Woodrow, who have gained widespread international acclaim in recent years. Born in London in 1950, Gormley studied archaeology, anthropology, and art history at Trinity College in Cambridge. Between 1971 and 1974, he traveled extensively through Turkey, Afghanistan, Pakistan, India, Iran, and Iraq, and studied Buddhist meditation at monasteries in India and Sri Lanka. In 1974, he attended London's Central School of Art, followed by two years at Goldsmiths School of Art, and finally, two years at the renowned Slade School of Fine Art. His sculpture was included in the Slade's post-graduate exhibition in 1979. Over the next few years, Gormley's work was featured in a solo exhibition in London, as part of group presentations at the 1983–1984 São Paulo Bienal and the 1986 Venice Biennale, and in exhibitions in Portugal, Mexico, Italy, and across England. His sculpture came to the attention of American audiences as part of a 1984 exhibition at the Museum of Modern Art in New York.

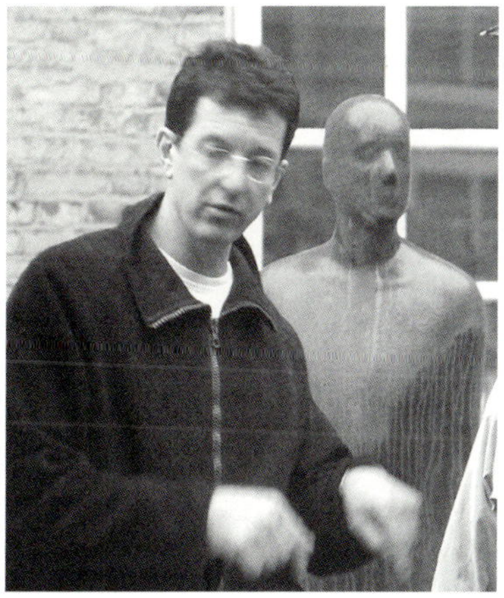

Antony Gormley at his London studio, March 2001

For Gormley, the course of the last fifteen years has been regularly punctuated by his inclusion in important exhibitions across Europe, Asia, and the United States, and highlighted by numerous significant commissions. In the early 1990s, his *Field,* an installation of thousands of hand-formed figurative statuettes, captivated the global art community. However, two recent commissions have undoubtedly secured the artist's position in the history of art. In 1998, Gormley unveiled *The Angel of the North,* a heroic winged figure of reinforced steel, sixty-five feet high, in Gateshead, England. Two years later, *Quantum Cloud,* a colossal ninety-eight-foot

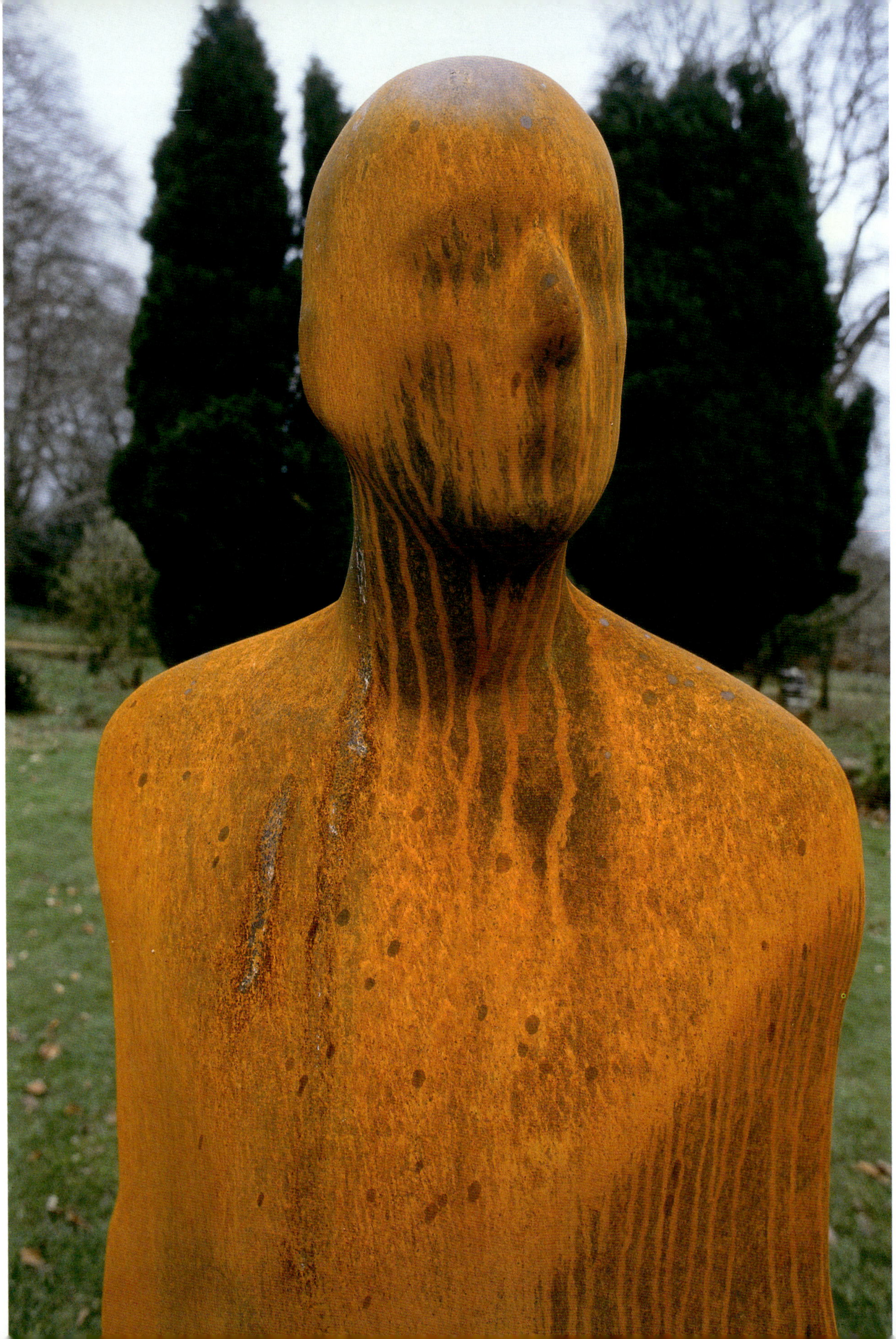

figure fabricated from an array of intersecting stainless steel bars, was installed at London's Millennium Dome.

In an era when abstract, nonfigurative modes of expression remain highly favored among sculptors, the human form has been the primary focus of Gormley's efforts. Indeed, he is often credited with influencing a growing interest in the human figure in contemporary sculpture. Frequently, the sculptor's own body serves as the basis for his work; his lead and iron figures often result from life casts. Likewise, enlarged and reduced versions of these casts have been employed in highly innovative ways. To date, the figures are characterized by poses of subtle, seemingly casual, activity or arrested motion through which ideas of profound introspection are clearly intended, even when the figures are exhibited in groups. The artist challenges audiences to reflect on states of being in these works, as well as a myriad of intellectual and emotional relationships between an object and a viewer.

One and Other is a life-size work in iron, cast from a mold of the artist's body. Specific detail is absent; the figure is granted anonymity, but spared androgyny. Anatomical contours have been distilled to form a sensuous vertical landscape. The arms, held close at the sides, meld with the torso, while the legs nearly merge as a single unit. Only the face, turned gently to the left, breaks the decidedly frontal orientation of the figure. In pose and attitude, echoes of ancient Greek and pre-Greek sculpture can be discerned. The form, with its solemn stance and chrysalis-like containment, offers itself as a meditative icon. Simultaneously, it exudes an earthy sensuality through the cast-iron medium. Although the choice of iron is in keeping with Gormley's repertoire, the material has not been widely used in contemporary art. The surface color, a natural patina developed through the process of oxidation, is at once jarring and at ease against the backdrop of nature's changing palette. Stains from the flow of precipitation over the oxidized surface further enhance its highly unique color and texture. A recent creation, *One and Other* can be viewed as an heir to both Western and Near Eastern traditions. It may also serve as a harbinger of directions in art yet to be encountered.

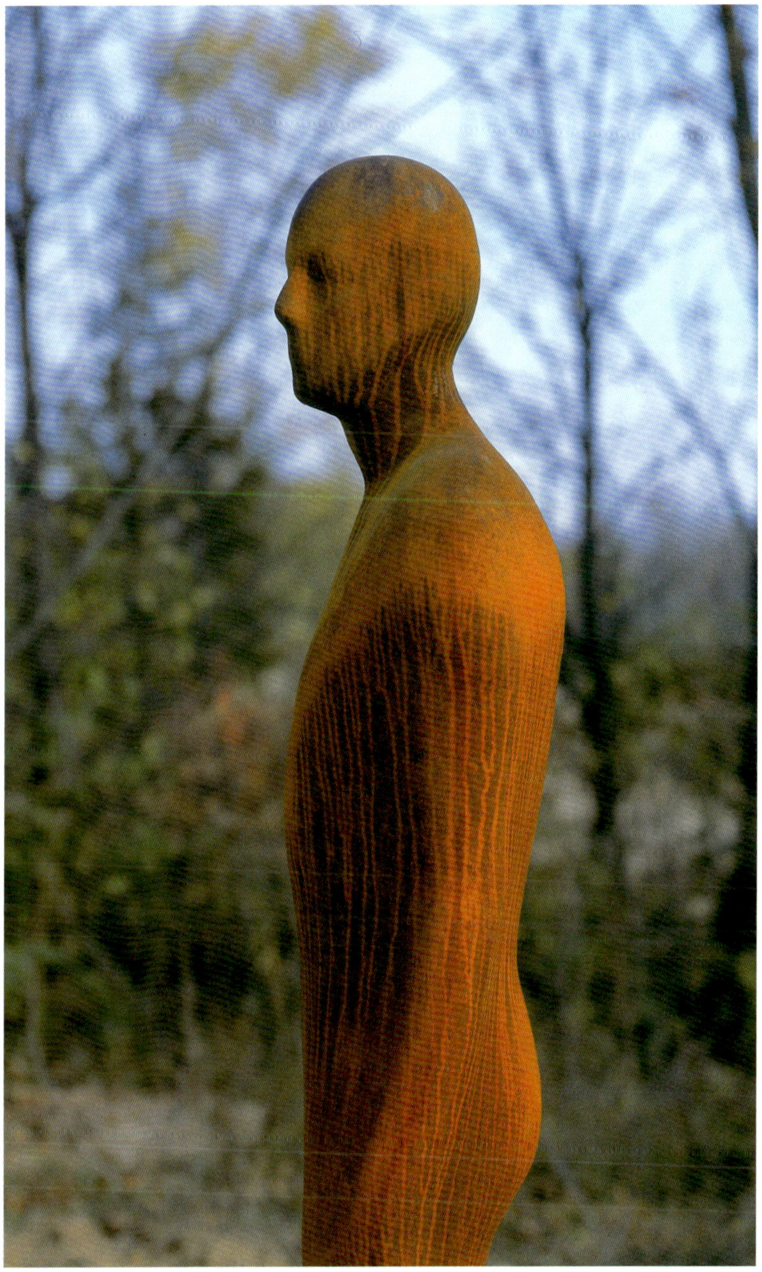

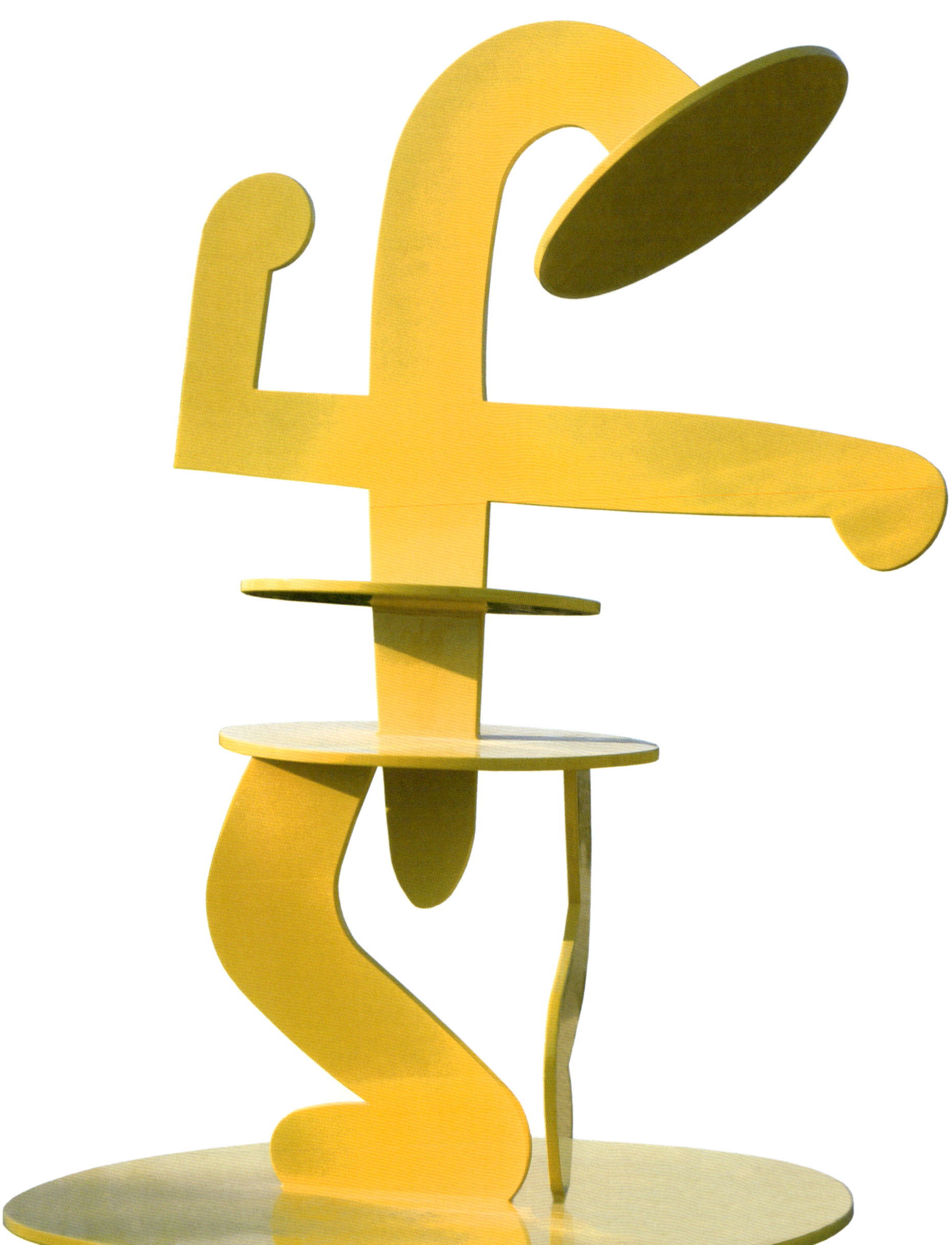

American, 1958–1990

KEITH HARING :: JULIA

1987

Painted aluminum, 4/5 (fourth in an edition of five), h. 96 inches (243.8 cm)

Gift of the Meijer Foundation, 2001.02

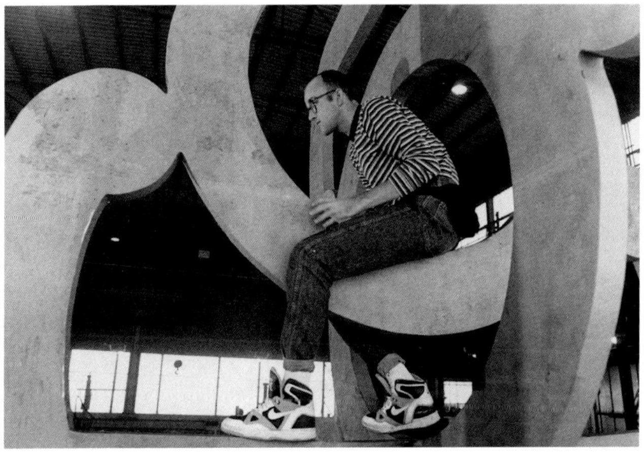

Keith Haring at Düsseldorf foundry, 1987

DURING THE COURSE of his brief career, Keith Haring quickly became one of the most significant and prolific American artists of the last quarter of the twentieth century. Haring was born in rural Pennsylvania in 1958, and trained in Pittsburgh before attending the School of the Visual Arts in New York. From the graffiti art and break dancing of the streets to the panorama of Western and non-Western art he experienced in numerous museums, the cultural and aesthetic dynamics of the city were a constant source of inspiration to the artist. While still an undergraduate, Haring secured the opportunity for a one-person show in 1979. He painted all the gallery surfaces, astounding faculty and fellow students with the energy and boldness of his murals. Shortly thereafter, he turned to the walls of the city subway system, where his stylized chalk drawings attracted the attention of millions. Throughout the 1980s, Haring's public art became a vibrant, inextricable thread in the fabric of New York's visual culture.

Haring's rise to international fame during the late 1970s and 1980s is frequently described as meteoric. Graffiti art, chalk drawings, paintings, prints, and electronic media were essential to his repertoire. His *Radiant Child* Spectacolor billboard in Times Square in 1982 heralded his emergence as one of the leading visionaries in the art world and was followed by numerous exhibitions and commissions across the United States, Europe, and Japan. References to children's art, Egyptian hieroglyphics,

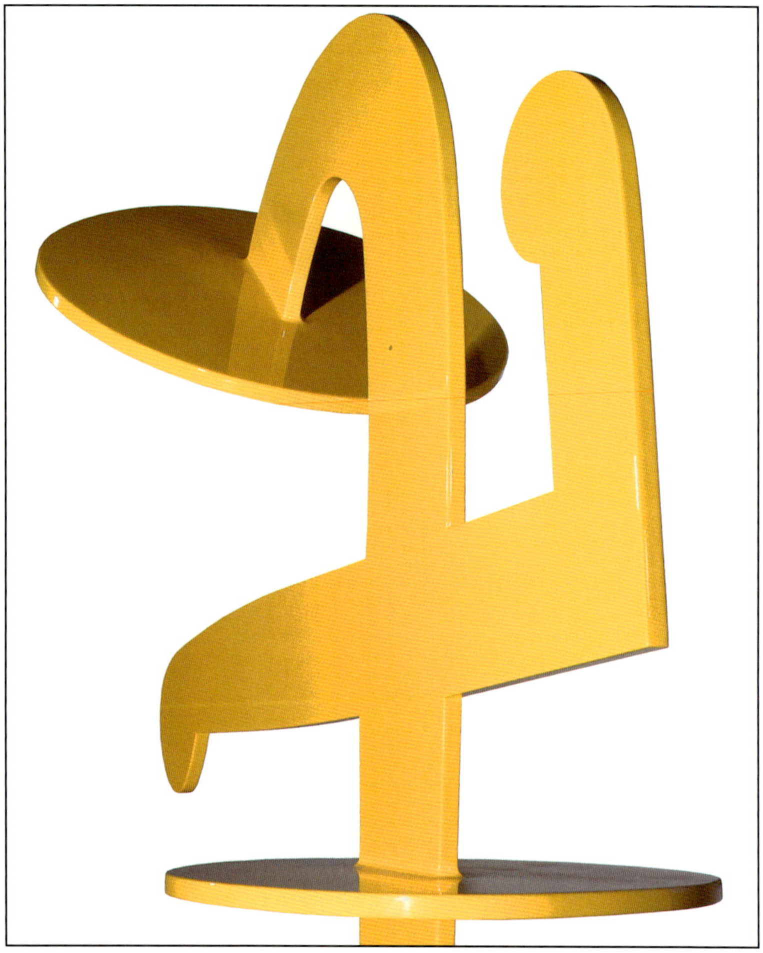

pre-Columbian murals, cartoon art, and American Pop Art found in Haring's works made a wide array of viewers comfortable with his imagery, even when the subject matter might be biting or controversial. Although the focus of Haring's work was largely joyous and life affirming, difficult subjects faced by American society, such as AIDS and drug abuse, did not escape his attention.

Whereas in previous years he frequently covered the surfaces of existing three-dimensional forms with his imagery, in 1985, Haring began to fabricate metal sculpture. Regardless of medium or scale, the artist's style, articulated in simple, strong, and animated forms, remained constant, as did the ability of his work to communicate to an astoundingly diverse audience of every age and origin. As a sculptor, Haring was indebted to Alexander Calder and Claes Oldenburg. In Calder, he was attracted to the bold, abstract compositions as well as the use of brightly painted metal; in Oldenburg, he deeply appreciated the lighthearted, monumental realism and social commentaries of Pop Art. Haring's sculptures are at once formal and lyrical; they merge the straightforward use of vertical and horizontal elements with the curvilinear contours of the individual metal plates he employed. Irony is also a critical factor. The bright colors and energetic poses of the figurative compositions carefully disguise the reality that each large-scale work is made up of literally thousands of pounds of metal.

Julia is one of a series of monumental sculptures that Haring executed during his final years. The inspiration for the work was Julia Gruen, the artist's longtime friend and now the executive director of the Keith Haring Foundation. Except for the self-portraits, *Julia* is the only Haring sculpture specifically linked to an individual. However, his sculpture is ultimately a visual essay about balance and movement through the relationship of forms in space. For an artist accustomed to creating two-dimensional work, Haring made the transition to sculpture through a familiar vocabulary of broad planes and largely geometric shapes. The artist's models, or maquettes, were critical to realizing his ideas for three-dimensional imagery. The intersections of horizontal and vertical elements were carefully planned, and enlivened with occasional diagonals. Although Haring's sculpture is figurative, an examination of works like *Julia* from all sides reveals challenging points of view that successfully venture beyond the representational toward abstraction.

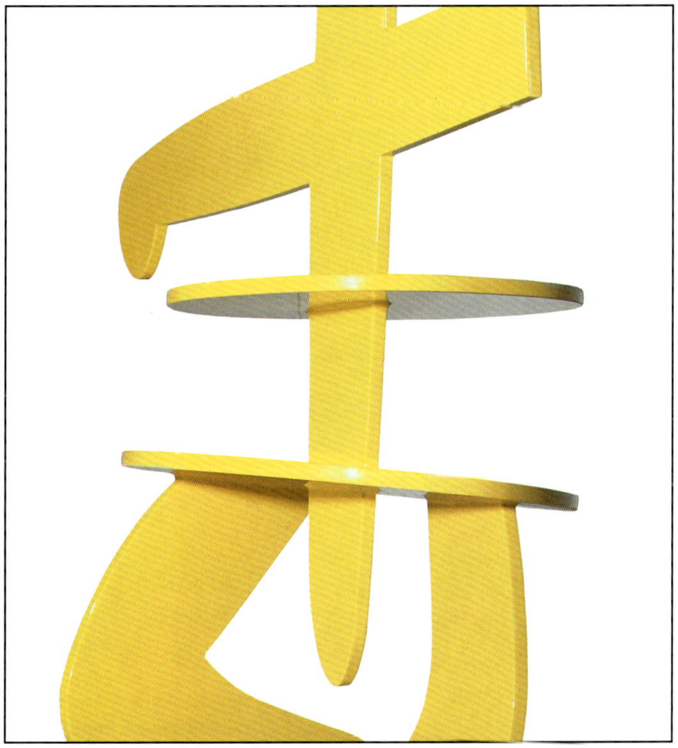

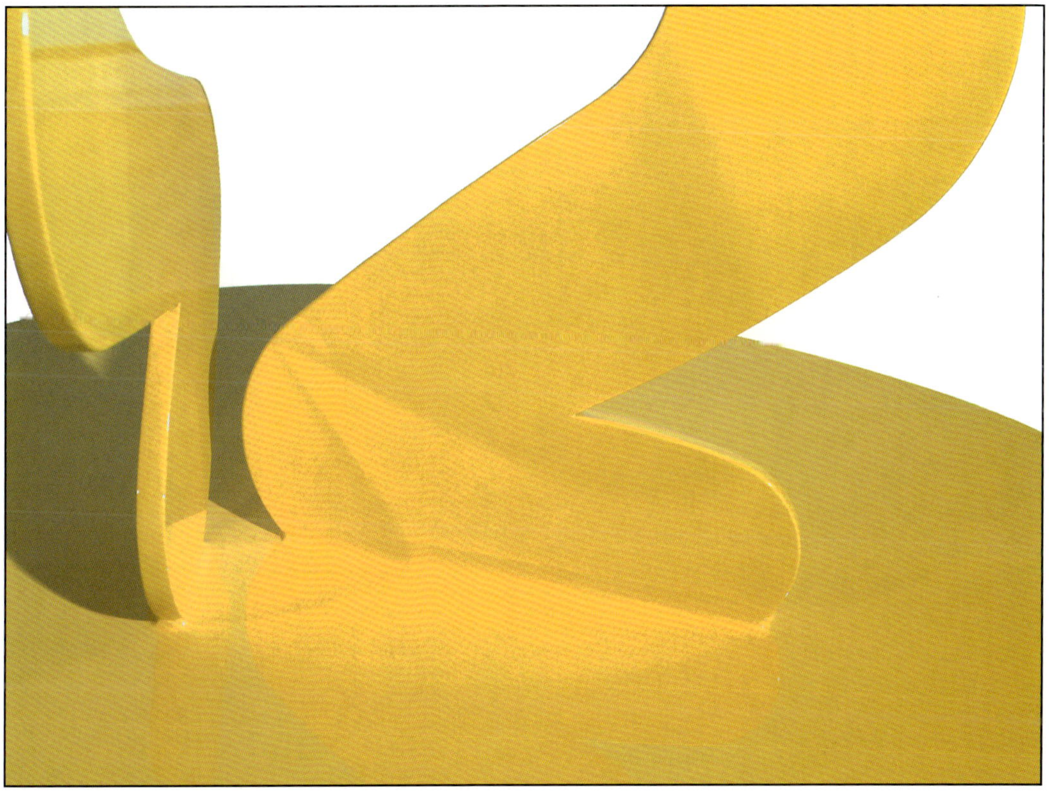

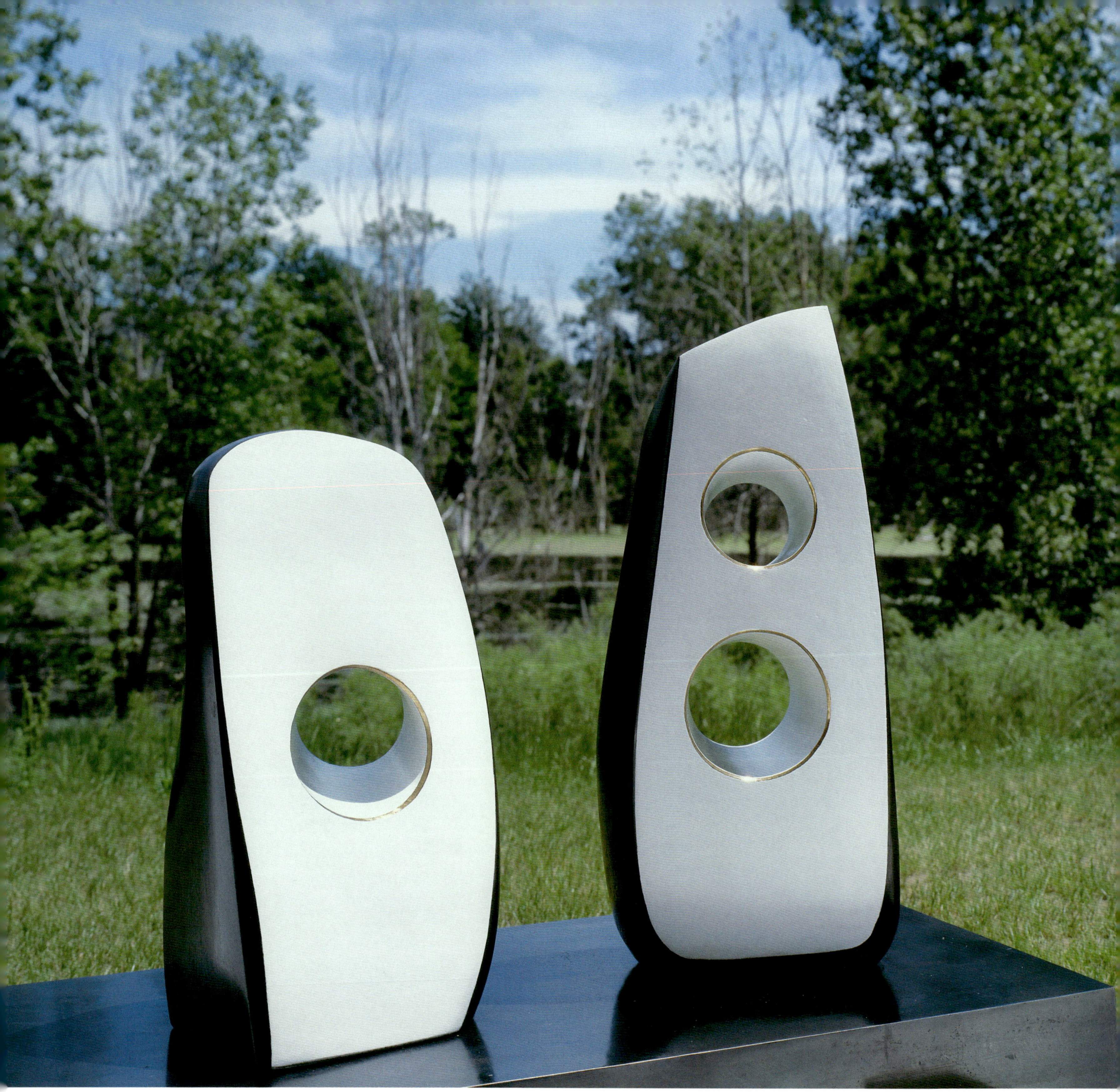

BARBARA HEPWORTH :: SUMMER DANCE

1971

Bronze, 1/6 (first in an edition of six), h. 35½ inches (90.2 cm)

Gift of the Meijer Foundation, 2001.13

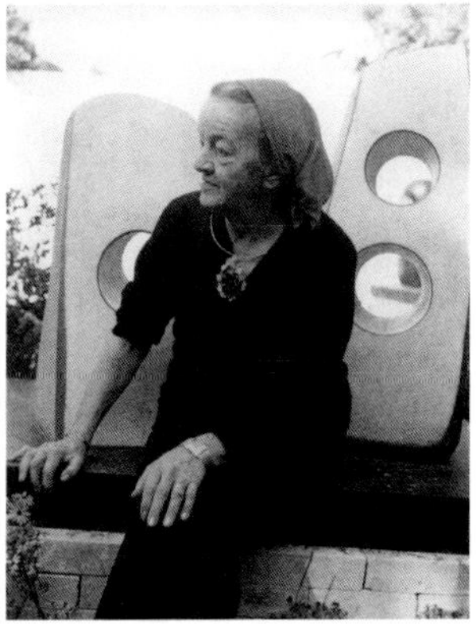

Barbara Hepworth with *Summer Dance*, early 1970s

FROM ITS ORIGINS until its untimely end, the career of sculptor Barbara Hepworth perfectly parallels the intense developments of mid-twentieth-century modernism to which she was an important contributor. Hepworth was born in Yorkshire, England, in 1903, and died in a tragic fire in her St. Ives studio in 1975. For five decades, her work was at the forefront of the British avant-garde, gaining international recognition in the postwar period. She attended the Leeds School of Art, where Henry Moore was also a student. Both received scholarships to the Royal College of Art in London, and Hepworth took a diploma there in 1923. However, the seminal experience of her training was arguably the opportunity to study drawing, painting, and marble carving in Italy the following year.

In 1926, she returned London with her first husband, the sculptor John Skeaping. Hepworth exhibited throughout the late 1920s and 1930s. Simultaneously, she found herself immersed in British modernism and had increasing contact with continental masters including Pablo Picasso, Georges Braque, Constantin Brancusi, Wassily Kandinsky, and Piet Mondrian. In 1935, one of her sculptures was acquired by the Museum of Modern Art in New York. Two years later, she exhibited alongside Moore, Alexander Calder, Naum Gabo, and Ben Nicholson, her second husband. Hepworth's imagery, almost exclusively carved and moderate in

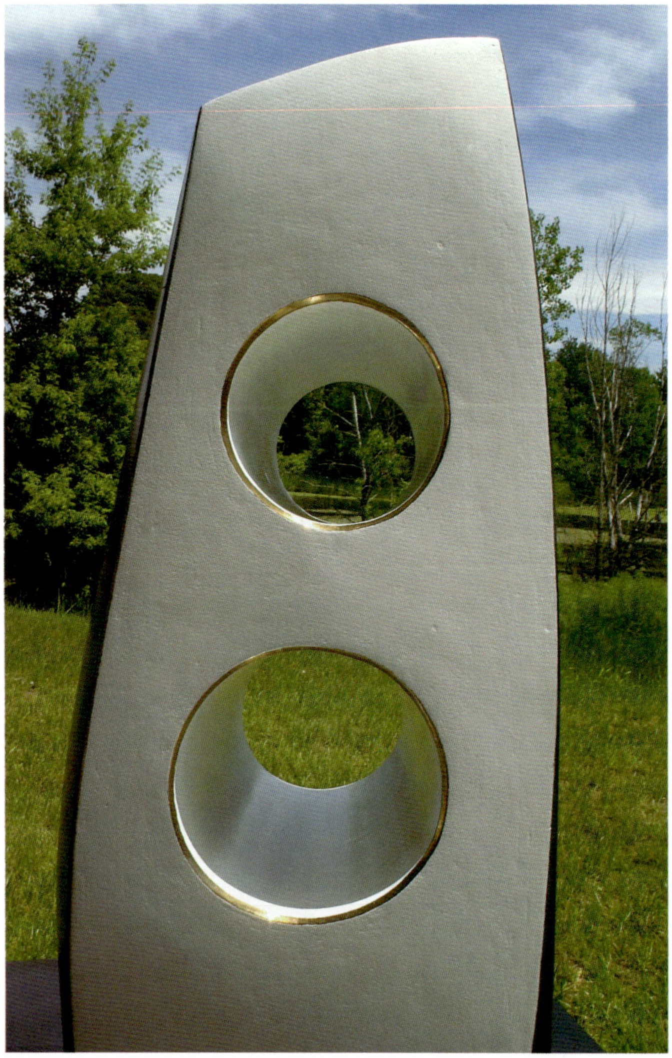

scale, had by this time moved from the figurative into abstraction. Just prior to the outbreak of World War II, she moved to St. Ives, opened a nursery school for her children and others, and worked on drawings and small plasters at night. Immediately following the war, she began to exhibit again, and a monograph of her work was published. In 1950, she represented England at the Venice Biennale, to great acclaim.

As her reputation grew throughout the 1950s, Hepworth was encouraged to experiment on a monumental scale. By 1956, she began to work in bronze, while continuing to carve in stone and wood. Monolithic upright forms, frequently pierced, became characteristic of her repertoire. Most significant among these was undoubtedly Hepworth's massive bronze of 1964 for the plaza of the United Nations Secretariat in New York. In the wake of its unveiling and widespread appeal, she worked tirelessly throughout the 1960s and early 1970s on ensuing commissions and projects.

Summer Dance is a lyrical work of 1971. Two upright forms that faintly echo the proportions of a human figure are featured on a single base. Although moderate in scale, the shapes suggest the monumentality of Hepworth's largest bronzes. The mass of each form has been characteristically opened up, alleviating the density of a solid object with controlled passages for light, shadow, and air. The face of each has been painted a matte white to accentuate the flatness of the plane, while the more voluptuous sides and backs are patinated a deep, forest green. Associations between the brilliance of summer sunlight that defies weight and the weightiness of corresponding shadows, or between the skin of ripened fruit and the exposed fleshy interior, abound and are in keeping with the artist's reverence for the natural world. Elegant contours are formed between the white and green surfaces by linear passages of highly polished bronze. More than lines of demarcation, these glistening edges enhance the organic quality of the forms and encourage the illusion of movement anticipated in a living object. Finally, the independence of the two elements that comprise *Summer Dance* cannot be challenged, but Hepworth intends a partnership between the two. Scale, form, color, and position create unity. Ultimately, *Summer Dance* calls to mind the timeless rhythm of relationships between living things.

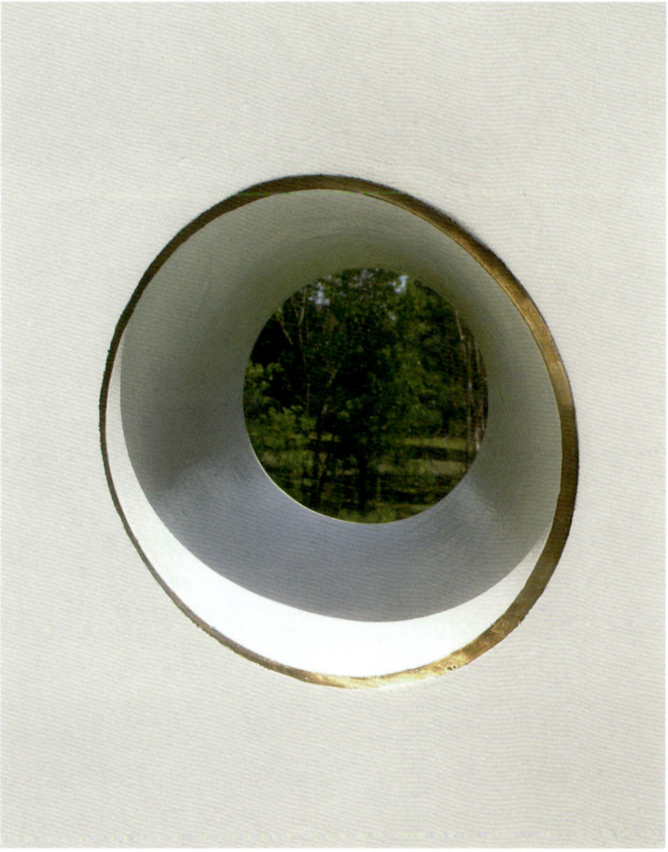

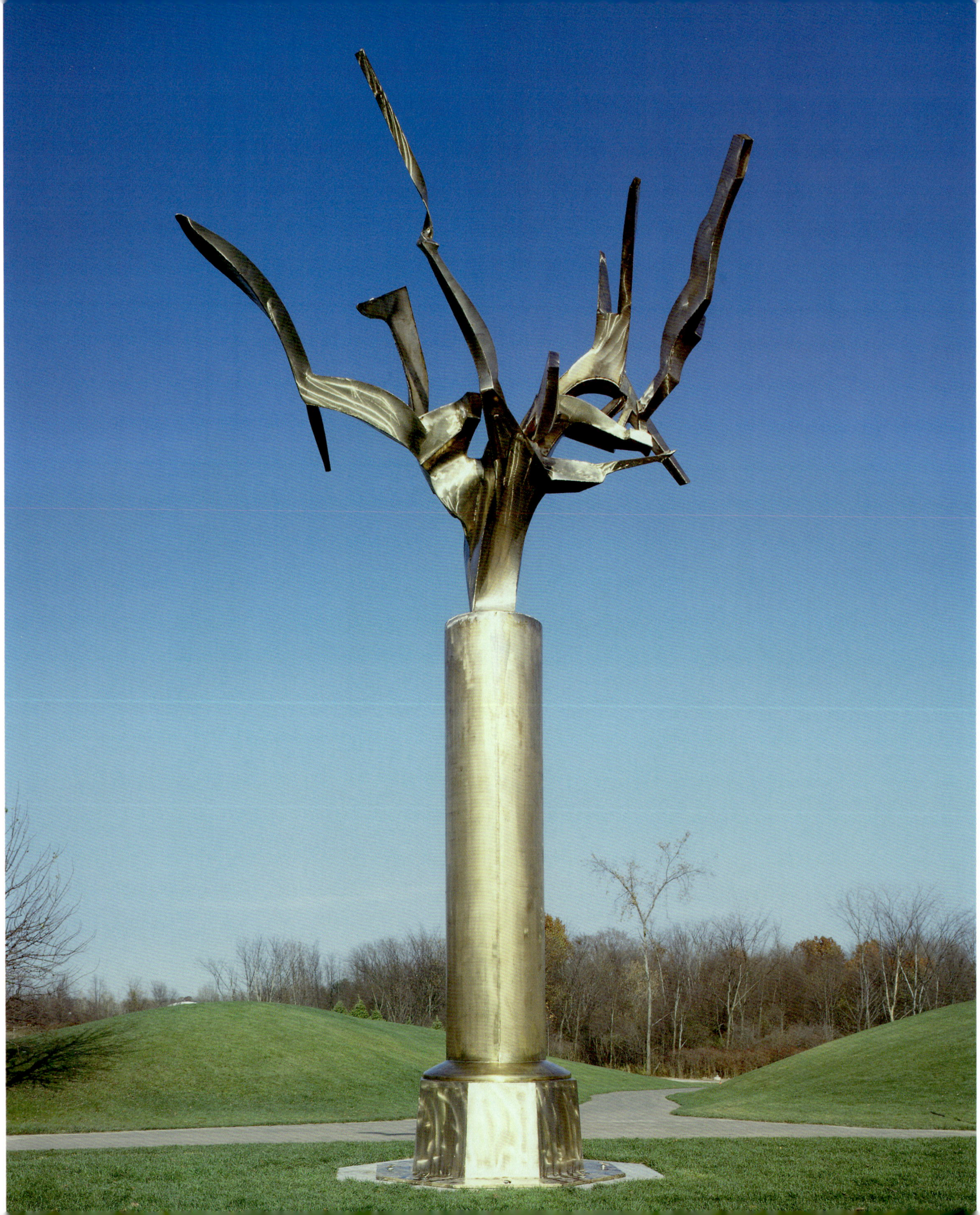

RICHARD HUNT :: COLUMN OF THE FREE SPIRIT

2000

Bronze, unique, h. 25 feet (762 cm)

Gift of the Meijer Foundation, 2000.10

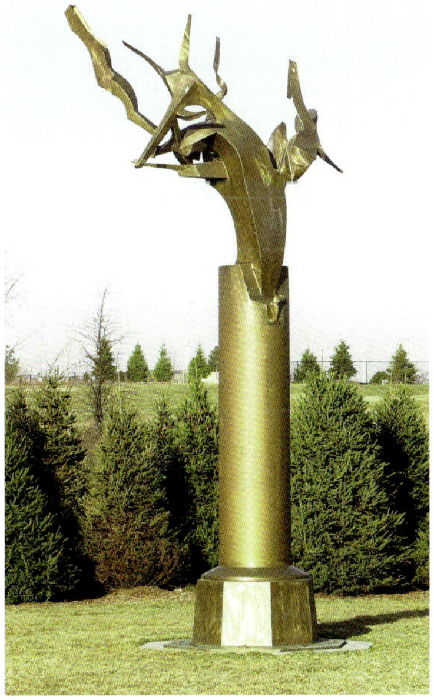

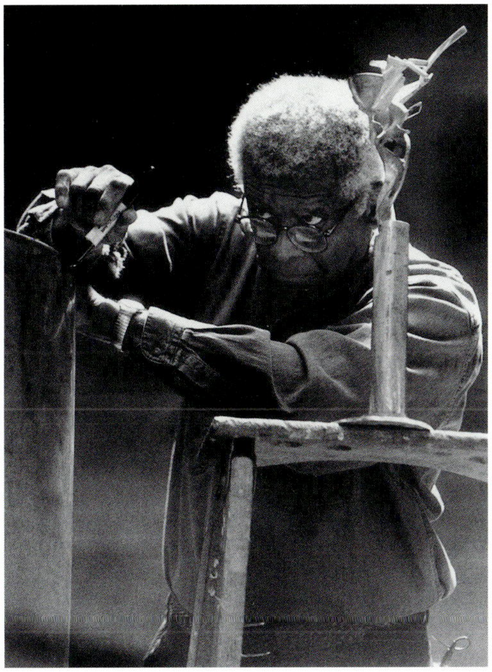

Richard Hunt at work on *Column of the Free Spirit* in his Chicago studio, 2000

RICHARD HUNT was born in Chicago in 1935. As a youth, he attended Saturday classes at the Art Institute of Chicago, but his interests then, as now, were not limited to art. Science, literature, history, and music have remained important to him. He earned a degree in art education from the School of the Art Institute in 1957. Following his education, he toured Europe to study both the great monuments of public sculpture and renowned museum collections. He then served in the U.S. Army for two years before returning to sculpture on a full-time basis in 1960. He has remained singularly committed to his craft for more than forty years. In 1971, Hunt was the subject of a retrospective at the Museum of Modern Art in New York that introduced his work to a national audience. Since that time, his work has been eagerly acquired by many of the leading public institutions across the United States, and he has completed more than 100 site-specific commissioned works.

Discussing his formative experiences and present endeavors, Hunt speaks reverently about a variety of important influences that, in varying degrees, are discernible forces behind his art. He mentions Cubism and the related movements within its orbit, Surrealism and Abstract Expressionism, with great frequency. The impact of Cubism came through Hunt's examination of the sculptural pursuits of Pablo Picasso and the direct-metal works of Julio González. The influence of Surrealism has been largely intellectual, as Hunt recognized the power of the subconscious and was

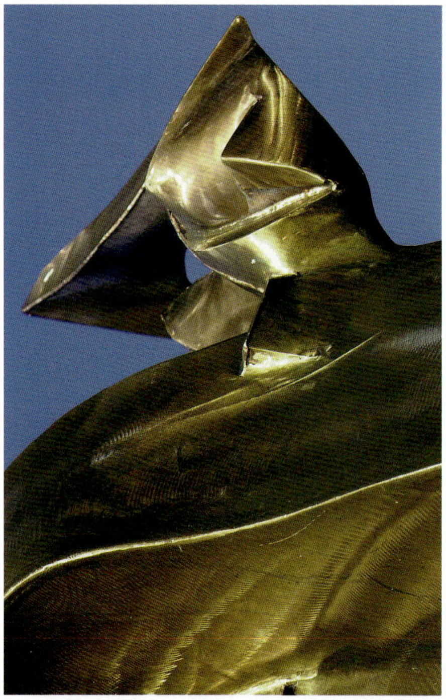

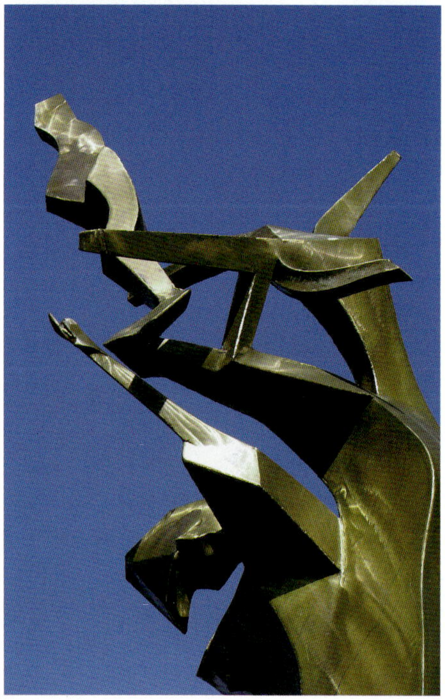

willing to let it be given form. Abstract Expressionism has affected Hunt through the significance of gesture (or gesturalism) and a desire to reveal the artistic process and the characteristics of a given medium. Simply put, Hunt intentionally records what he has done and with what materials. It is difficult to find a singular movement within the confines of contemporary art in which to place the sculpture of Richard Hunt, although he has light-heartedly referred to himself as a "surreal expressionist."

Column of the Free Spirit is the first large-scale work commissioned for the Sculpture Park. Discussions with the sculptor regarding a monumental piece began in 1998. A group of three maquettes was presented the following year. The version selected and the resulting full-scale sculpture are part of a series of celebratory columns that Hunt has pursued over the course of the last decade. Works from this series recall numerous urban monuments across the history of Western art, from Egyptian obelisks and Roman triumphal columns forward. In addition, the influence of non-Western, primarily African, art is felt in the forms and meaning of any number of staffs and tools from the sculptor's extensive personal collection.

In essence, there are three distinct components to the *Column of the Free Spirit* that, combined, create a work measuring twenty-five feet in height: a large octagonal base with gently sloping panels, a columnar shaft, and a cluster of numerous individually fabricated elements. The substantial base and shaft provide the vertical power for the work as it extends upward. As the eye rises, a metamorphosis occurs. Gestural bands branch out from the sleek industrial volume of the column. The column's architectonic restraint is brought to life with the energetic expanse. The undulating projections, with their jagged and burnished contours, bear witness to an additive welding process. Freedom seems to have perched atop a dedicated, long-serving sentinel. Such juxtapositions are critical elements within Hunt's oeuvre and help define his hybrid imagery. Although a singular interpretation of the work was never intended, ideas that derive from burning flames, wings in flight, and the branches of trees are most frequently encountered in the sculptor's own discussions of the piece.

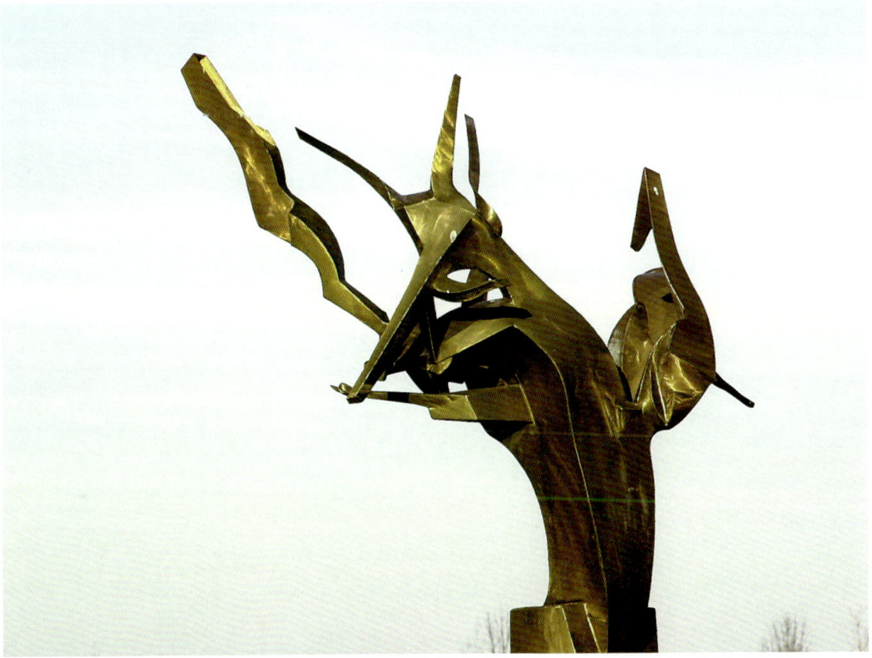
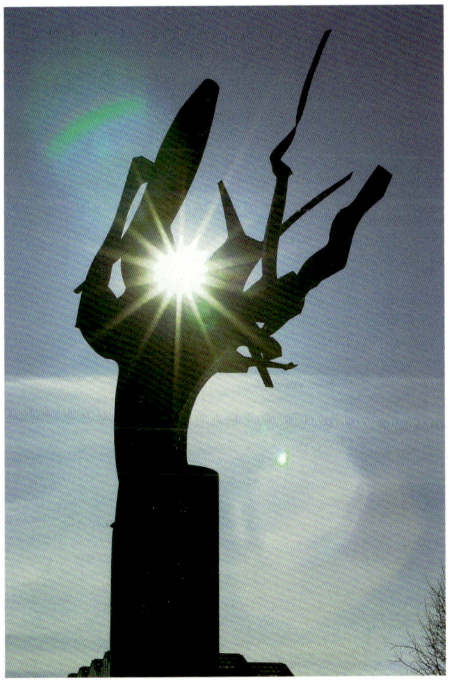
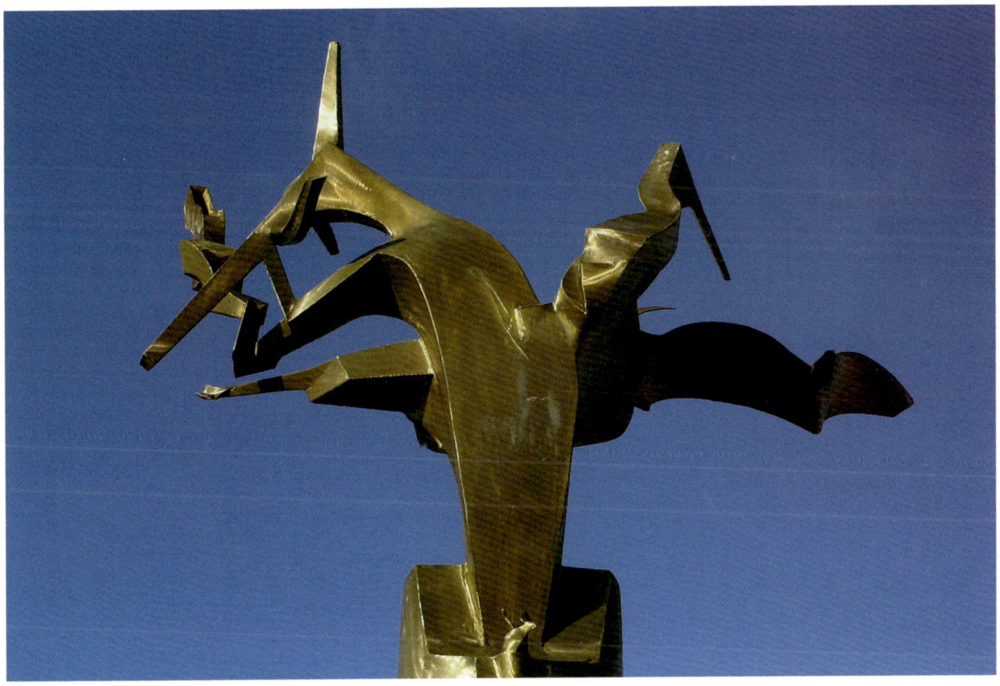

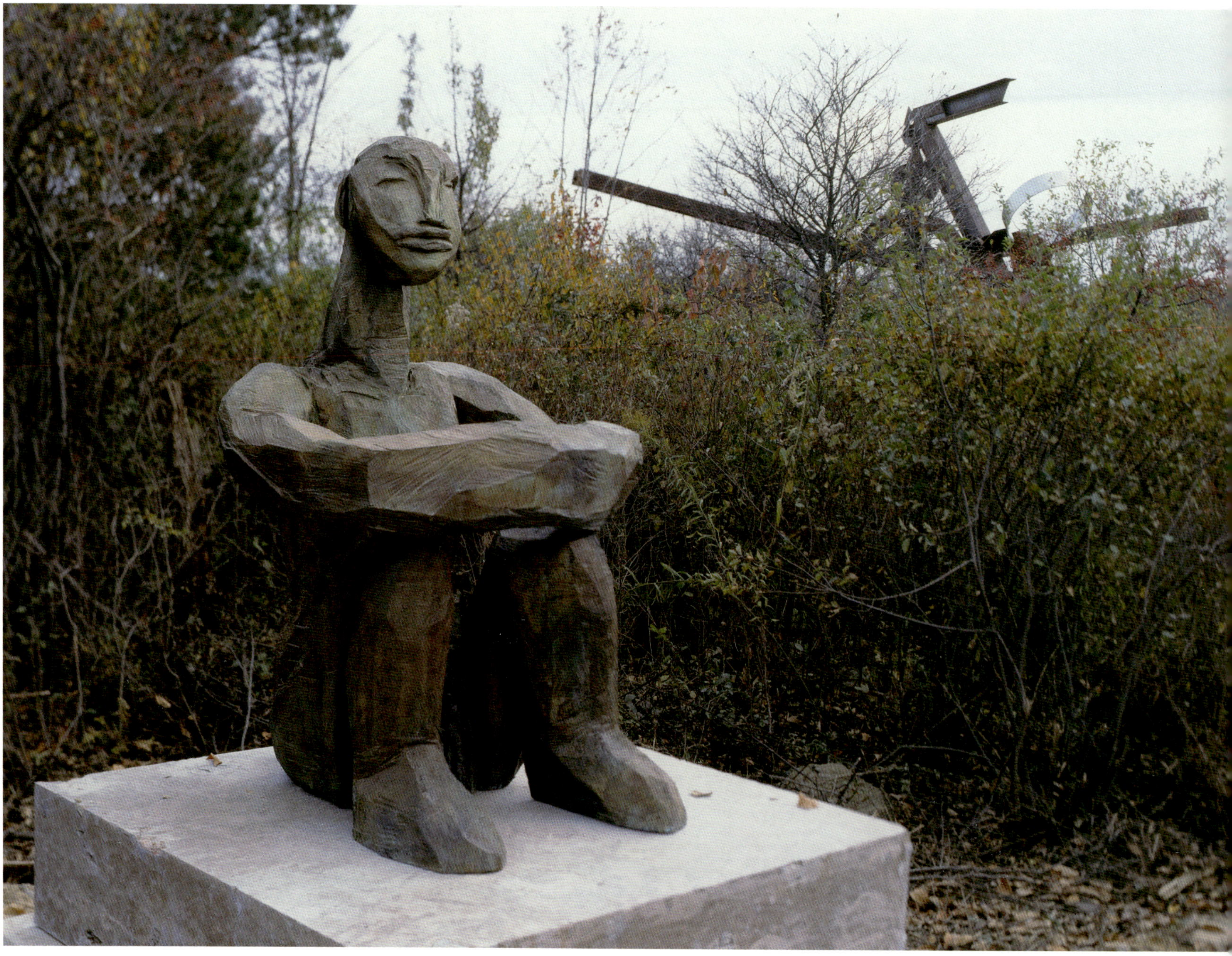

German, born 1954

DIETRICH KLINGE :: GROSSER TREFREE

2000

Bronze, 4/6 (fourth in an edition of six), h. 56½ inches (143.5 cm)

Gift of the Meijer Foundation, 2001.10

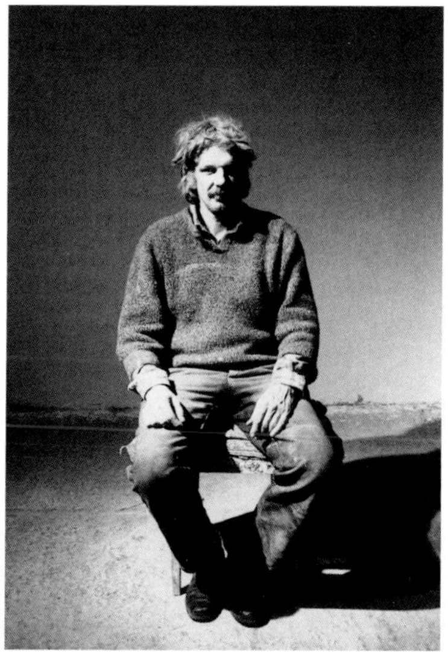

The artist, Dietrich Klinge, in his studio

THE HUMAN FIGURE has been central to the development of European art since the dawn of the classical world. Even when abstract and nonrepresentational art emerged as a focal point for many twentieth-century artists, innumerable European painters and sculptors held fast to the tradition of representing the human form. Dietrich Klinge, born in 1954 and trained in Germany, is among a group of influential young European sculptors whose figurative works have captured recent critical acclaim. The artist attended Stuttgart's renowned art school, the Staatlichen Akademie der Bildenden Künste, and received traditional training in drawing and printmaking from 1973 to 1980, and in sculpture from 1980 to 1984. After completing his education, Klinge established a studio in Stuttgart and, more recently, one near Weidelbach. In 1990, he had his first major exhibition in Berlin. Immediately following, his work was shown throughout Germany and was included in the prestigious Cologne and Hamburg Art Expos. His first international exposure came at the Basel International Art Fair in Switzerland in 1992, and his work began to be acquired by important private and public collections in Europe. Although Klinge is best known in Europe, his reputation has grown significantly. In 2000, the first major exhibition of his work outside Germany and Switzerland was held in Spain.

Klinge works primarily as a sculptor, although he continues to make drawings, prints, and photographs. Regardless of medium, the artist has pursued numerous interpretations of the human figure. In sculpture, Klinge frequently initiates an idea in wood using large woodland branches and rough-hewn timber. Integral to the sculptor's design are the natural graining and knots of the wood and the irregular striations and planes that carving brings forth. Following the carving process, the perishable wood object is given greater permanence in bronze. Molds are made of the original form, and it is then carefully cast. Once the metal has been chased and cleaned, the surface is given a rich, variegated patina of ochers, browns, and greens to suggest, rather than imitate, natural distressed wood. Drawing is critical to Klinge's efforts, and numerous studies are often made in anticipation of his carving. In both drawing and sculpture, the artist's concern for bold forms, textured surfaces, and contrasting roles of light and dark recall the traditions of German Expressionism of the early twentieth century. These concerns are also kindred to certain non-Western, especially African, carving traditions.

The large seated male figure, *Grosser Trefree,* is just over life size. It is among the first of Klinge's works to enter an American public collection. There is no exact English translation for the title; it is an anagram: *grosser,* meaning grand or great, is paired with *trefree,* itself a combination of the words *tre,* or three, and *free,* or liberty, creating the namesake of this character—a type of grand arbor deity. Like other examples of Klinge's figures, this work calls to mind Germanic legends of woodland spirits and tree gods. The figure is seated in a frontal position, its back decidedly erect, and its knees drawn up and held with arms joined in an unbroken circle. The neck is elongated, elevating the head well above the concentrated mass of the body. The figure, with eyes closed, may at first appear to be poised in some primeval moment or trance, but it is actually planted firmly on the ground in deep contemplation. Its overall symmetrical composition and pensive aura is in balanced contrast to its distorted proportions, raw texture, and varied patina. The stylized elements and compelling irregularities may be unique to Klinge, but the authoritative, even ritual, pose calls to mind an array of seated, stately, and deified personalities from throughout the history of art. *Grosser Trefree* ultimately emerges as a significant, contemporary representative within the historical traditions of figurative sculpture.

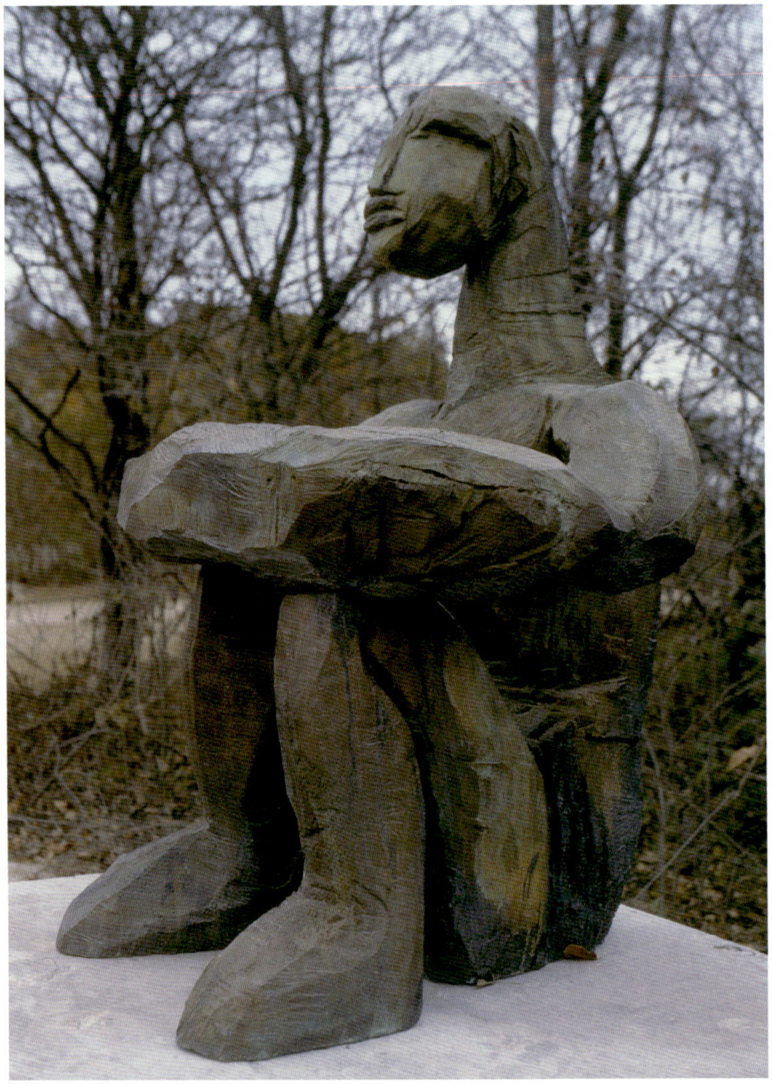

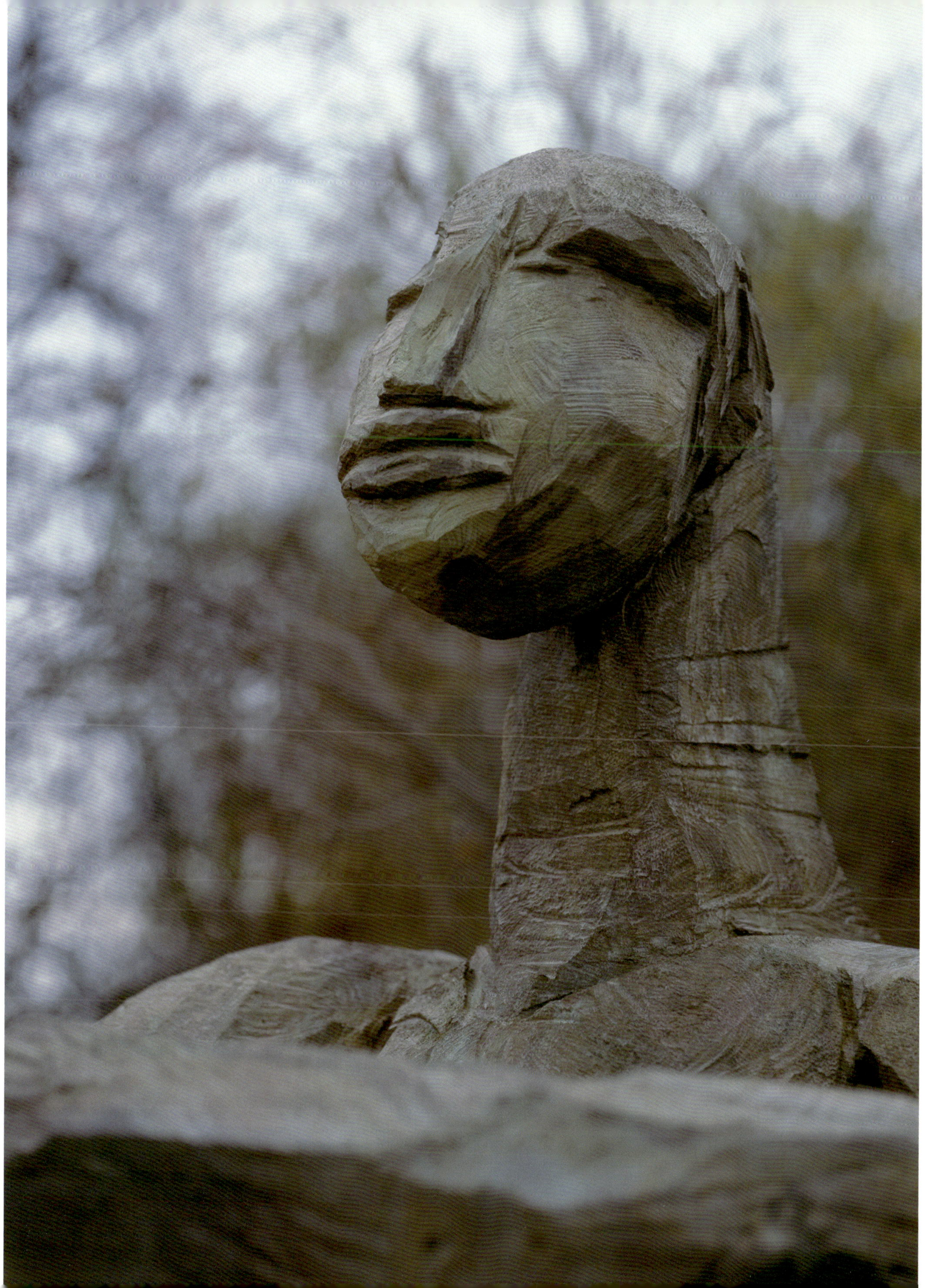

American (born Russia), 1912–1999

ALEXANDER LIBERMAN :: ARIA

1979–1983
Painted steel, h. 42 feet (1280.2 cm)
Gift of the Meijer Foundation, 1999.03

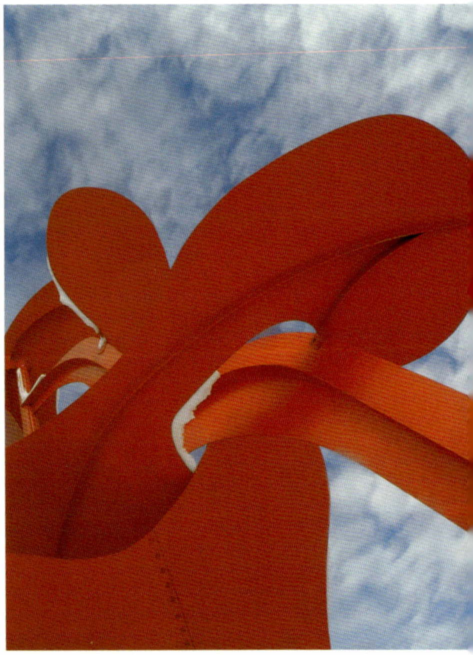

AT THE TIME of his death in 1999, Alexander Liberman was recognized as one of the twentieth century's most influential figures in American and European fashion and culture. He was equally regarded among the most notable individuals to emerge on the American art scene since 1950. For the enormity of his success in the United States, Liberman's origins were decidedly international. He was born in 1912 in Kiev, Russia, where his father worked for the imperial family. He left Russia in 1921 to attend school in England, and in 1924 moved to France. There he studied philosophy and mathematics at the Sorbonne and architecture and painting at the École des Beaux Arts. During his studies, he began to work part-time for the avant-garde magazine *VU* in Paris, and became its managing editor in 1936. Due to the changing political orientation of the magazine, he eventually resigned. In 1941, he left Paris for Spain and Portugal and then emigrated to New York. He pursued a career in publishing, beginning with *Vogue* in 1941, and was appointed art director of the magazine two years later. Liberman was named editorial director of *Vogue*'s parent company, Condé Nast Publications, in 1962. He played a pivotal role in the company's trendsetting success and defined the aesthetics of its numerous publications for more than forty years. He was lauded for his unfailing concern for design and detail and for introducing modern and contemporary art and artists to a broader public.

Alexander Liberman with *Aria* in progress at his Warren, Connecticut, studio

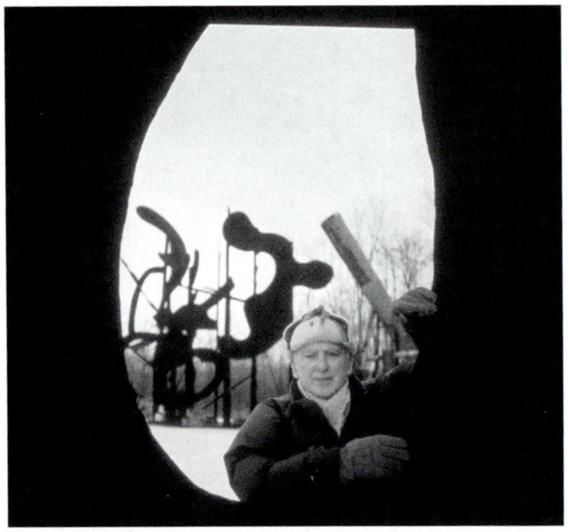

Concurrently with his career in publishing, Liberman was actively engaged as an artist. He returned to painting

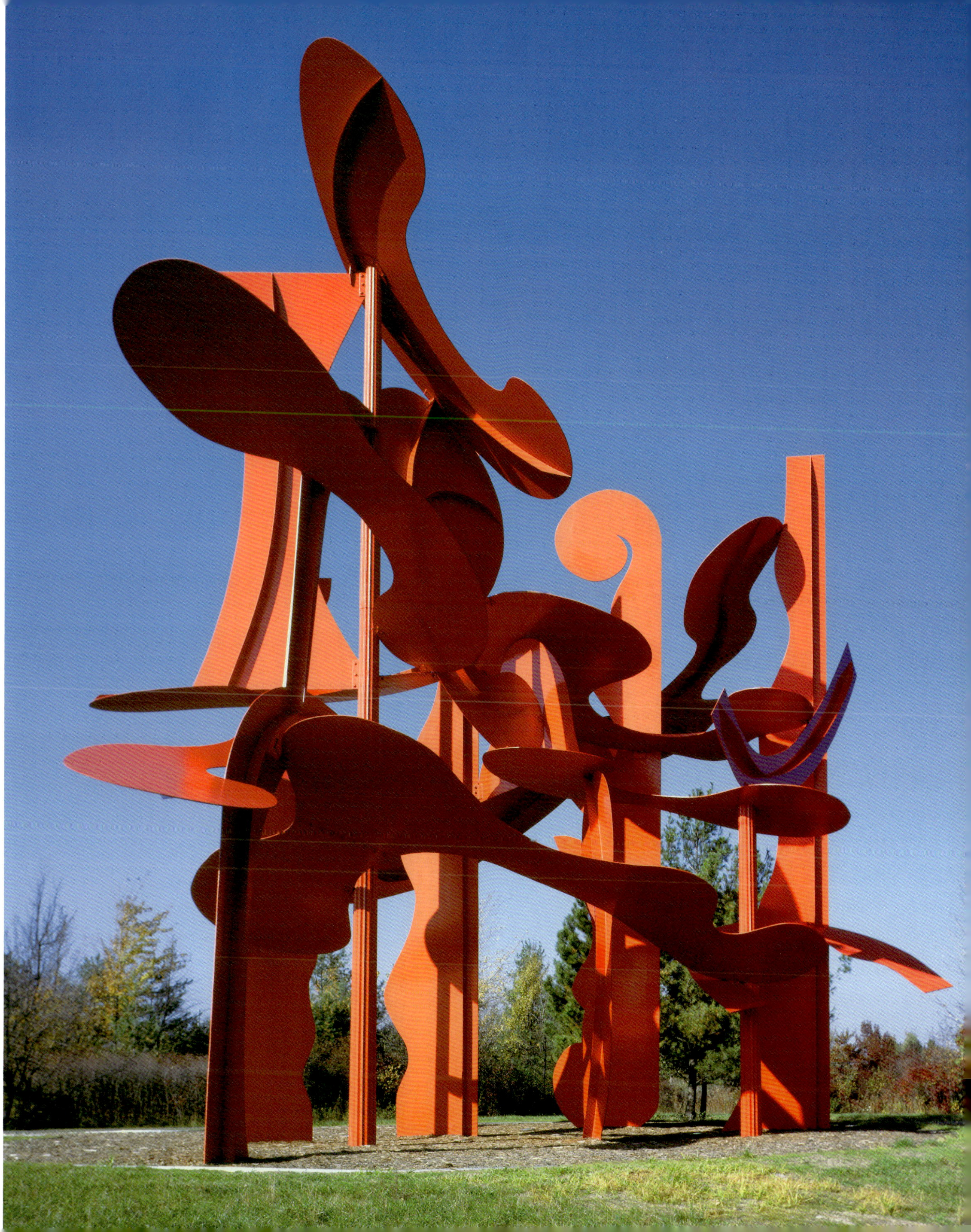

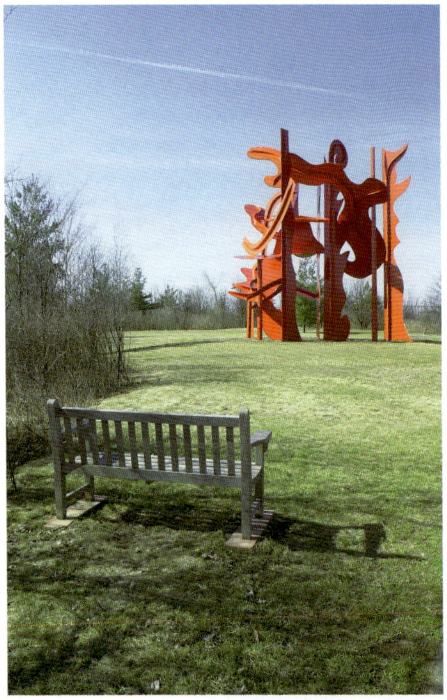

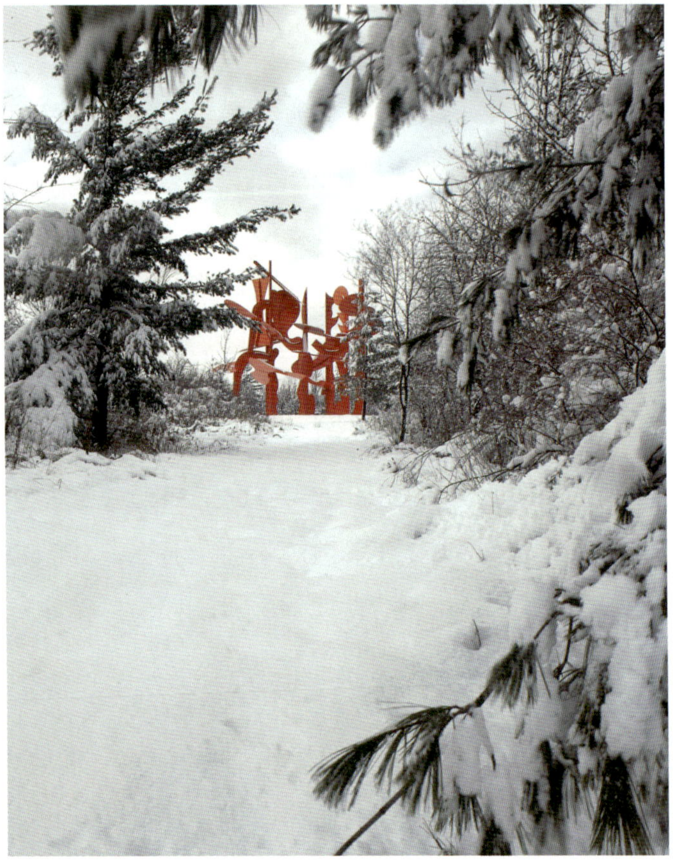

after World War II with a period of gestural abstraction. This was followed by hard-edge paintings of geometric shapes that he initiated in the late 1940s and continued through the next decade. His geometric paintings are regarded as precursors to the minimalist aesthetics of the 1960s. However, Liberman's most enduring legacy to the art world is his sculpture. He had learned arc welding by 1960, and began to fabricate his first welded pieces. Two years later, he exhibited his sculpture together with his paintings. In 1964, he was commissioned by the celebrated American architect Philip Johnson to create a monumental public work for the New York World's Fair, and in 1965, he exhibited his first large sculpture at the Museum of Modern Art in New York. Liberman liked to work on a monumental scale. He transformed industrial materials ranging from steel beams, machinery parts, gas storage tanks, and old boilers into colossal abstract constructions. He frequently painted these a single color (white and "Liberman red" are most common), granting his vision further unity and clarity. Well suited to either urban settings or stretches of natural terrain, these sculptures have been heralded by critics and embraced by general audiences. His works are found in cities, museum collections, sculpture parks, and college campuses across the United States and abroad. Liberman is thus acknowledged among the most prolific public artists of his time.

Aria, at a height of forty-two feet, is an expansive, architectonic sculpture. There are no preliminary models or maquettes for the work, at least in the formal sense, as Liberman preferred to allow an immediate interpretation of form and perspective to evolve in monumental scale. Liberman drew directly on sheets of steel and sometimes made sketches. In addition, he used cardboard or metal shapes to finalize the engineering and construction process. Three drawings for *Aria* are included in the permanent collection of the Frederik Meijer Gardens. The sculpture was originally constructed at the artist's studio in Warren, Connecticut, of a lighter gauge steel than that ultimately used for the Gardens' piece. After refining the design and consulting with engineers, Liberman had the work fabricated in its final form at the Tallix Foundry in Beacon, New York.

Aria is a nonrepresentational work that ascends, treelike, in a crescendo of radiant red. A grove of vertical elements—some ribbed columns, others flat cutouts shaped into calligraphic sweeps and curls—are linked by horizontal and diagonal forms. The vertical parts grant stability to the structure. They also act as foils for the connectors that, radiating in lyrical arcs and flourishes around the uprights, are responsible for the overwhelming sense of movement appropriate to the musical reference implied by the title. A melodious relationship, emphasized among the fluid shapes, is further enhanced by the play of positive and negative space and the movement of light and shadow among the surfaces. Standing beside *Aria*, or walking beneath its grand forms, reinforces our experience of the acute sensibility the artist had toward sculpture and its setting. Light and air are as critical to the success of this work as are its curvaceous contours and brilliant color. The sculpture is arguably among Liberman's finest and serves as a witness to his enduring passion for architectural monumentality, clarity of design, and the invigorating intrusion of three-dimensional forms into their surroundings.

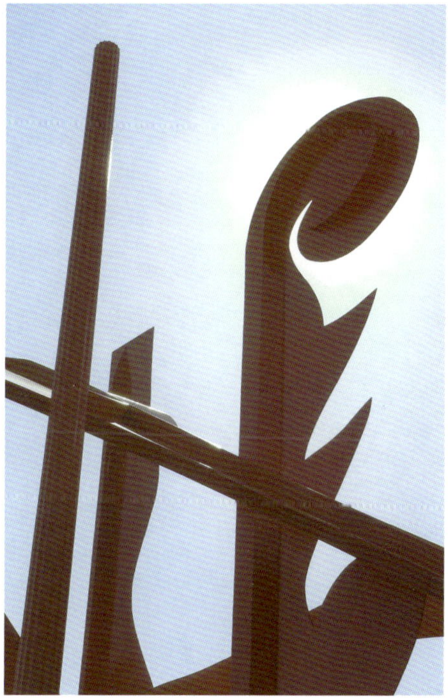

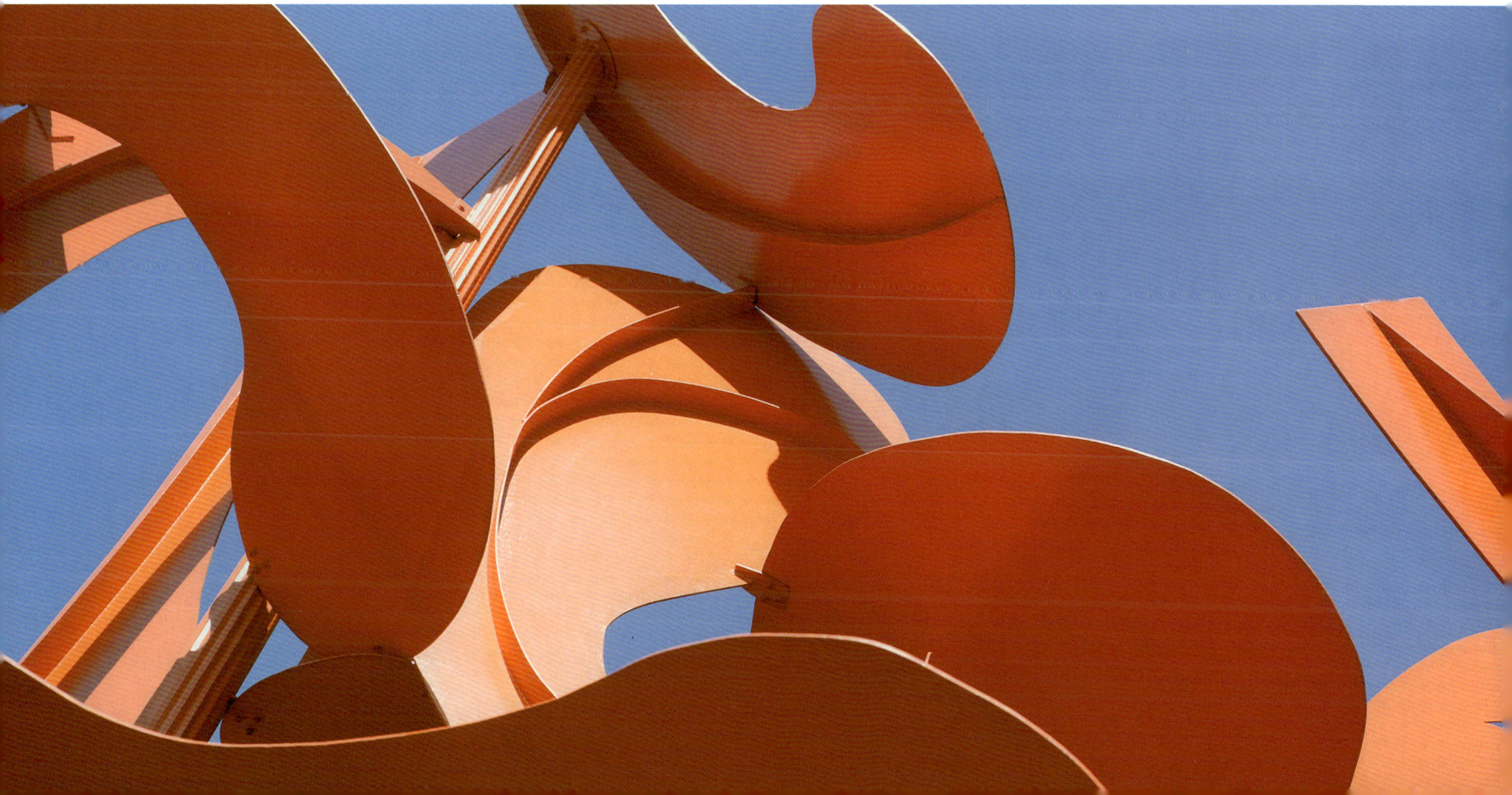

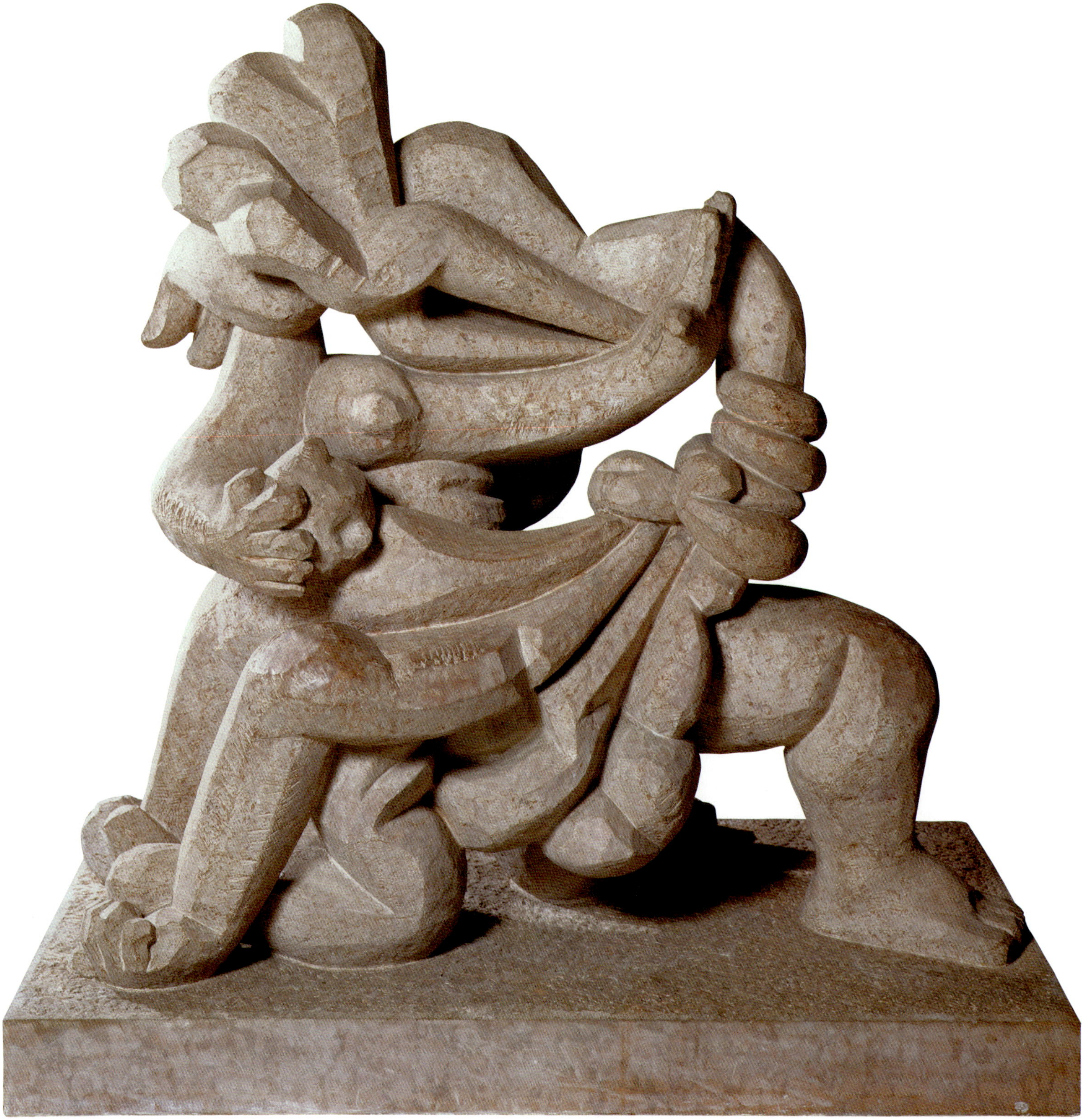

JACQUES LIPCHITZ :: HAGAR

1971

Granite, h. 72 inches (182.9 cm)

Gift of the Meijer Foundation, 2000.05

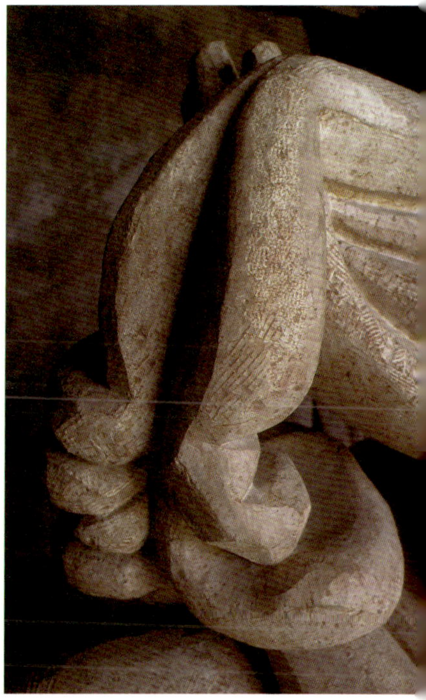

JACQUES LIPCHITZ is revered as one of the pioneers of modern sculpture. He is credited with providing a complete three-dimensional expression for Cubism, as pioneered by colleagues Pablo Picasso and Georges Braque, but his distinguished and prolific career spanned more than six decades and greatly expanded upon the Cubist vocabulary. Born Chaim Jacob in Duskieniki, Lithuania, in 1891, he traveled to Paris in 1909 to study sculpture. He endeavored first at the École des Beaux Arts before transferring to the Académie Julian. In 1911, he made an important trip to St. Petersburg, Russia, and was captivated by the vast collections of the Hermitage Museum, which initiated, among other things, a lifelong interest in African and other non-Western art. Through the rest of the decade, Lipchitz was closely associated with Picasso and Braque, and he began to exhibit his sculpture. He was among the first sculptors to experiment with abstraction, but ultimately he preferred a representational style that, indebted to Cubism, realized forms through a series of fragmented surfaces and a complex arrangement of planes.

The artist at work with the sculpture *Hagar* in his studio in Italy

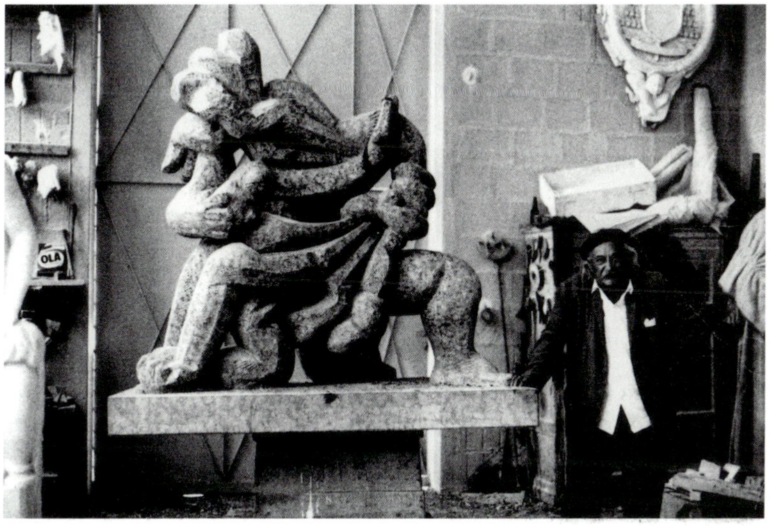

In the period between World War I and World War II, Lipchitz experimented with open, lyrical

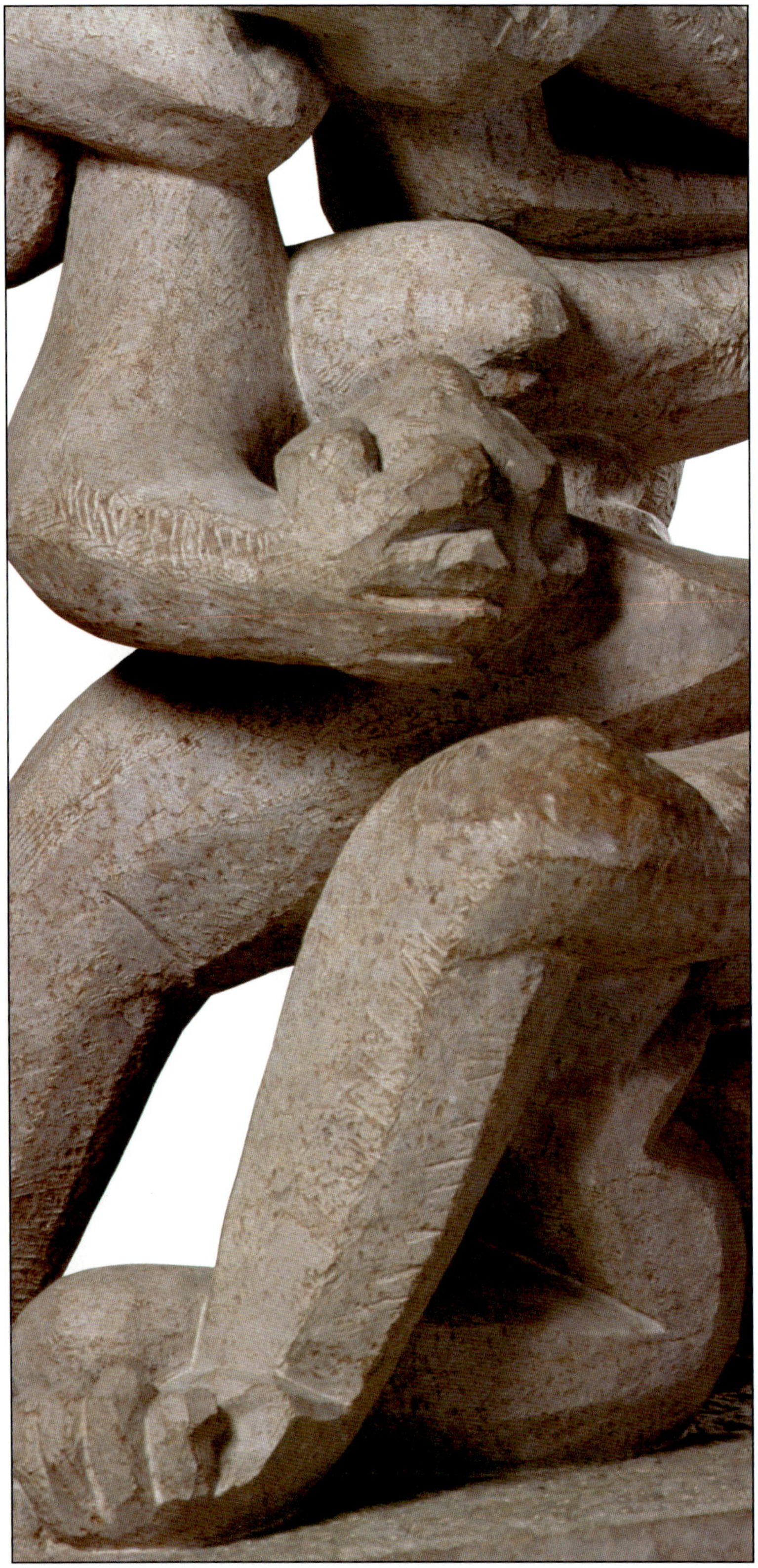

constructions and began to work on a monumental scale. He frequently utilized mythological, literary, and biblical subjects, whose themes both connected his sculpture with the historical traditions of Western art and allowed for commentaries on contemporary society. His most powerful work of this genre, *Prometheus Strangling the Vulture* of 1936–1937, was an attack on the Nazis. Lipchitz fled France for the United States in 1941. Although he returned briefly to Paris following the war, New York would remain his primary residence. From the 1940s onward, Lipchitz's work was deeply personal and frequently autobiographical, expressing his hopes and fears for humanity. Much of this work can be related to the sculptor's increasing awareness of Jewish causes and his own Jewish identity. Lipchitz received a wide variety of commissions from cities and universities, private collectors, and architects. During the final decade of his life, he began to spend time in Italy, where the renowned bronze foundries and marble carving studios of Pietrasanta sustained a prolific late period.

Hagar is a massive granite work that held great personal meaning for Lipchitz, and he portrayed the subject three times. It represents the Old Testament heroine Hagar and her young son, Ishmael, who was Abraham's firstborn. In this biblical story, Hagar was an Egyptian maidservant to Abraham's wife, Sarah. Because Sarah was childless, Hagar acted as surrogate mother and bore Ishmael to Abraham. Later, in her old age, Sarah bore Abraham a son, Isaac. After the miraculous birth, Sarah insisted that Hagar and Ishmael be expelled from the household. Abraham banished them to the desert, where, nearly dying of thirst, mother and son were saved by divine intervention. Hagar and Ishmael are seen at the cornerstone of Arab tradition and genealogy, whereas Sarah's son, Isaac, is held as the heir to Abraham in Judeo-Christian history. The theme is one that spoke to the artist of a desired brotherhood between Arabs and Jews. Moreover, it can be seen as part of the sculptor's mother and child imagery in general and, by some scholars, as a reflection of his own personal relationships with his wife, mistress, and son. The sculpture, dated 1971, is Lipchitz's third and final version of this relatively unique subject. It is his last monumental work and was also inspired, on several levels, by his extended stays in Italy.

Lipchitz was known for the stone carvings of his early career, but he also developed a reputation for his bronzes. During his later years in Italy, he once again returned to carving, inspired by the abundance of stone quarries, carving studios, and historical carvings that extended back through the Renaissance and Baroque periods to antiquity. Both his autobiography and photographs of the period reveal Lipchitz's renewed interest in and energy for such a demanding undertaking. In this *Hagar,* Lipchitz portrays the mother cradling her son as he lies dying in the desert. The complex arrangement of forms and attention to planar details are reminiscent of Cubism, yet the challenge to decipher the action of the protagonists among a multitude of curvaceous elements suggests the dynamism of the Baroque. The upright placement of *Hagar* at the back of the composition, with her son lying across its center, calls to mind Michelangelo's *Pietà,* while suggestions of physical struggle and emotional anguish through a myriad of interlocking limbs evokes the power of the ancient *Laocoön* group. More than a personal commentary on contemporary events, the *Hagar* beckons further consideration among several of the most powerful movements and monuments in the history of art.

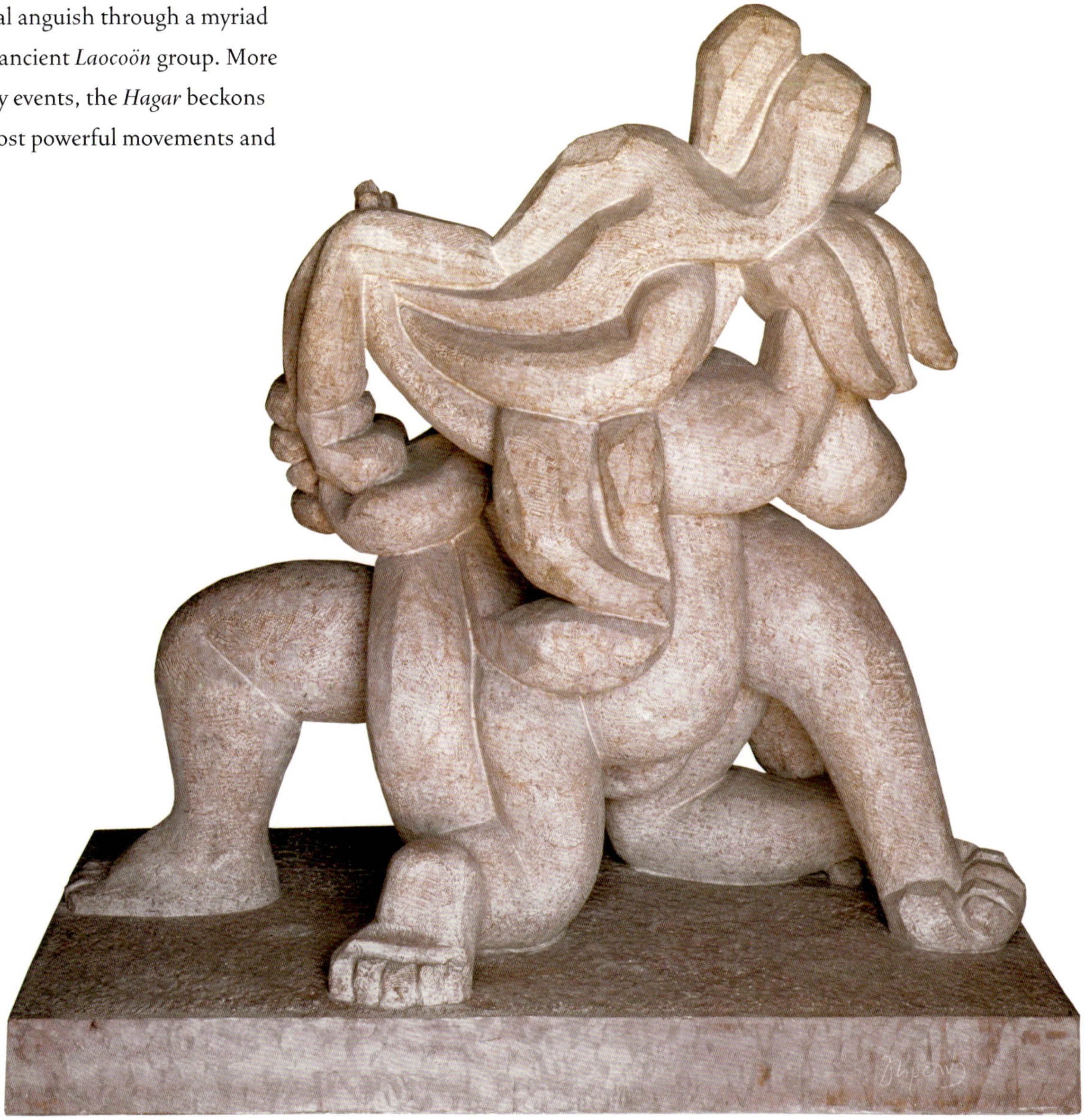

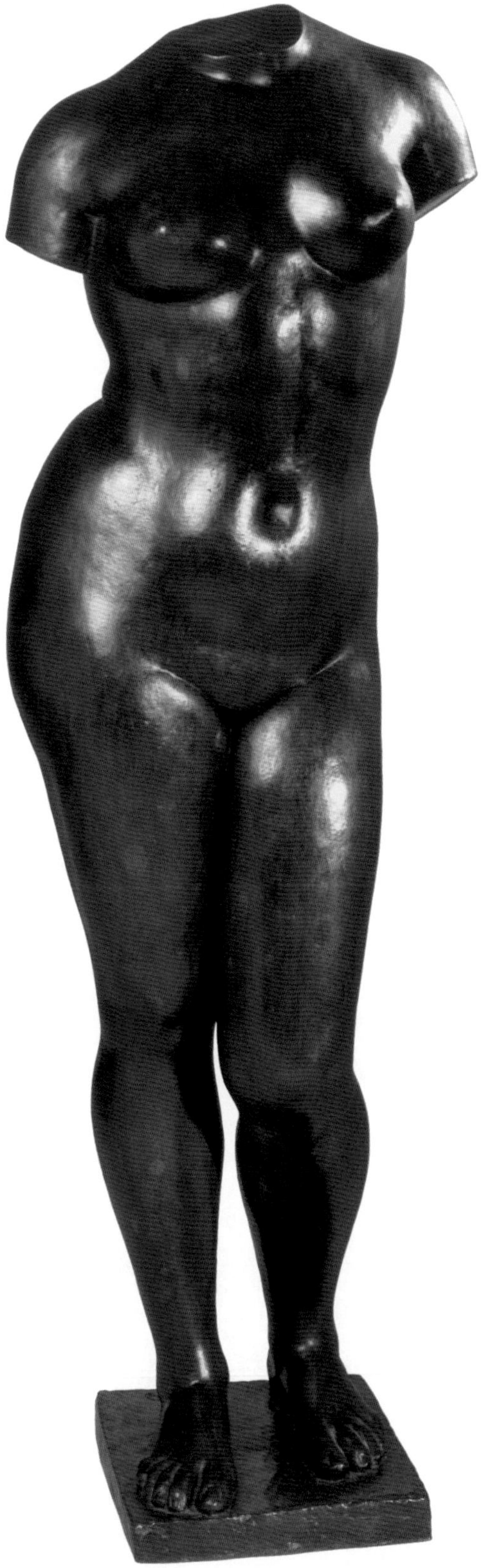

ARISTIDE MAILLOL :: TORSO OF SUMMER (TORSE DE L'ÉTÉ)

1911

Bronze, 2/6 (second in an edition of six), h. 56 inches (142.2 cm)

Gift of the Meijer Foundation, 2000.03

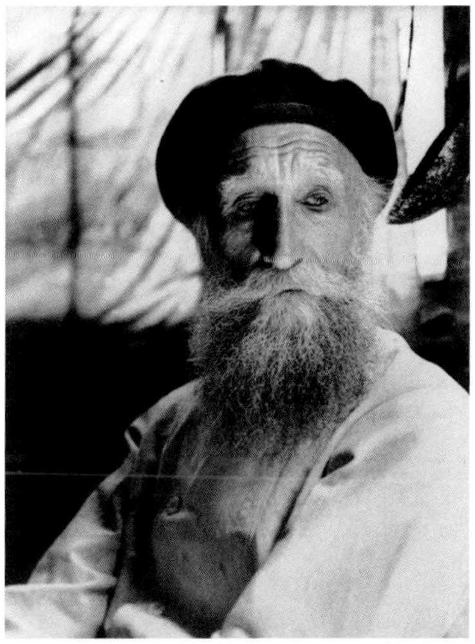

Aristide Maillol at Banyuls-sur-Mer, France, 1942

THE IMAGERY of Aristide Maillol focuses almost exclusively on the female figure as a sensuous vehicle for addressing issues of form, composition, texture, and movement in a tradition reminiscent of the ancient Greeks. Considering the sheer classicism of Maillol's forms, it might surprise contemporary audiences that Auguste Rodin referred to him as the greatest of modern masters. Born into humble conditions at Banyuls-sur-Mer in the south of France, the young Maillol desired to study art in Paris. Although no family member had ever been a professional artist, he moved to the French capital in 1881 to study painting, and was accepted into the École des Beaux Arts two years later. By the end of the decade, he had grown familiar with the avant-garde painting styles of the day, including that of Paul Gauguin, and had also developed an interest in tapestries. Maillol returned home by 1893, and set up a small tapestry studio to execute works after his own designs. It was during this period that he began to create small sculptures in wood and clay.

In 1901, Maillol was introduced to the famed art dealer Ambroise Vollard, who represented Paul Cézanne, Gauguin, Pierre-Auguste Renoir, and the young Pablo Picasso. Vollard bought several of Maillol's small sculptures, and others were acquired by Rodin. By 1903, Maillol's failing eyesight forced him to abandon tapestries in favor of sculpture. Within two years, his work was exhibited in Germany and France, including the revolutionary Salon d'Automne, which launched the career of his friend Henri Matisse. Considering Maillol's intense interest in the human form, it is not surprising that he traveled to Greece, but he also developed an affinity for Egyptian, Indian, and Far Eastern sculpture. His concern for volume and the relationship of forms in space intensified in a series of

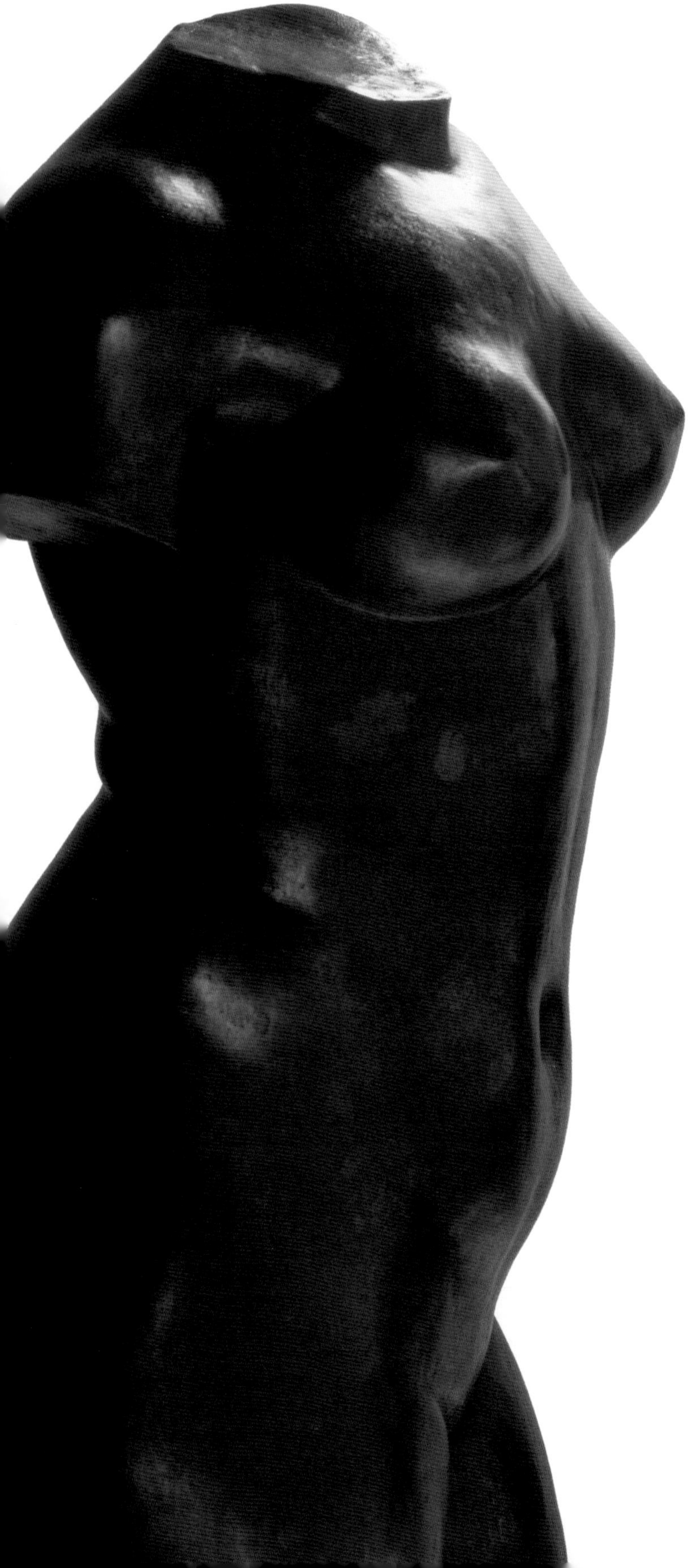

allegorical and symbolic subjects. In the years preceding World War I, his career was firmly established at the forefront of European sculpture. Following the death of Rodin in 1917, Maillol was regarded as the world's leading sculptor.

The bronze *Torso of Summer* of 1911 is a significant example of Maillol's work. In the broadest terms, it represents the sculptor's concern for subjects free from narrative or portrait constraints. As an allegory, it is a reflection on the fullness and fecundity of summer. The work must be seen in connection with a small group of sculptures the artist created around the theme of the four seasons. For Maillol, the female form was a timeless vehicle through which he could express his reverence for the beauty of the natural world. He made two related versions of the subject, both life size. One features an entire figure, including a turbaned head; the other, as represented in the collection of the Frederik Meijer Gardens, concentrates on the body, without the inclusion of the head or arms.

Torso of Summer provides a remarkable link to a classical past and serves as a gateway to a modernist future. Certainly the absence of a head and arms calls to mind innumerable examples of ancient statuary from both Western and Eastern traditions that have survived in a fragmentary state. Without the presence of a face, the sculpture is given an anonymity that focuses attention on the compositional concern of a form in space and neutralizes issues of gender and sexuality. In *Torso of Summer,* Maillol has employed the contrapposto, or weight-shift position, favored since ancient Greek times. This pose, which releases the figure from a strictly frontal stance and increases its animation, enables the sculptor to fully examine the three-dimensional power of sculpture, explore issues of mass and volume, and, in this instance, capitalize on the dynamic relationship between open and closed space. The voluptuousness of the female figure, while symbolic of the season represented, confers levels of subtlety to notions of the form in space that can be understood only if the figure is examined in the round. The exploration of such formal concerns became standard for the history of twentieth-century sculpture. Maillol's use of the human figure to both call upon and reinvent historical tradition not only set an example for sculptors and painters of his own time, but his work will also undoubtedly continue to inform new generations of figurative artists in the twenty-first century.

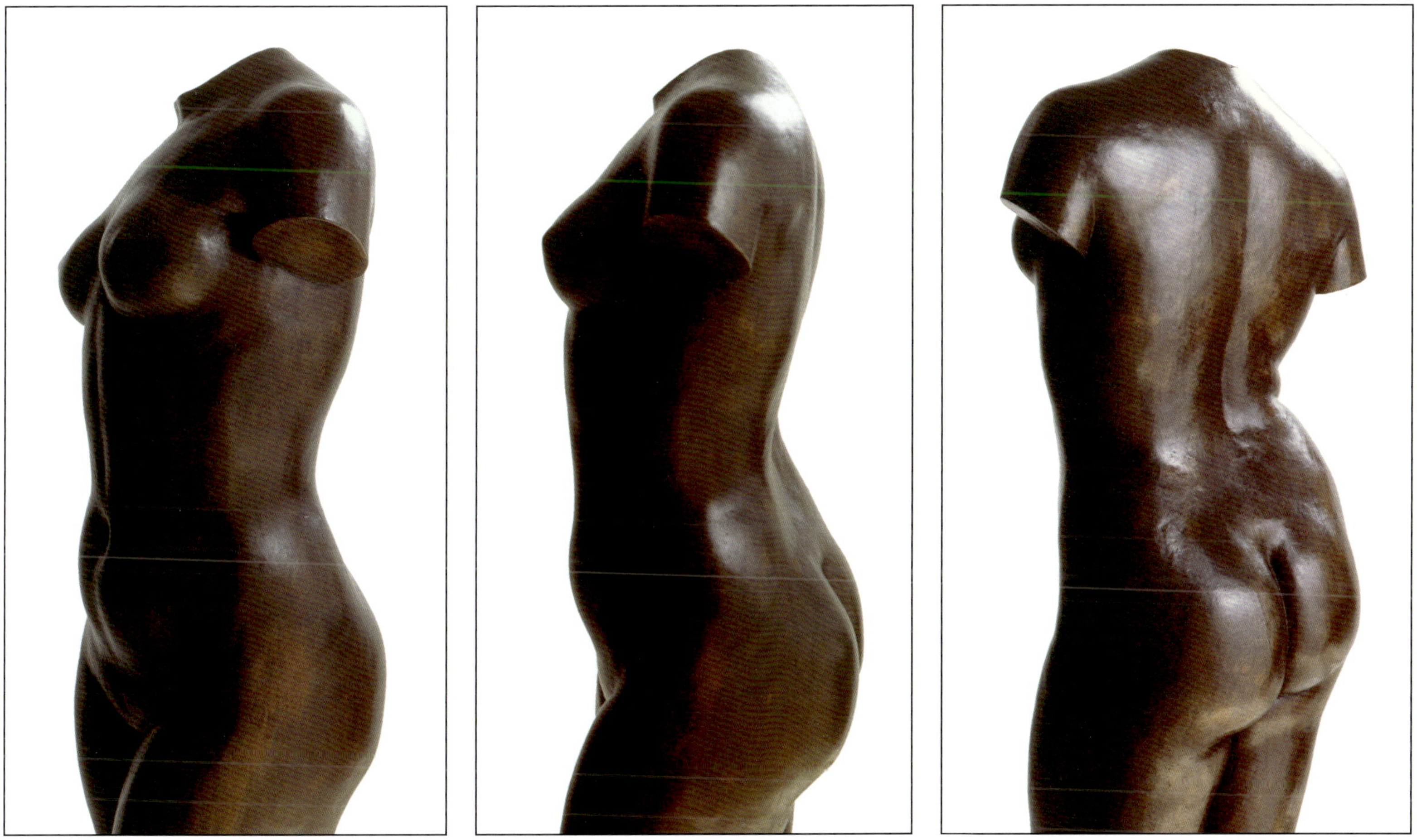

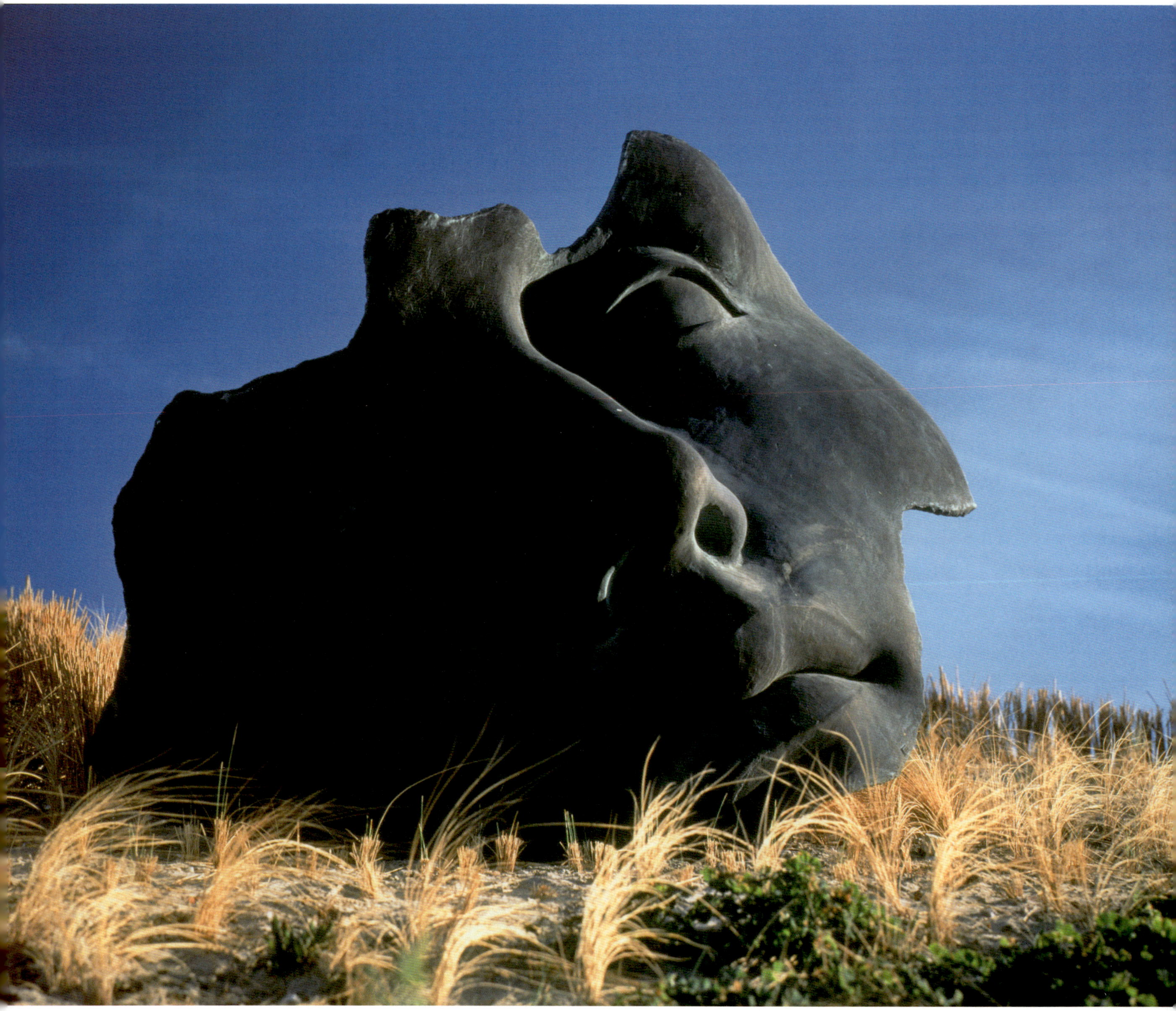

IGOR MITORAJ :: LIGHT OF THE MOON (TSUSKI-NO-HIKARI)

1991

Bronze, A/P (artist's proof for an edition of three),
h. 11 feet, 10 inches (360.7 cm)

Gift of the Meijer Foundation and the Frederik Meijer Charitable Trust,
2002.2

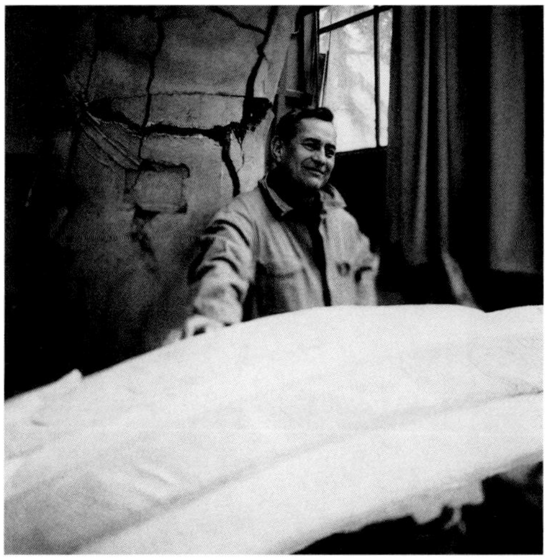

Igor Mitoraj in his studio, Pietrasanta, Italy, 2001

ALTHOUGH RECOGNITION and appreciation of his oeuvre is now developing in the United States, the classically allied yet psychologically penetrating work of Igor Mitoraj has captivated European and Japanese audiences for more than two decades. The overt historicism of Mitoraj's style firmly places him as a direct descendant of a sculpture tradition that originated in ancient Greece, was sustained throughout the Roman era, reasserted itself during the Renaissance, and flourished in the late eighteenth and nineteenth centuries under the rubric of Neoclassicism. Such associations have contributed to the large number of installations and exhibitions of his sculpture at institutions devoted to archaeology and history, in addition to those dedicated to the visual arts. It is understandable, then, that the artist's creations have engaged broad and diverse audiences well beyond the confines of art museum and gallery attendance.

Mitoraj was born to Polish parents in Oderan, Germany, in 1944. He studied painting at the Krakow Academy of Fine Arts, under the direction of Tadeusz Kantor, and at the Krakow Art School. After exhibiting his paintings in Poland, including the 1968 Krakow Biennale, Mitoraj moved to Paris. He began to make sculpture in 1974, and was the subject of a highly successful exhibition in Paris the following year. From 1975 to the present, the artist has focused primarily on sculpture. He has traveled widely across Europe and North and South America, and has made regular trips to Greece. Although his travels and vast knowledge of the history of art informs his work, Mitoraj remains relatively isolated from the trends and schools of contemporary art. Following a visit to the famed marble quarries in Carrara, Italy, he established a studio in that country. Since 1983, he has divided his time between Italy and France.

The monumental bronze *Light of the Moon* portrays the central portion of a human face. Smooth, sensual contours gently undulate across the forehead and from jawline to cheekbone, outlining the remains of a perfectly proportioned countenance. Carefully delineated almond-shaped eyes and full lips are held in balance with the strong triangular nose. Such large-scale interpretations of the human face in fragmented terms are an important motif within Mitoraj's repertoire. This work is unique in that the face is posited on its side, along a strong diagonal, instead of being set on a more typical vertical axis. The suggested momentum of the angled format is nonetheless stabilized by the symmetrically allied features. From a distance, *Light of the Moon* resembles a poignant remnant of ancient statuary that collapsed, became embedded in soft earth, and later emerged as part of the modern landscape. Close inspection, however, reveals that rather than succumbing to the ravages of time, the sculpture's carefully modulated surfaces have been realized through acute attention to casting, texture, and patina, according to the artist's design.

The representational clarity of *Light of the Moon* secures its connection to Classical and Neoclassical art. The sleek and supple surfaces, punctuated by the strong linear articulation of stylized eyes and mouth, further such associations. It is in the sculpture's overall sensuality, however, that Mitoraj's style hovers near the timeless androgyny that echoes the work of such artists as the ancient master Polykleitos, the Renaissance sculptor Donatello, and the Neoclassical sculptor Antonio Canova. Classical traditions are points of departure for Mitoraj; this segment of the human visage suggests multiple interpretations. The idea of the fragment recalls concepts of lost civilizations and the passage of time, and concurrently implies the presence of both original and contemporary audiences, as well as the artist himself. The masklike face, with its exposed concave reverse, calls to mind the iconography of the theater and hints at Surrealist-inspired fantasy and dream imagery. Recognizing the tension between past and present, movement and stillness, drama and fantasy, we begin to fathom Mitoraj's art. Ultimately, his compositional control, economy of presentation, and description of surfaces enhance our complete understanding of Mitoraj's ongoing dialogue with the masters and monuments of the past.

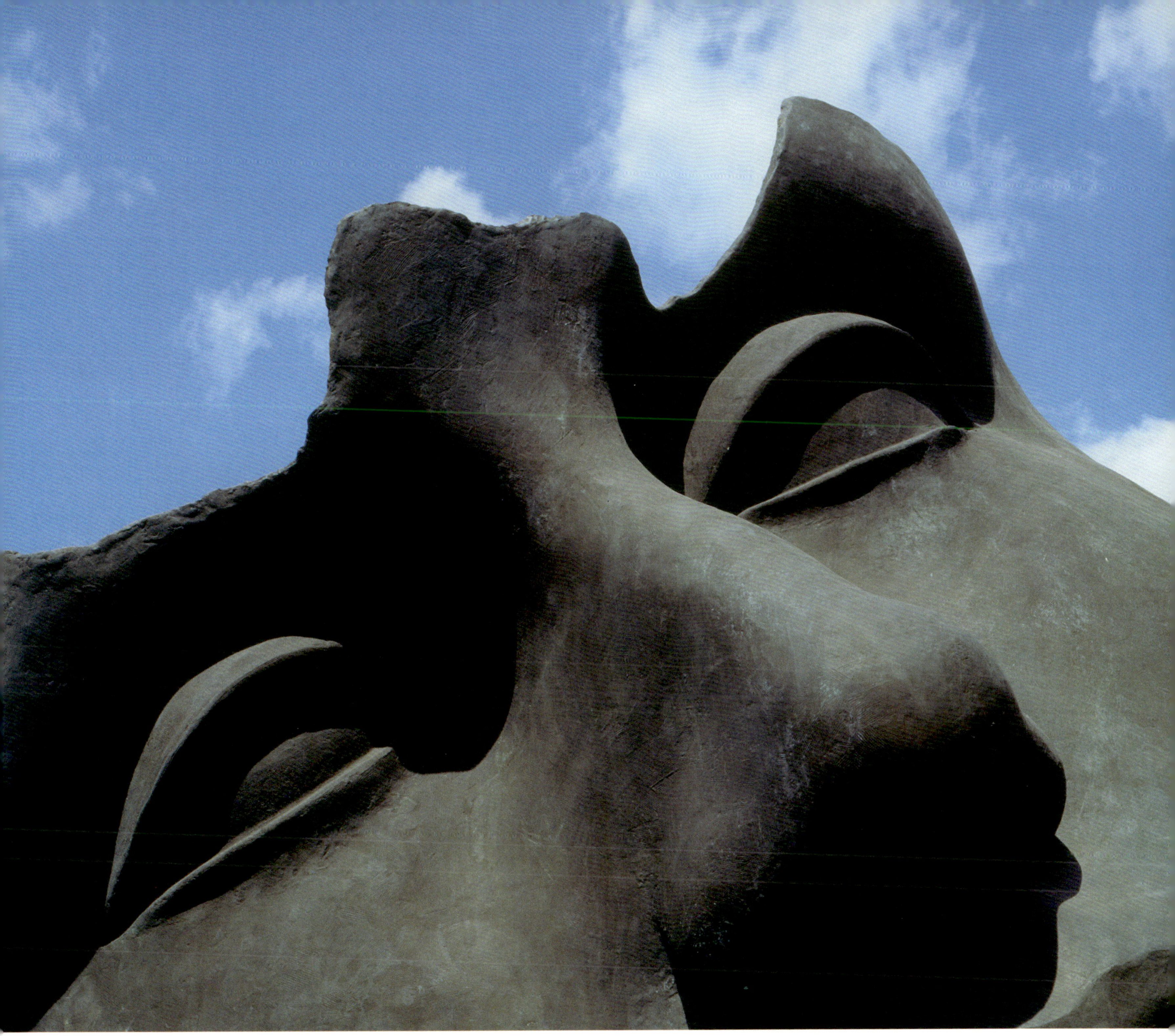

HENRY MOORE :: WORKING MODEL FOR DIVIDED OVAL: BUTTERFLY

1982

Bronze, 6/6 (sixth in an edition of six), h. 21½ inches (54.6 cm)

Gift of the Meijer Foundation and Peter C. and Pat Cook, 2000.08

HENRY MOORE is among the most prodigious and influential sculptors of the twentieth century. Recognized as the single most important figure in the history of British art during the last century, his work has been of critical importance internationally for more than fifty years. He was born the seventh child of a self-educated miner in northern England in 1898. To oblige his father's wishes, Moore became an elementary school teacher before pursuing art as a vocation. Following his service in World War I, Moore began a two-year program at the Leeds School of Art in 1919. During this period, he had his first extensive contact with Post-Impressionist painting and non-Western art forms. Two years later, he received a scholarship to the Royal Academy in

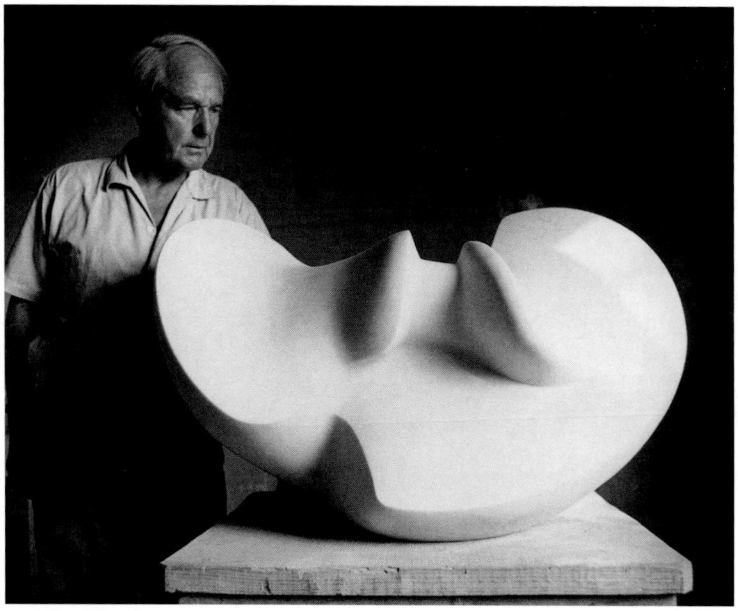

Henry Moore with the marble original of *Divided Oval: Butterfly*, Forte dei Marni, Italy, 1967

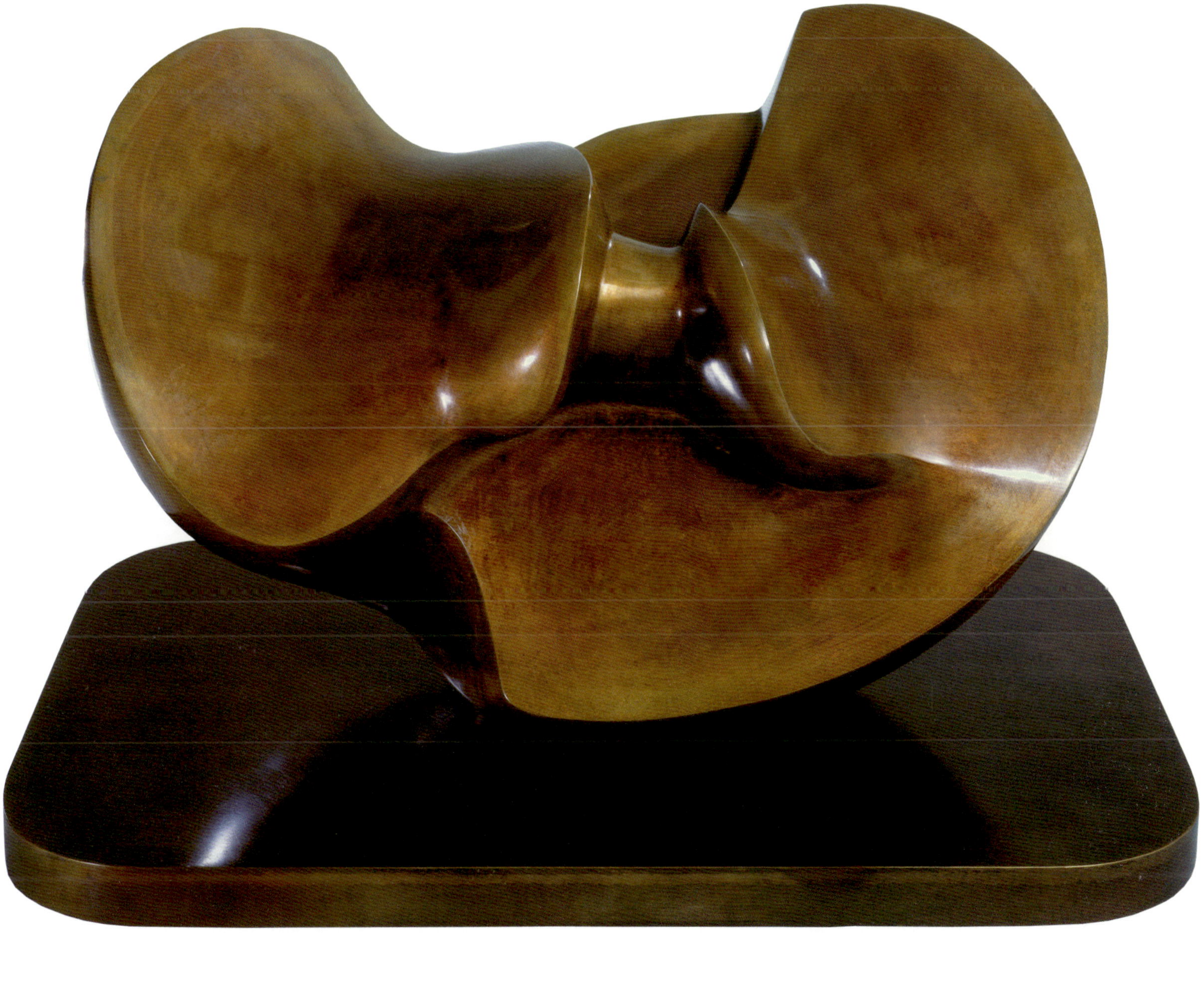

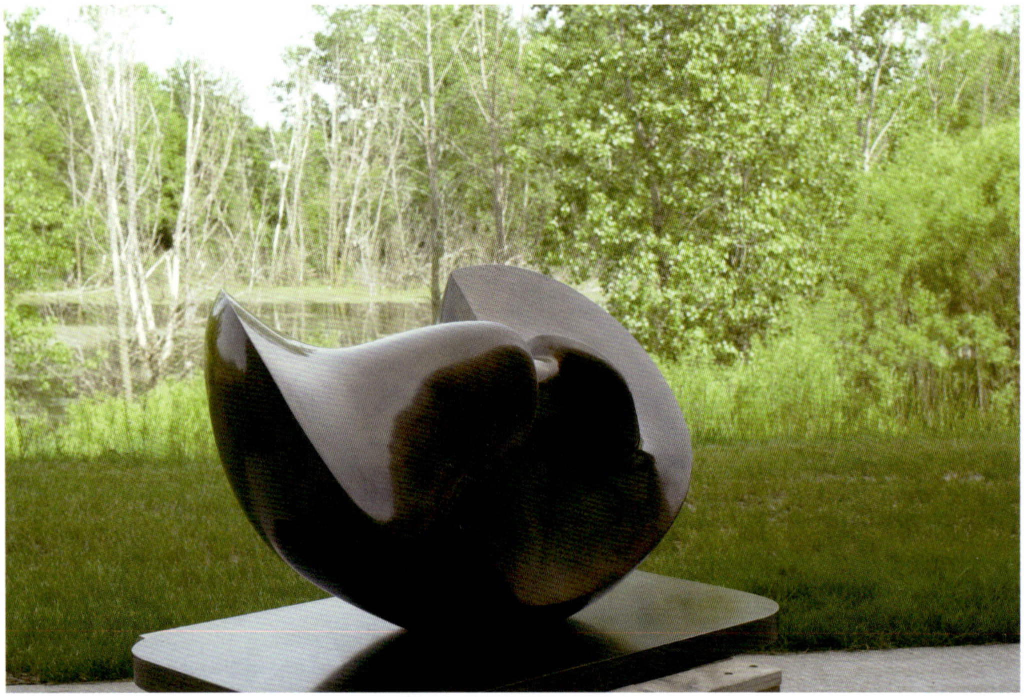

London, and became a frequent visitor to the British Museum, where the renowned collections of ancient Greek, African, Oceanic, and, in particular, pre-Columbian art had a profound influence on him. The period from the mid-1920s through the late 1930s was critical to Moore's development. It marked his extensive travels throughout Italy and France; his exposure to the work of Pablo Picasso, Jean Arp, Alberto Giacometti, and the Surrealists; and, finally, his association with British avant-garde artists like Barbara Hepworth, with whom he attended the Leeds School, and Ben Nicholson.

Although Moore showed his sculpture prior to World War II, in exhibitions including an international Surrealist exhibition in 1936, he came to national attention during the war through his drawings of Londoners taking refuge from air raids in the Underground stations. The concern for volume and form in these drawings is seen as an integral part of his development as a sculptor. Following the war, the landmark event in his career was the monumental sculpture he exhibited in the 1951 Festival of Britain, where it drew the attention of international audiences. Moore's work was initially representational, but he gradually moved toward a vocabulary of organic, simplified forms that, however abstract, were frequently drawn from nature. After years of investigation, his academic training, reverence for non-Western art, Surrealist compatibility, and interest in the human figure and other natural forms were distilled into a unique personal vision. Moore's highly organic sculpture fully explored the three-dimensional power of form from the 1960s onward, often on a monumental scale. When, in 1972, he was honored with a major exhibition at the Forte di Belvedere above the city of Florence, Moore was heralded as the leading sculptor of the second half of the twentieth century.

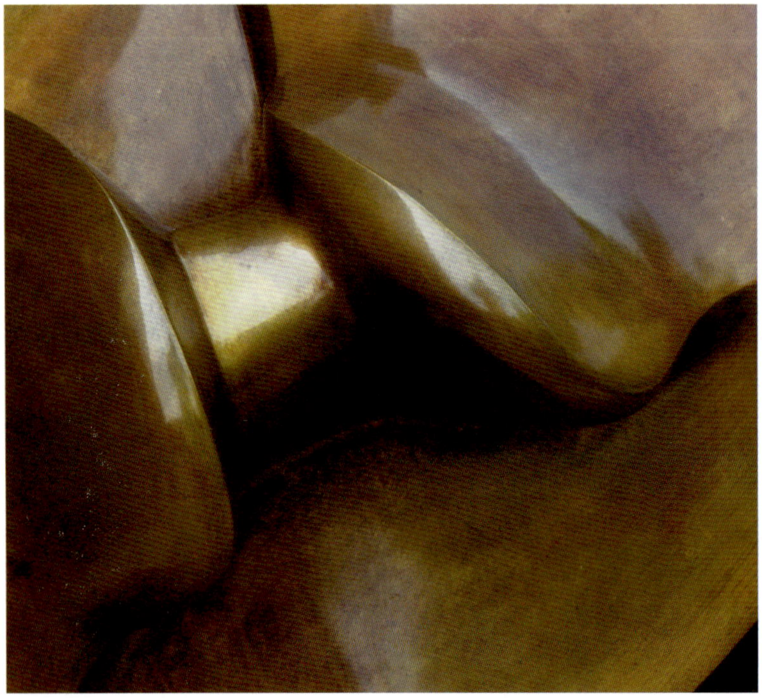

Working Model for Divided Oval: Butterfly was originally conceived in marble in 1967. Pleased with the harmonious, well-balanced form, Moore later created a plaster model and cast the work in bronze in an edition of six in 1982. The natural world was an important source of inspiration for the artist. Bones, shells, and stones, for example, were among the objects that prompted a myriad of ideas. Furthermore, references to human, animal, and insect forms abound in Moore's oeuvre. The plaster model of *Working Model for Divided Oval: Butterfly* and numerous bones, including vertebrae, that in part sparked the formation of this and other sculptures are preserved in the artist's studio outside London.

While not a literal interpretation of a butterfly, the work suggests the general contours and symmetry of wings and the grace and beauty of their movement. The planes of the sides slope downward and inward, encouraging the illusion that the sculpture is hovering above the base rather than resting solidly upon it. From the gently upraised central elements of the upper face to the graceful contours that guide the eye around the sculpture, one quickly perceives the artist's fully realized concept of form and volume. Considering this in combination with its inherent monumentality, it is not surprising that Moore had a twenty-six-foot version cast—one of his largest works. Finally, it is critical to note the rich, golden-brown patina. The warm tones unify the form, yet the play of highlights and shadows suggests a voluptuousness found in many living things that in sculpture is usually reserved for figurative pieces.

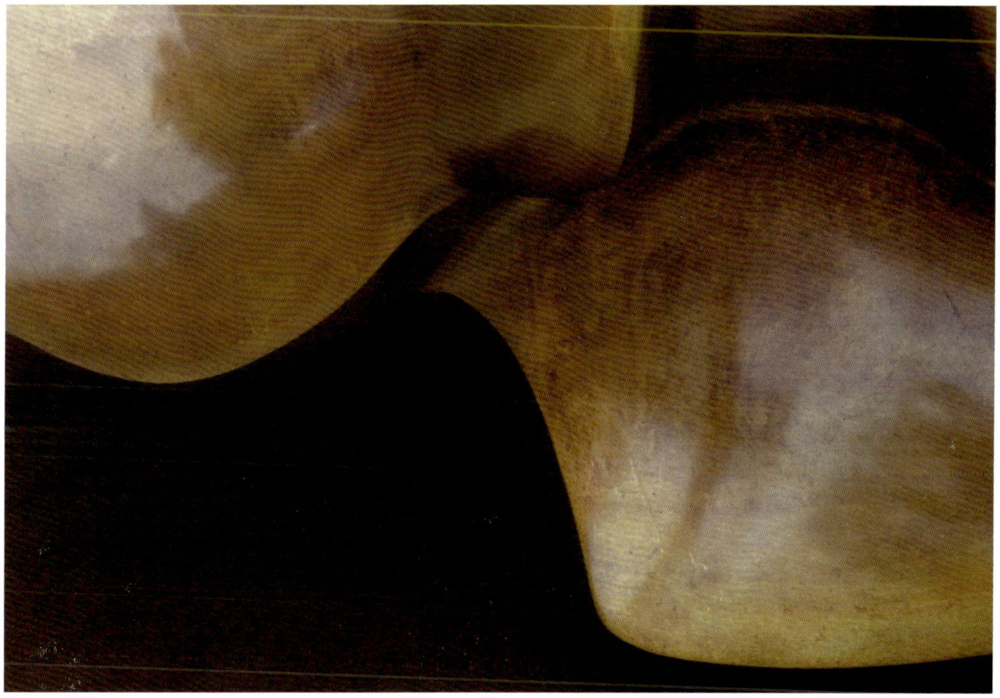

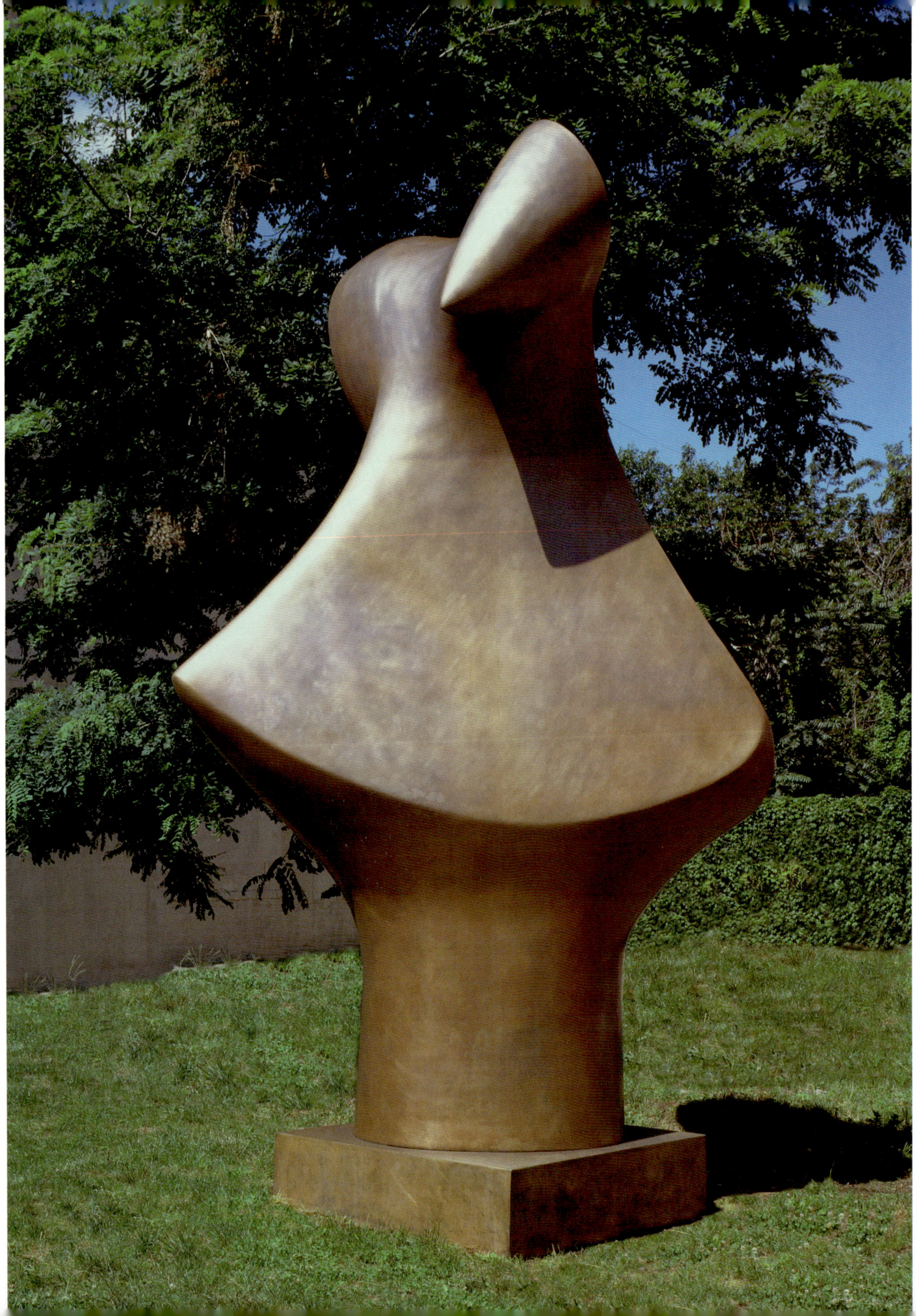

HENRY MOORE :: BRONZE FORM

1985–1986

Bronze, 1/6 (one in an edition of six), h. 14 feet, 6 inches (442 cm)

Gift of the Meijer Foundation, 2001.15

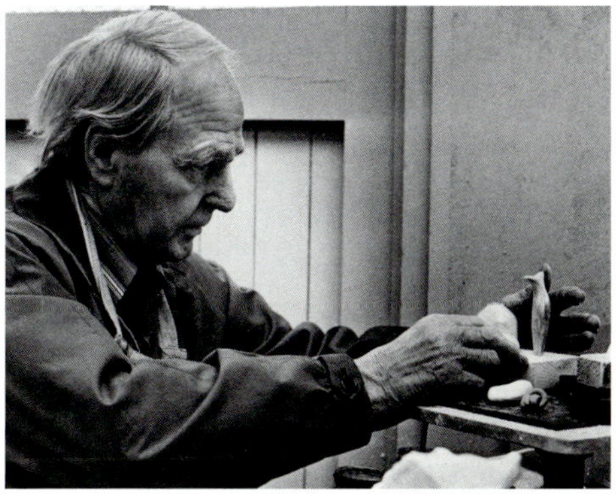

Henry Moore in his studio in 1976, working on a plaster sketch model comparable to early maquettes from which *Bronze Form* was derived

AS THE TWENTIETH CENTURY enters the realm of historical periods, critics and scholars are better able to discern those individuals who set the course of major developments in the visual arts during this time. There is little doubt that the British sculptor Henry Moore is among the most illustrious artists of the post–World War II era. The critical and public acceptance of his work was instrumental in reminding the world of the profound role that monumental public sculpture holds for audiences of every age and experience. Recent well-received retrospective exhibitions in the United States and an unprecedented touring exhibition of Moore's large outdoor work throughout China suggest an enduring, universal appeal that few artists enjoy.

Moore received traditional academic training in England, following his service in World War I. His exposure to non-Western art and to contemporary avant-garde trends in continental European painting and sculpture were also highly influential to his artistic development. He gained initial recognition during World War II for his drawings, but garnered international attention for his monumental bronzes in the 1950s. In the ensuing decades, Moore's prolific career is revealed in a vast number of public and private commissions, exhibitions, books, and print projects. The organic character of the sculptor's aesthetic, his sensitivity to materials, and his acute awareness of the relationship between object and viewer quickly emerged as hallmarks of his work, whether the forms are representational, abstracted, or nonrepresentational. Because of the mellifluous nature of his concerns, it can be argued that Henry Moore convincingly welcomed a

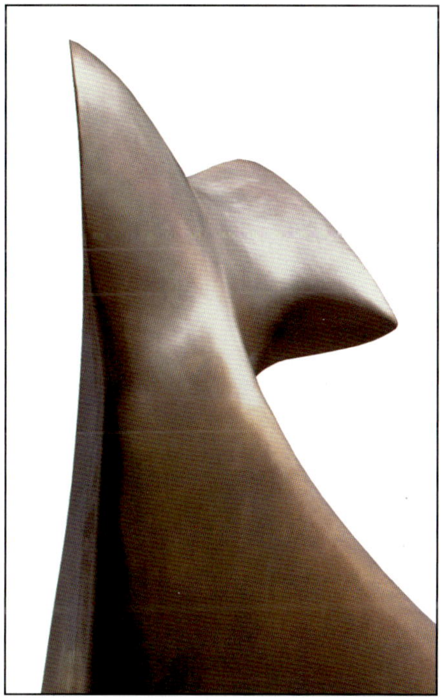

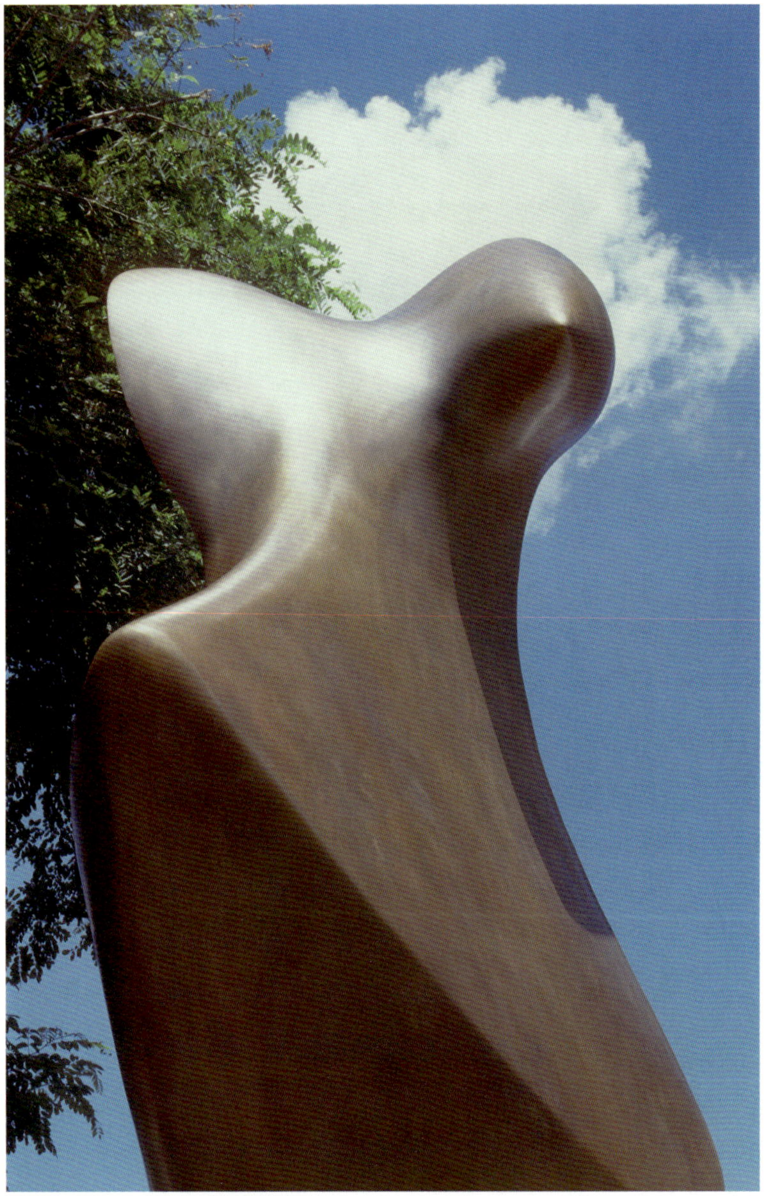

broader audience to the merits of abstract and nonrepresentational sculpture—more than any other artist of the last century.

Moore worked until his death in 1986, at the age of eighty-eight, producing nearly 140 sculptures from 1980 through 1986 alone. Among these are a surprising number of large-scale pieces. The monumental *Bronze Form,* cast in 1985–1986, is one of the last sculptures the artist completed. The history of this piece begins in 1975, with a series of three maquettes in which a diminutive element, clearly anticipating *Bronze Form,* is featured within a semicircular niche, or as Moore referred to it, a shelter. Customarily, Moore enlarged his maquettes, making adjustments according to changes in scale and often singling out specific elements for further development. One of the 1975 maquettes was realized in a bronze edition at five feet high in 1983, and called *Figure in a Shelter.* In the following year, a unique granite carving approximately nine feet in height, known as *Stone Form,* was created based on the central element of *Figure in a Shelter.* In 1985 and 1986, Moore enlarged these sculptures: *Large Figure in a Shelter* was cast at twenty feet, and its internal element inspired *Bronze Form,* which was cast at fourteen-and-one-half feet. These and other similar works based on the shelter motif ultimately derive from Moore's helmet head series—protective hood or cavelike forms that recall the helmets of ancient warriors and often house a figurative or an abstract object.

The majority of Moore's monumental sculptures were envisioned for a public context. Most are horizontally oriented, derived from his popular motif of the reclining figure. In *Bronze Form,* the sculptor instead emphasized the vertical axis. The columnar lower third of the work gently rises, converging with a broad expanse whose contours dramatically ascend inward and then flare out, climaxing in two slightly asymmetrical, rounded forms. Moving around the work magnifies the effect of these visually uplifting, interrelated elements. Experiencing the sculpture in the round also highlights Moore's powerful command of a visual vocabulary that is both planar and angular, organic and sensual. These diverse elements not only coexist, but also inform one another. *Bronze Form* may be viewed as nonrepresentational. However, in its compliance with general human proportions and in its genealogical link to the aforementioned works of the helmet head series, understanding this sculpture as an abstraction of the human figure is equally compelling.

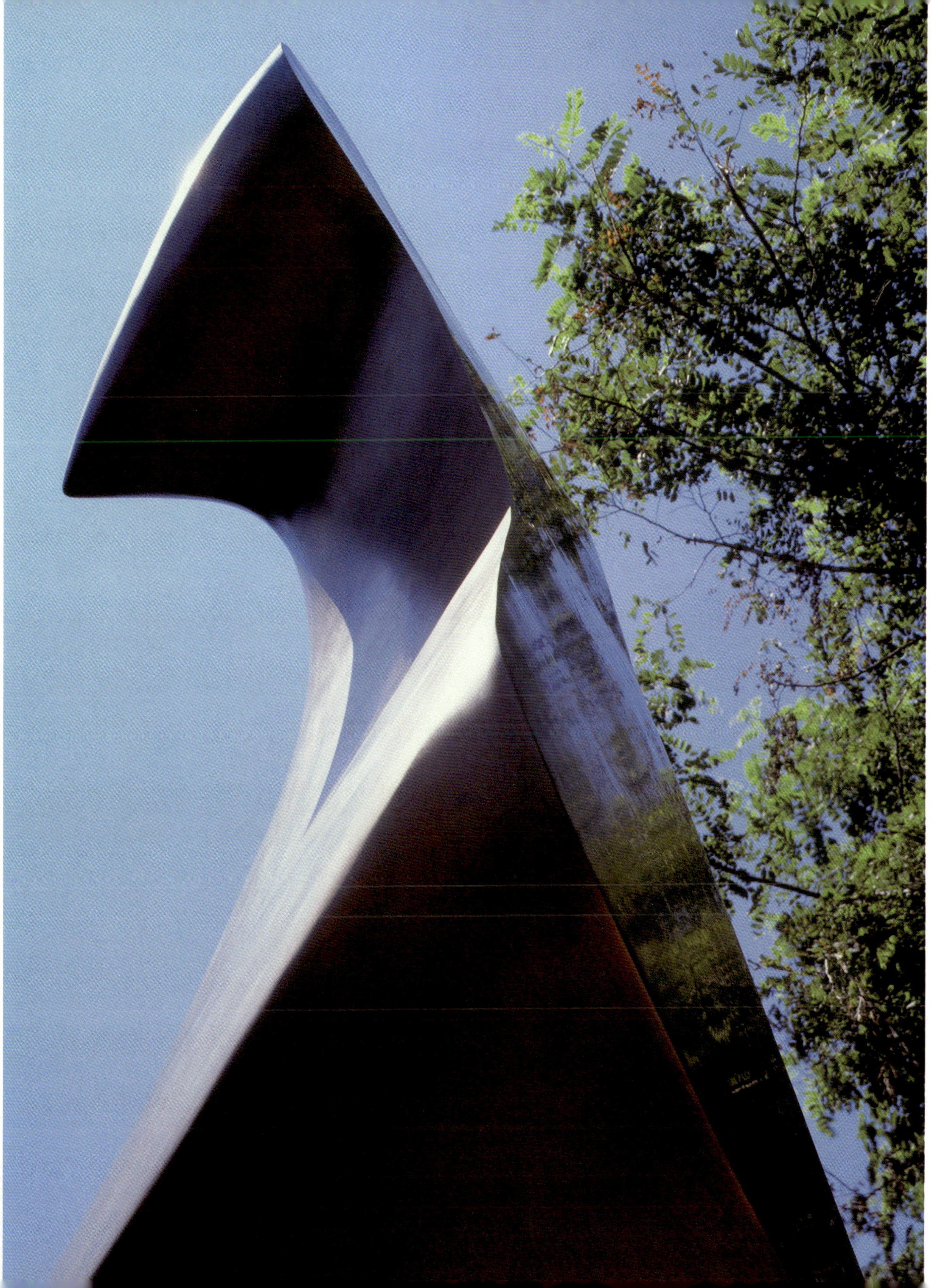

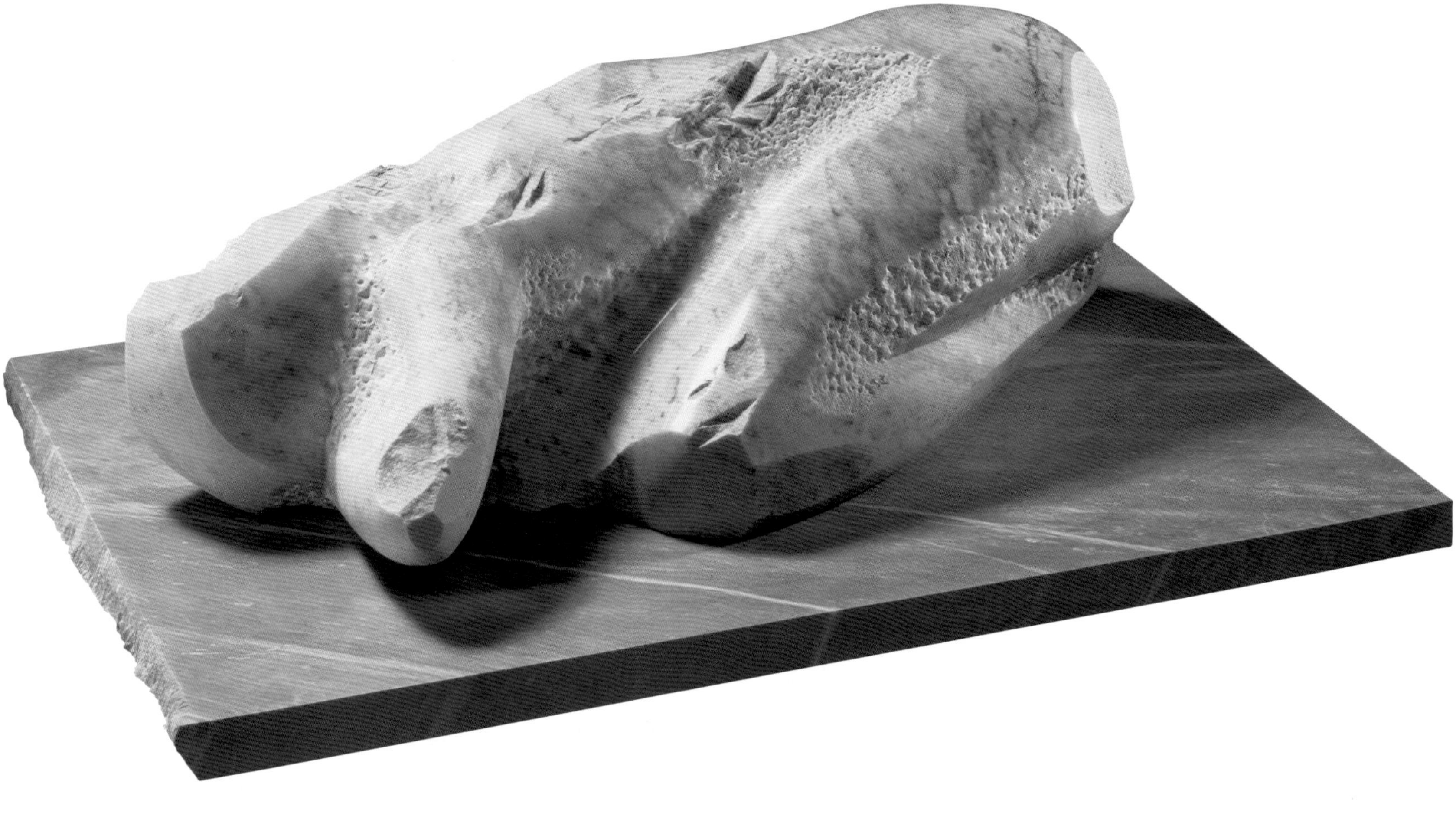

American, born 1930

MANUEL NERI :: ODALISQUE IV

1994

Marble, h. 18 inches (45.7 cm)

Gift of the Meijer Foundation, 2002.3

REGARDED AS one of the leading contemporary American sculptors, Manuel Neri has for more than four decades engaged audiences with his plaster, bronze, and, more recently, marble figures. The artist's two-dimensional works have also been eagerly collected and exhibited. National recognition came to Neri in the 1950s and 1960s, as the only sculptor of note to be part of the acclaimed San Francisco Bay Area Figurative movement. The achievements of the Figurative artists—comprising primarily painters, including Elmer Bischoff, Richard Diebenkorn, and Nathan Oliveira—surged beyond regional importance and bore witness to some of the most fruitful and innovative passages in the history of American art. Unquestionably, Neri's penetrating series of female figures, given form in roughly textured plaster—sometimes with stark surfaces, but frequently energized by broad swaths of applied color—are particularly celebrated, and reflect the legacy of Abstract Expressionism, Funk Art, West Coast Minimalism, and other avenues of Bay Area visual expression. In recent years, Neri's stone carvings have attracted significant critical attention while

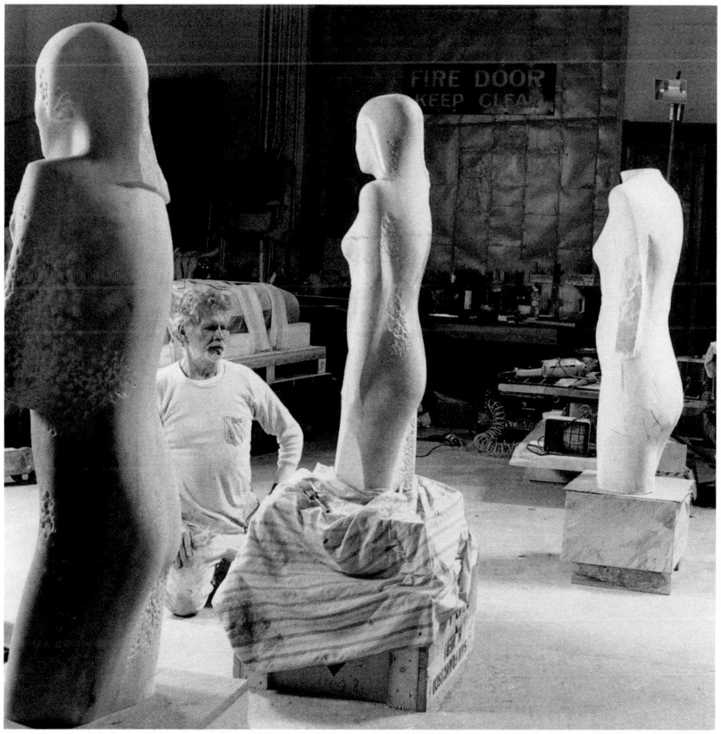

Manuel Neri in his Benicia, California, studio, 1977

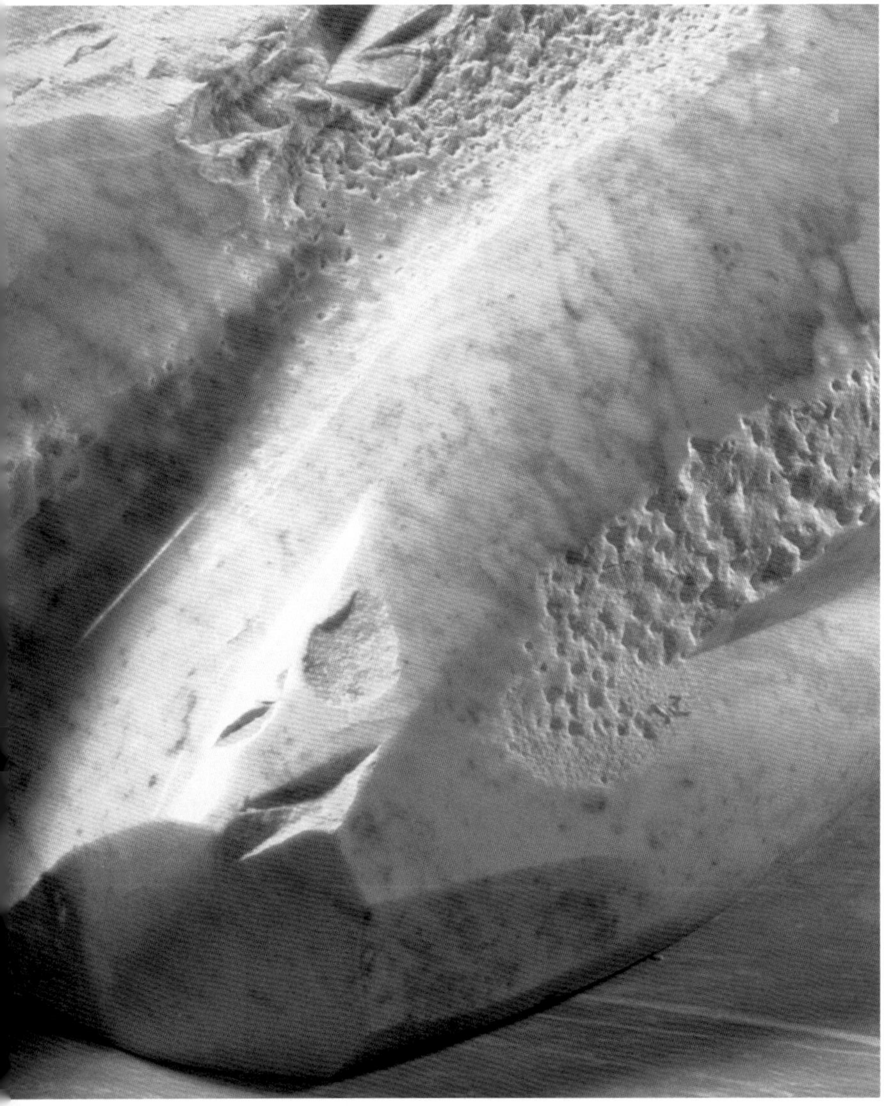

laying claim to historical traditions that reach back to the statuary of ancient cultures and the Renaissance.

Neri was born in California's San Joaquin Valley in 1930. Although he intended to become an engineer, his exposure to the highly innovative ceramics of Peter Voulkos captured Neri's interest and encouraged his pursuit of art. He studied at the University of California, Berkeley; the California College of Arts and Crafts, Oakland; and the California School of Fine Arts, San Francisco (now the San Francisco Art Institute). Between 1959 and 1990, teaching played an important role in the artist's career. Neri taught at the California School of Fine Arts; the University of California, Berkeley; and the University of California, Davis. As early as 1953, he received his first award for sculpture, followed by an award for painting in 1957. Also in 1957, he was given his first solo exhibition. Since these achievements, Neri has been the subject of numerous museum and gallery exhibitions worldwide. He has also received several prestigious grants and awards, including a National Art Foundation award in 1965, a Guggenheim Foundation fellowship in 1979, and a National Endowment for the Arts grant in 1980. Additionally, he has completed several important commissions over the course of the last two decades.

Within his repertoire as a sculptor, Neri began working in plaster in 1957. He was attracted to its raw, and consequently expressive, mutability. The relatively fluid medium could be easily built up, boldly manipulated, and even alarmingly cropped. In the late 1970s, the artist began casting some of his plasters in bronze, following an important sculptural tradition best exemplified in the work of Auguste Rodin. Through bronze, Neri explored the transformation of his original plasters, still impulsively gouging and severing the figures and obscuring the metal under splashes of enamel paint.

During the 1980s, the artist became increasingly engaged with stone, due to his experiences at the legendary marble quarries of Carrara, Italy. In addition to its rich historical associations with masters such as Michelangelo, marble from Carrara is highly prized for its color, luster, and veining. The expressive potential of these formal qualities, as well as the stone's hardness and strength—and thereby its resistance to the artist's intervention—were attractive to Neri. Working in marble is singularly subtractive, requiring chiseling, hammering, and grinding—in essence, cutting away the stone without recourse to rebuilding forms. Such methodology is in direct opposition to Neri's process-oriented plaster aesthetic, which allows for the spontaneous addition and reduction of forms time and again. Neri thrives on the challenge of marble, however. He holds the stone in high esteem, but is less in awe of its preciousness, confronting the unique character of the block and manipulating the medium with a certain abandon not unlike his approach to plaster.

The marble *Odalisque IV* is a case in point. This work depicts a female figure with knees drawn up to her chest in an intimate reclining position. Attention to the female form is entirely in keeping with Neri's oeuvre, although it is more customary to encounter his standing or striding figures. The unpretentious planes of the head, arms, back, and legs are immediately discernable in the roughing out of the stone. Exquisite fields of stippling along the neck, under the torso, and between the recumbent thigh and calf speak the language of process fully exposed, and act as a type of three-dimensional *sfumato*—gradations of light and dark that enhance both the volume of the object and the mystery of the subject. Some surfaces are highly polished to bring out the beauty of the whites and pale grays in the marble, the color and sheen corresponding to the highlighted or shaded areas of the figure. In dynamic contrast to such sympathetic treatment of the form, Neri has made several trenchant and abrupt cuts to the elbow and knee and along the back.

Although all these markings may initially hold the allure of antique statuary, they are above all in keeping with the stylistic vocabulary the artist first introduced in his plasters. *Odalisque IV* is a contemporary fragment, compelling in its serene and sensual yet disquieting multiplicity. It harkens to art historical conventions of the reclining female nude and the odalisque, and pays homage to masters and monuments of the past. It also makes palpable the imprint of time and poignantly reflects the scars of physical loss or emotional burden. It is through his subtle but rigorous communication in stone, as well as his highly potent handling of plaster and bronze, that Manuel Neri has gained recognition as one of figurative sculpture's most important practitioners.

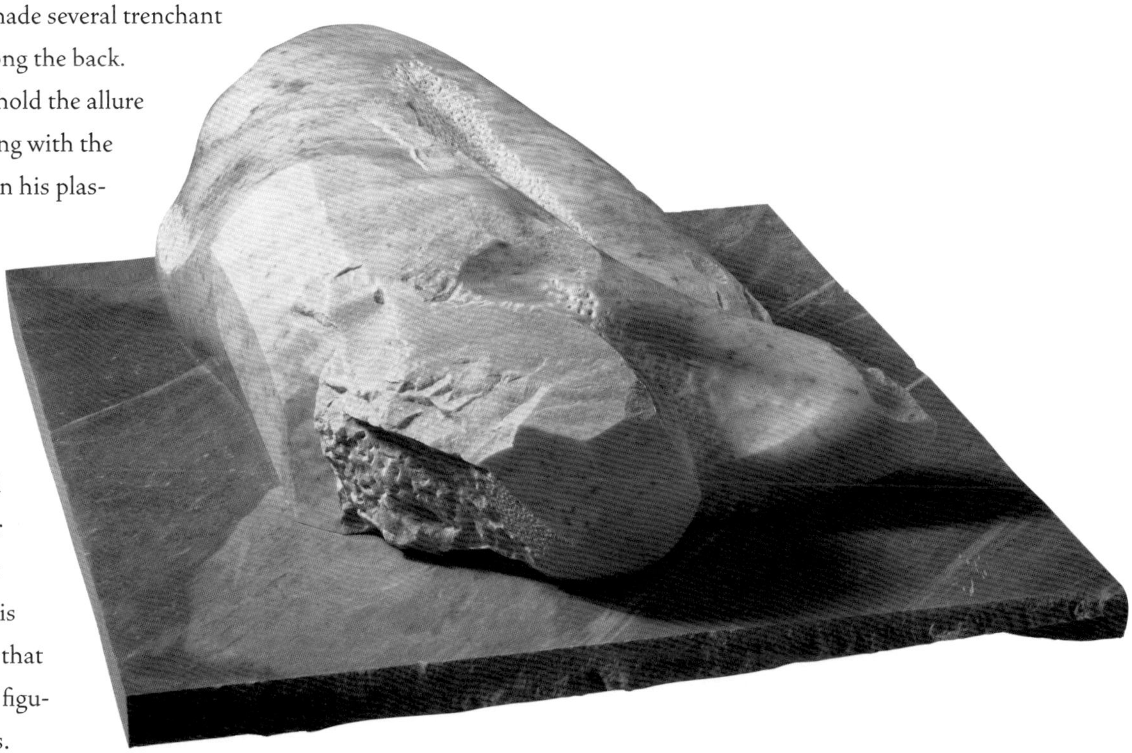

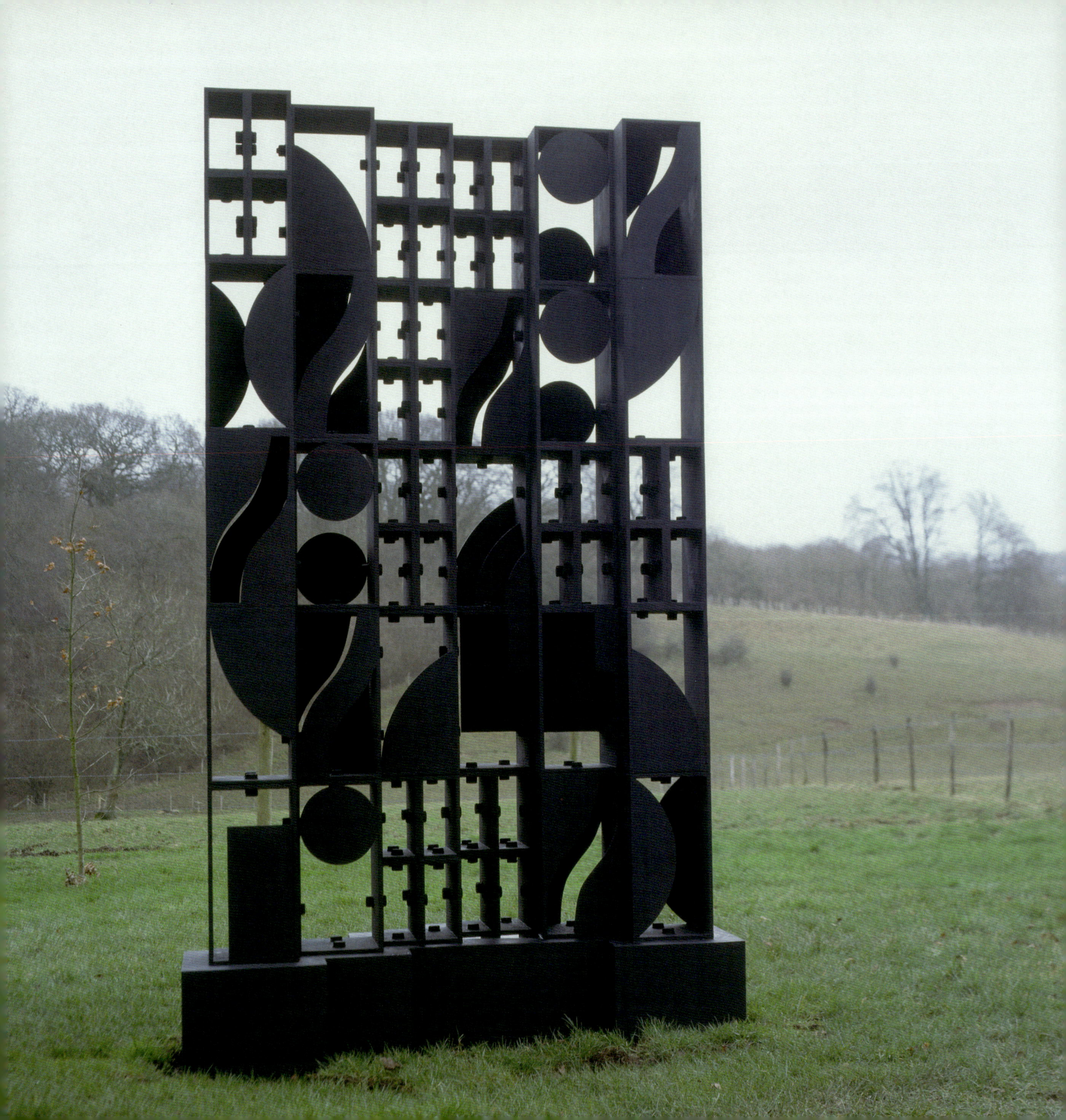

American (born Russia), 1899–1988

LOUISE NEVELSON :: ATMOSPHERE AND ENVIRONMENT XI

1969

Painted weathering (corten) steel, 1/3 (first in an edition of three), h. 9 feet, 3 inches (281.9 cm)

Gift of the Meijer Foundation, 2001.12

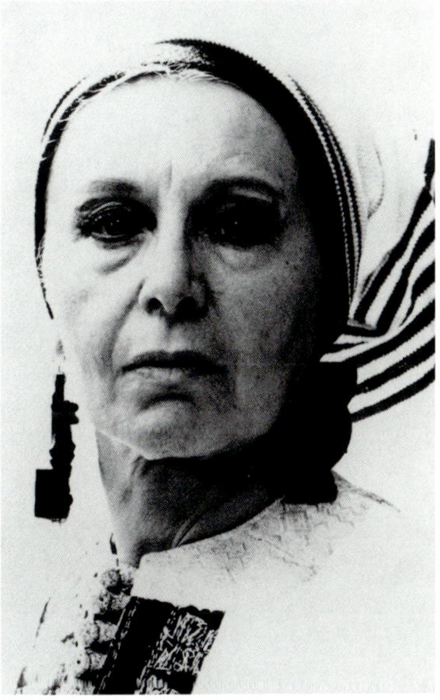

Portrait of Louise Nevelson, 1968

IN THE HISTORY of twentieth-century art, the highly individualized work and aesthetic contributions of Louise Nevelson are of great critical importance. During the course of her long career, she worked as a painter, printmaker, and ceramist, but sculpture is her most important and enduring legacy. Nevelson was born in Kiev, Russia, but her father moved the family to Rockport, Maine, in 1905, where he had established a successful lumber business. Following high school, she married shipowner Charles Nevelson in 1921 and moved to New York, where she immersed herself in the city's cultural life. Ten years later, she separated from her husband, traveled throughout Europe, and settled briefly in Germany to study with Abstract Expressionist painter Hans Hofmann. Upon her return to New York, she enrolled at the acclaimed Art Students League. Nevelson had the opportunity to work with the mural painter Diego Rivera, and to resume study with Hofmann, a recent émigré. She had also begun to seriously consider the work of Pablo Picasso and Cubism at large.

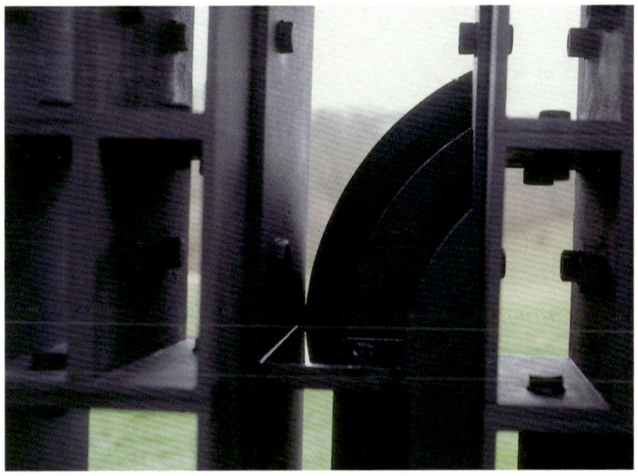

By the mid-1930s, the aspiring artist exhibited both her paintings and terracotta sculptures. Within a decade, she focused primarily on sculpture and began to use found, primarily wooden, objects in her work. Assemblage, the formal organization of these objects, quickly became the focus of her efforts. Nevelson took great pains to bring order and structure to her assemblages through balance, repetition, and subtle variations of pattern. Unity was ultimately achieved by painting the entire surfaces a single color: black was first employed and is most commonly

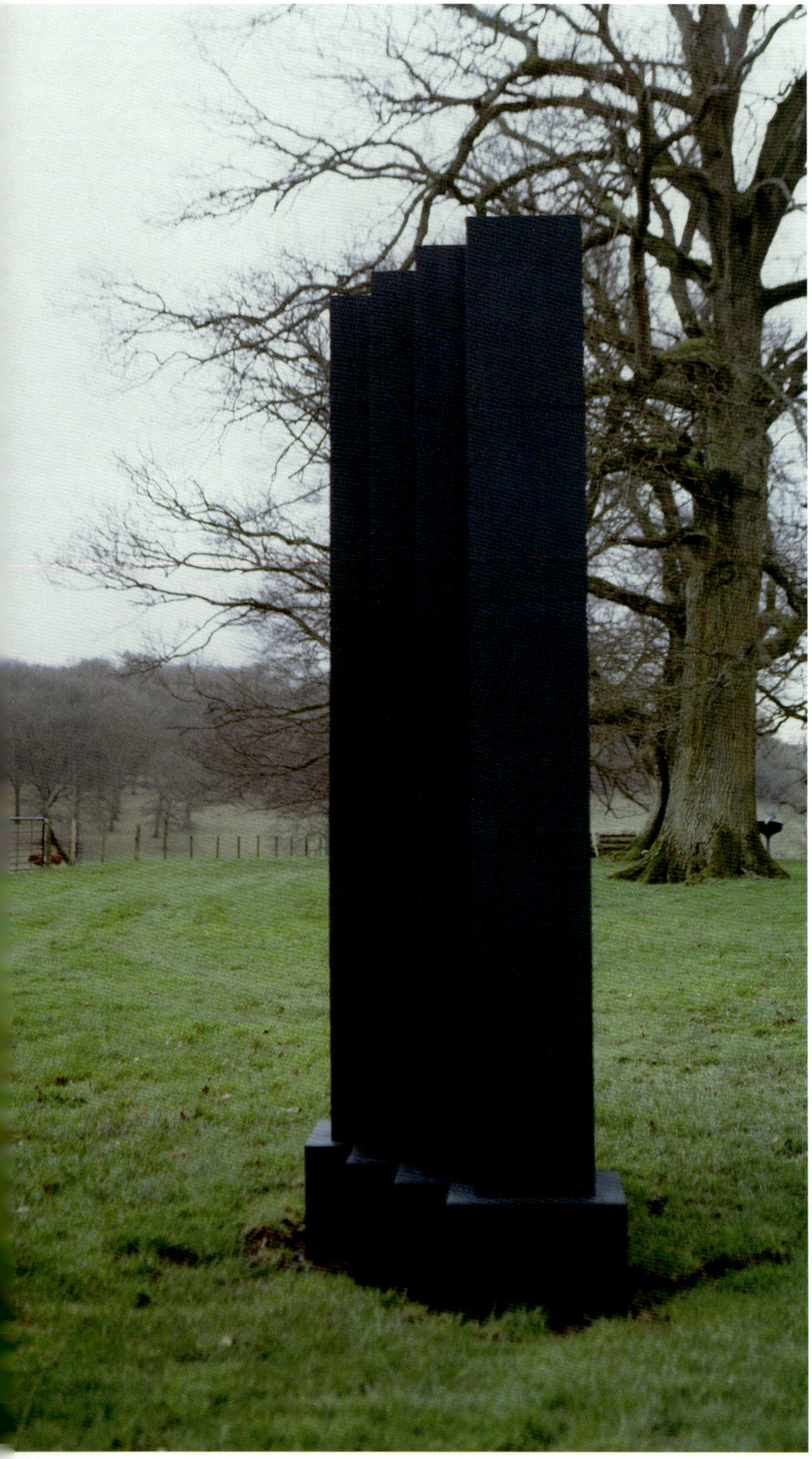

associated with her sculpture, but white and gold were also utilized. Throughout the next three decades, Nevelson perfected her techniques and worked on an increasingly large scale, with indoor designs that ranged from elaborate installations to stage settings and complete interiors. Consequently, her sculptures could be contributions to an existing environment or become environments in themselves.

Nevelson's sculpture was the subject of numerous important exhibitions about the mid-twentieth-century modernism that had emerged by the mid-1960s. At this point, she began to experiment with new materials, fabricating sculpture in aluminum and working with plexiglass. In 1969, she received her first outdoor commission from Princeton University and began to work with weathering (corten) steel. *Atmosphere and Environment XI,* also from 1969, is one of a series of structures based on gardens and natural environments. The work is a result of Nevelson's exploration of the weathering steel medium and her desire to investigate numerous aspects of sculpture unavailable in a gallery setting or studio interior.

The work is composed of a series of open, cubic units, creating a geometric organizational fabric. Arranged in a rectilinear and totemic fashion, these units firmly establish the architectural presence of the sculpture. When viewing *Atmosphere and Environment XI* from a distance, the front and rear facades may appear to be flat surfaces, but Nevelson has created a work that functions as a type of folding screen. Each vertical row either advances or recedes from the rows to which it is attached. This ebb and flow is more pronounced at a moderate distance or when viewed from the sides, where decidedly vertical steps can be seen and the true depth of the piece is understood. A pattern of circular and curved forms are poignantly positioned across the units, adding visual texture and variety to the composition. The curves and arcs suggest motion and growth in response to the currents and forms of the surrounding landscape. As the title *Atmosphere and Environment* implies, the sculpture explores issues of light and shadow, climate and context. The uniformity and carefully arranged structural variations of the design elements present themselves differently according to the time of day, weather, and season. The simplicity of the composition, enhanced by the black painted surface, is deceiving, for both the boldness and the nuances of Nevelson's design literally unfold as the sculpture is experienced in the round.

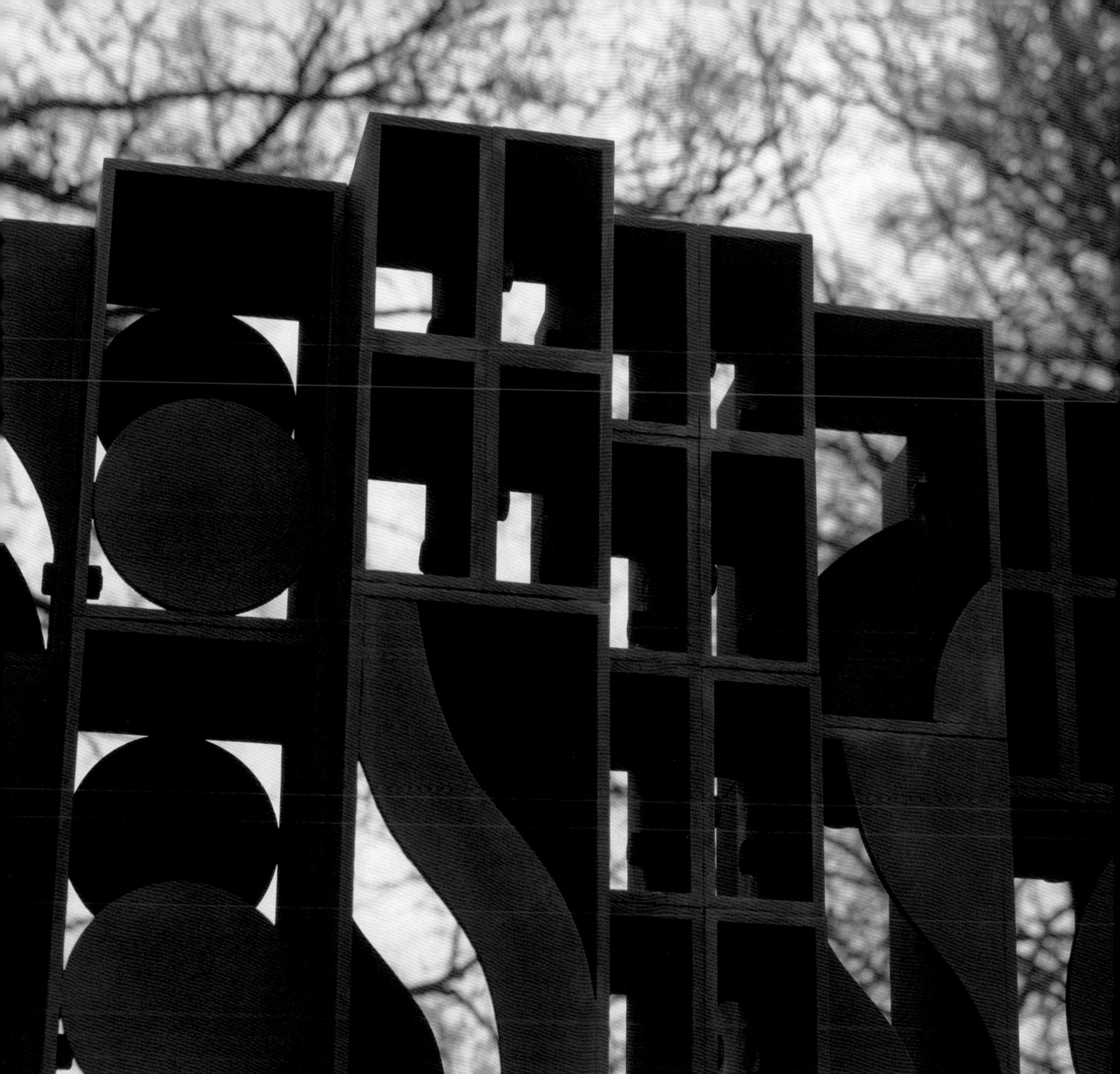

American (born Sweden), 1929
American (born The Netherlands), 1942

CLAES OLDENBURG AND COOSJE VAN BRUGGEN :: PLANTOIR

2001

Stainless steel, aluminum, and fiberglass, painted, A/P (artist's proof for an edition of three), h. 23 feet, 11 inches (729 cm)

Gift of the Meijer Foundation, 2002.1

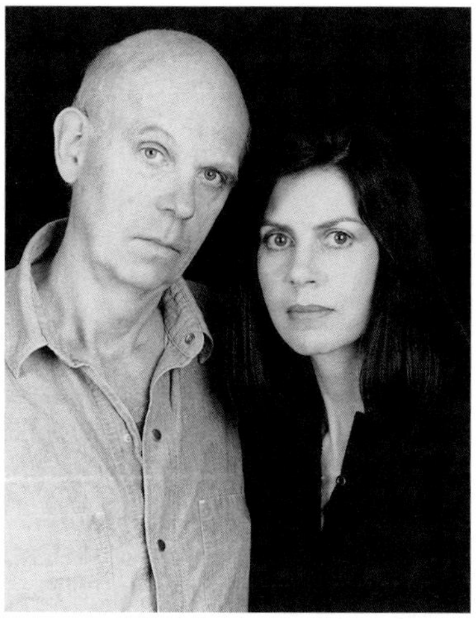

Claes Oldenburg and Coosje van Bruggen, 1986

CLAES OLDENBURG AND COOSJE VAN BRUGGEN have worked together in equal partnership on large-scale projects since 1976, when they placed the giant blue *Trowel* (1971–1976) in the sculpture garden of the Kröller-Müller Museum in Otterlo, The Netherlands. To date, the artistic team has executed more than forty monumental sculptures that are installed at various sites in Europe, Asia, and the United States. Oldenburg and van Bruggen are celebrated internationally for their transformation of everyday objects into colossal works that are realized with meticulous attention to aesthetics and engineering. Humor and irony welcome the most casual of viewers to these sculptures through unexpected scale, materials, and color. A deeper appreciation of the formal considerations of design, fabrication, and placement and the subtle discernment of meaning therein unfold through the continued examination of Oldenburg and van Bruggen's works over time.

Oldenburg was born in Stockholm in 1929. In 1936, he moved with his family to Chicago. He studied at Yale University, returning afterward to Chicago to work as a reporter for the City News Bureau of Chicago. During this period, he also attended the School of the Art Institute of Chicago. In 1956, he settled permanently in New York and had his first one-person show there in 1959. In the following year, he exhibited his installation *The Street,* with Jim Dine, and staged the first of his Happenings—a potent early example of performance art. In 1961, he exhibited *The Store,* a series of brightly painted plaster reliefs and sculptures of domestic and commercial mass-produced objects typical of an American consumer society. He quickly emerged at the very center of New York's cultural avant-garde and Pop Art

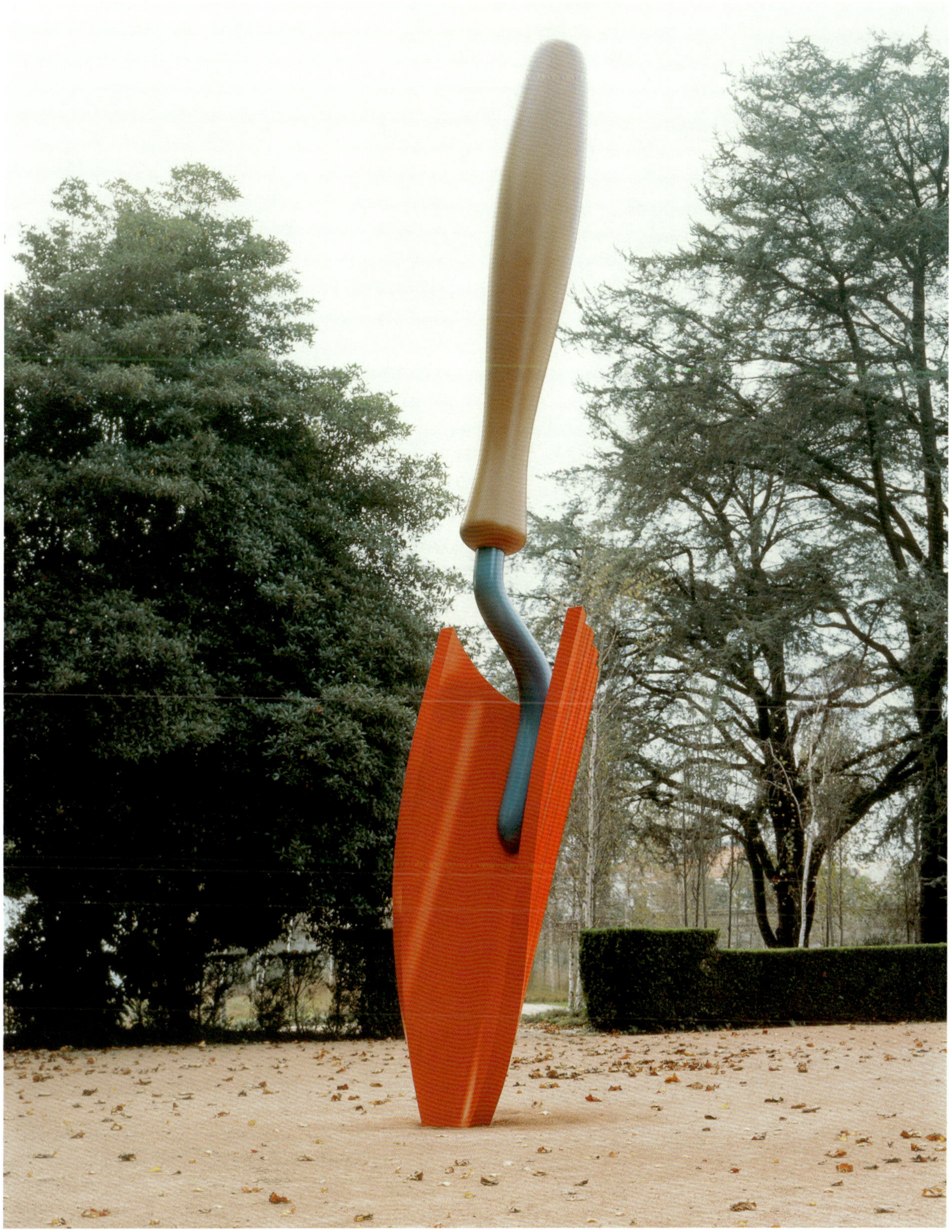

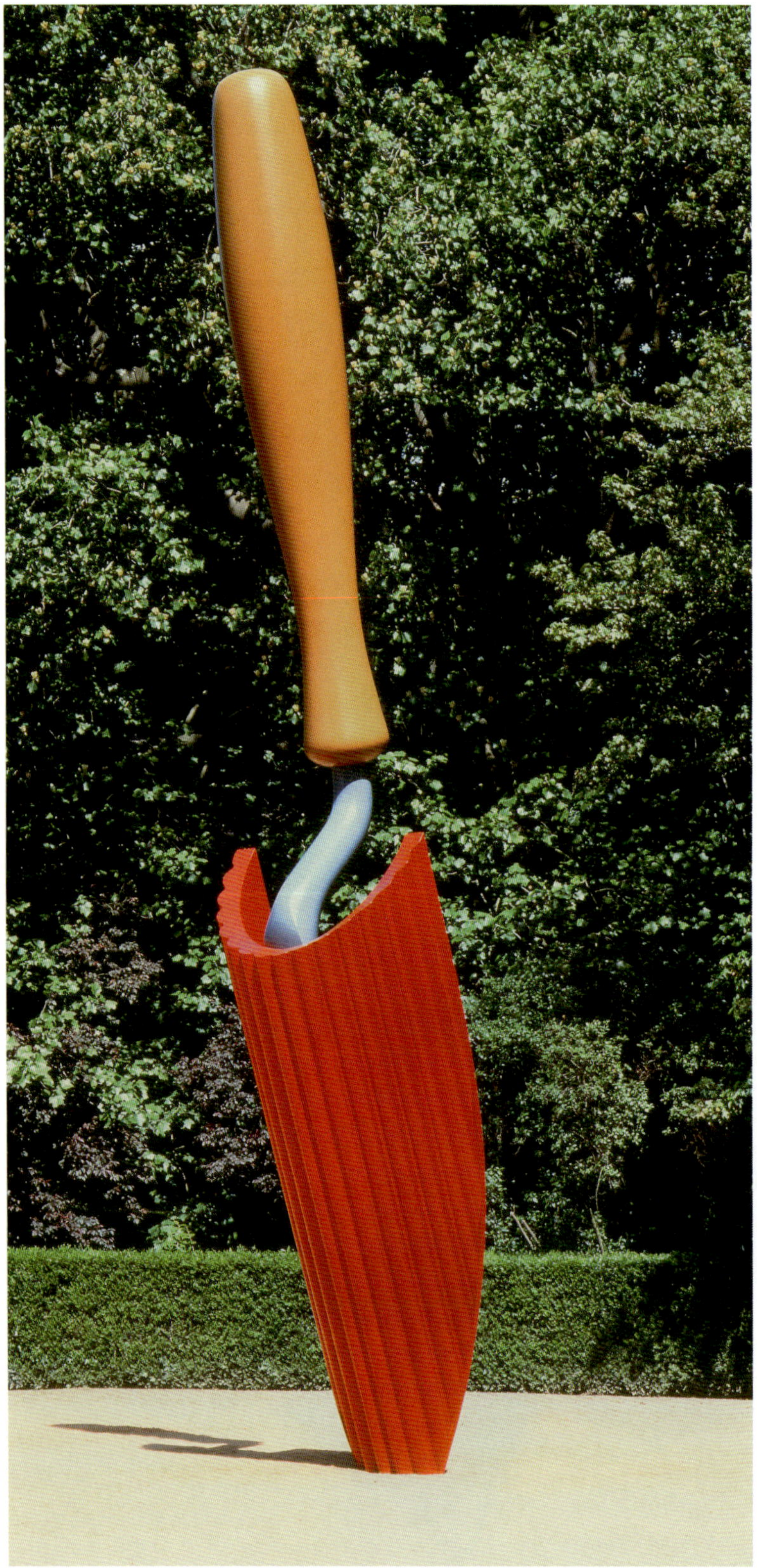

movement. In 1962, Oldenburg revolutionized the history of art with his large soft sculptures of normally hard objects. The sculptures' pliable, collapsing forms were alien not only to our expectations of the size, substance, and function of common things, but also to the anticipated use of metal, stone, or other solid material for the creation of three-dimensional works. By the end of the decade, he turned his attention to imaginary architectural projects based on mundane objects, and in the early 1970s, he began to focus almost exclusively on the larger-than-life outdoor works that continue to this day.

The writer and art historian Coosje van Bruggen began to work with Oldenburg in 1976. After receiving her doctorate in the history of art from the University of Groningen in 1967, Coosje van Bruggen became a member of the curatorial staff at the renowned Stedelijk Museum in Amsterdam, and later taught at the Academy of Fine Arts in Enschede. In 1979, she published *Claes Oldenburg: Mouse Museum/Ray Gun Wing,* one of her many highly regarded art historical writings. She has also written influential books on other artists, including Hanne Darboven, Bruce Nauman, John Baldesarri, and the architect Frank O. Gehry. In her capacity as a curator, van Bruggen has been involved in multiple museum projects and was the first female independent curator to serve on the selection committee for Germany's highly influential *Documenta* exhibitions devoted to contemporary art. She has lectured widely and has taught at Harvard University's Graduate Center for Architecture and at Yale University's Department of Sculpture. She continues to write, in addition to her sculptural collaborations with Oldenburg.

The Frederik Meijer Gardens' *Plantoir,* of 2001, is an exaggerated version of a French-style garden trowel of the same name. Standing nearly twenty-four feet high, it is the first monumental sculpture created by Oldenburg and van Bruggen specifically for a garden setting. It was originally featured as the majestic centerpiece of an outdoor display of their work on the grounds of the Serralves Foundation in Porto, Portugal. The artist's proof for the sculpture is permanently sited at the very center of the Sculpture Park.

Plantoir is viewed by the artists as a feminine counterpart to the more masculine *Trowel* at the Kröller-Müller Museum. A call and response is communicated over distance and time—feminine to masculine, domestic to industrial, curved to angular, scoop shaped to flat bladed. A common object expanded to nearly sacred proportions, *Plantoir*'s sheer size draws immediate attention to its aesthetic presence. The surface of the sculpture is glossy and smooth, like lacquer. Besides its recognizable imagery, *Plantoir*'s slender, elongated blade of gleaming red brings to mind associations with architectural niches found in formal garden settings, or suggests the sensuality of an unfolding flower. The neck of the tool is a sinuous curve, resembling the joint of a vigorous vine. With graceful ease, the neck transitions to the handle, which extends toward the open sky like a powerful exclamation point and invigorates the monolithic presence of the entire sculpture.

Profiled against the landscape and literally rising beyond familiar experience, *Plantoir* unquestionably alters our consciousness of ordinary things. Characteristic elements are exploited: the sculpture maintains the normal form of a trowel, and through its upright position and garden setting preserves a believable context. On the other hand, irresistible novelty resides in its shiny newness, reinforcing notions of mass consumerism. Whimsy is captured in the dramatic balance with which the sculpture is engineered to stand at an angle and remain secure with only a tiny fraction of the scoop embedded in the ground. With dynamic visual and narrative force and decisive sculptural presence, *Plantoir* is destined to be a fertile symbol of the Gardens' full and equal dedication to both horticulture and sculpture.

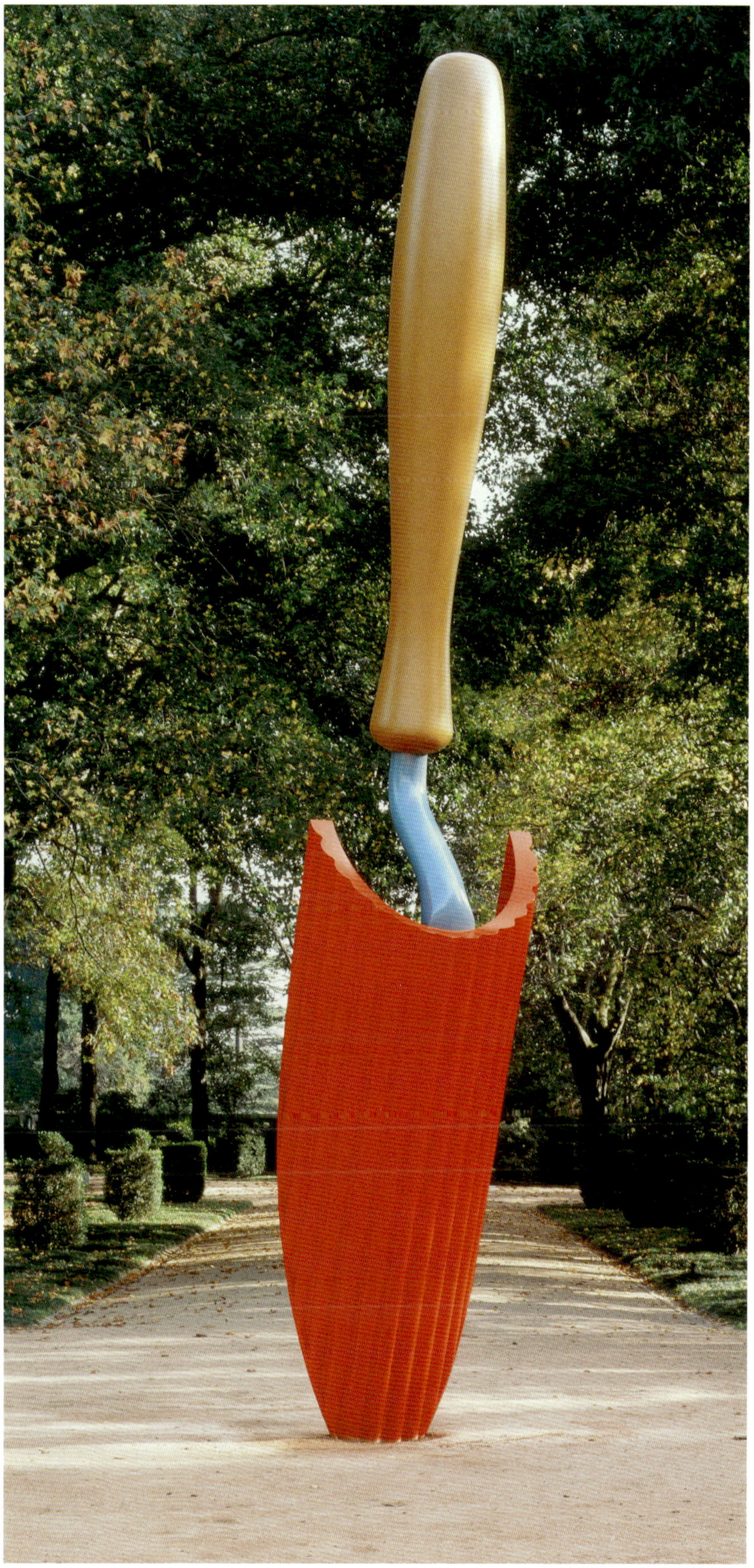

American, born 1960

CAROLYN OTTMERS :: FULL CIRCLE

1999

Industrial porcelain, h. 7 to 15 inches (17.8 to 38.1 cm)

Gift of the Meijer Foundation, 1999.04

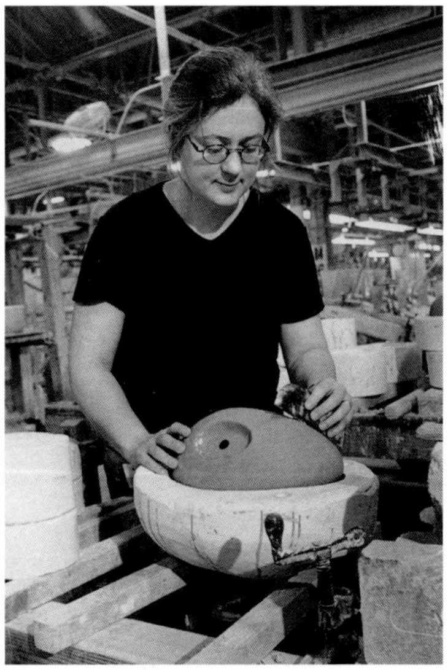

Carolyn Ottmers pulls a wet clay egg from a plaster mold

CAROLYN OTTMERS is one of two artists, along with Richard Hunt, who, to date, have been commissioned by the Frederik Meijer Gardens to create works of art specifically for the Sculpture Park. Ottmers was born in Austin, Texas, in 1960. She attended Southwest Texas State University and then transferred to the University of Texas, Austin, where she received a bachelor of fine arts degree in 1984. She continued her studies at the School of the Art Institute of Chicago and earned a master of fine arts degree in 1989. She currently teaches in the sculpture program at the School of the Art Institute. Ottmers has exhibited since the late 1980s across the United States and internationally. Her work is especially admired by critics and general audiences in the Midwest, where her expanding oeuvre is perhaps best known. She has been the recipient of several grants, including those from the Ford Foundation and the City of Chicago. In addition to her teaching and exhibition schedule, Ottmers has received a number of public commissions. The first, titled *Intersect,* was completed in 1989 for the exterior plaza of Chicago's Emergency Communications Center. Seven monumental cast-aluminum leaves, whose vein structure traces cartographic details of the city, are scattered across the

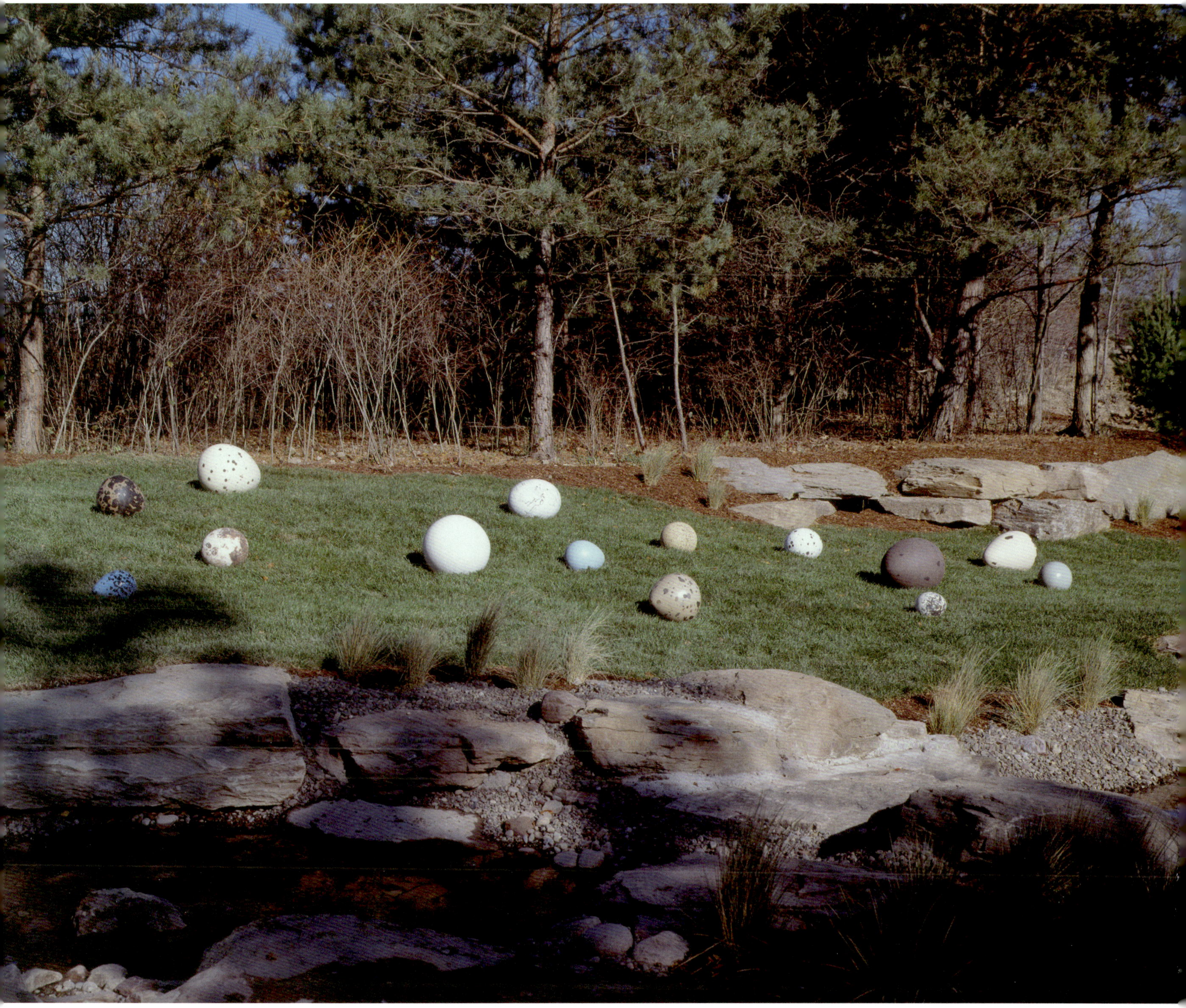

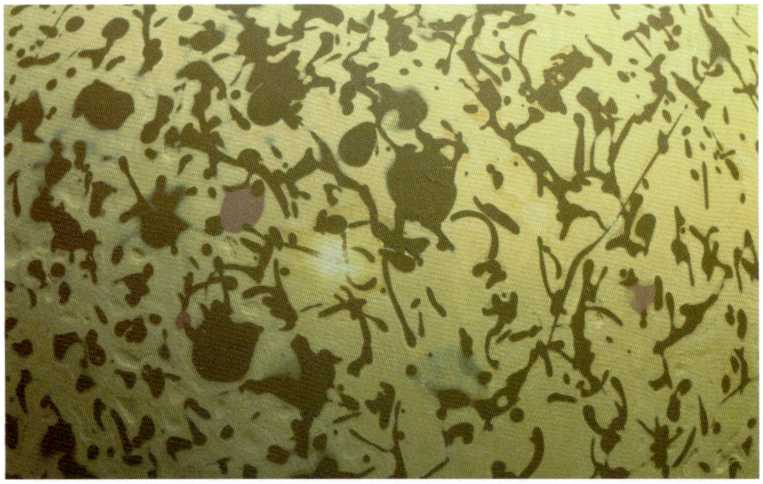

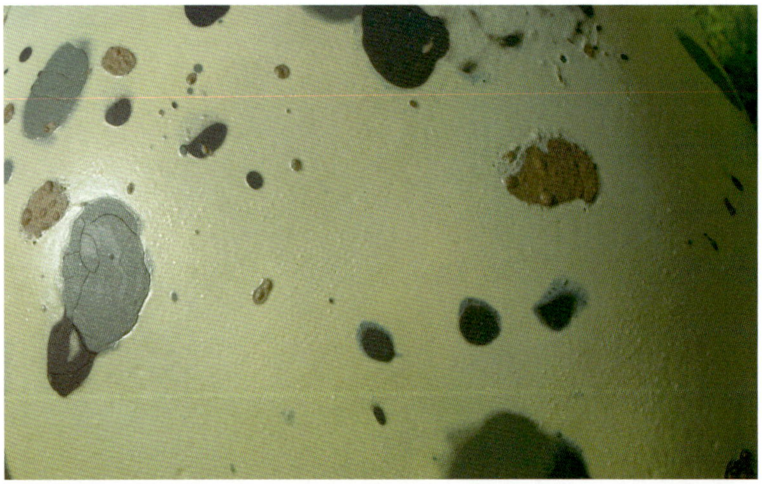

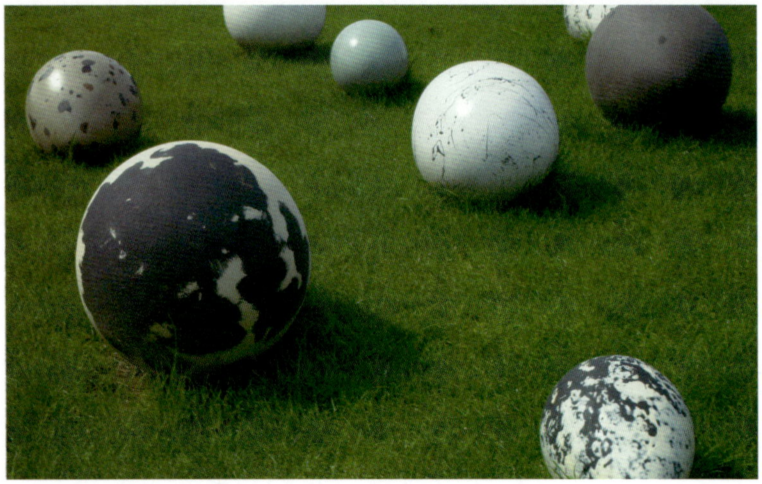

plaza. A second commission, for the Frederik Meijer Gardens, resulted in *Full Circle.*

Ottmers' contribution is the product of the first Meijer Sculpture Competition, initiated in 1997. The competition was open to artists living in one of the four states adjacent to Lake Michigan: Michigan, Wisconsin, Illinois, and Indiana. In the summer of 1998, Ottmers' proposal was selected from those of six finalists out of more than ninety entrants. The artist envisioned creating eleven eggs to be slipcast in clay and colored and patterned according to eleven species of birds indigenous to Michigan. The preliminary prototypes were produced in diminutive size, and then intentionally exaggerated in scale for the final work. Ottmers' concept was strongly influenced by the natural habitat at the Frederik Meijer Gardens, and the project would continue to evolve as matters such as scale, placement, and interpretation were considered.

To realize *Full Circle,* Ottmers worked with the staff of the Frederik Meijer Gardens and Sculpture Park to record the species of birds that had been documented on the grounds in the preceding year. The artist studied the birds selected and the characteristics of their eggs and first created the respective egg shapes in styrofoam at her Chicago studio. Then, at the Kohler Company's Pottery in Sheboygan, Wisconsin—the largest pottery studio in the world under one roof—Ottmers brought her idea to fruition. The Kohler Company, renowned as a leading manufacturer of plumbing and specialty products in the United States, annually invites artists, through application, to their clay and iron studios to work with the equipment and materials traditionally employed for the manufacture of industrial and commercial objects. Ottmers was awarded a residency there through the Arts/Industry program for visual artists administered by the John Michael Kohler Arts Center. With studio space, factory equipment, technical assistance, and a research laboratory at her disposal, the artist developed the clay prototypes and glazes for the eggs. She then slipcast, glazed, and fired the full-scale components in industrial porcelain (a strong, off-white vitreous china clay).

In its final form, *Full Circle* is composed of fifteen individual eggs arranged on the ground. The two smallest, representing the American crow and the killdeer, are ten inches in length, while the largest, that of

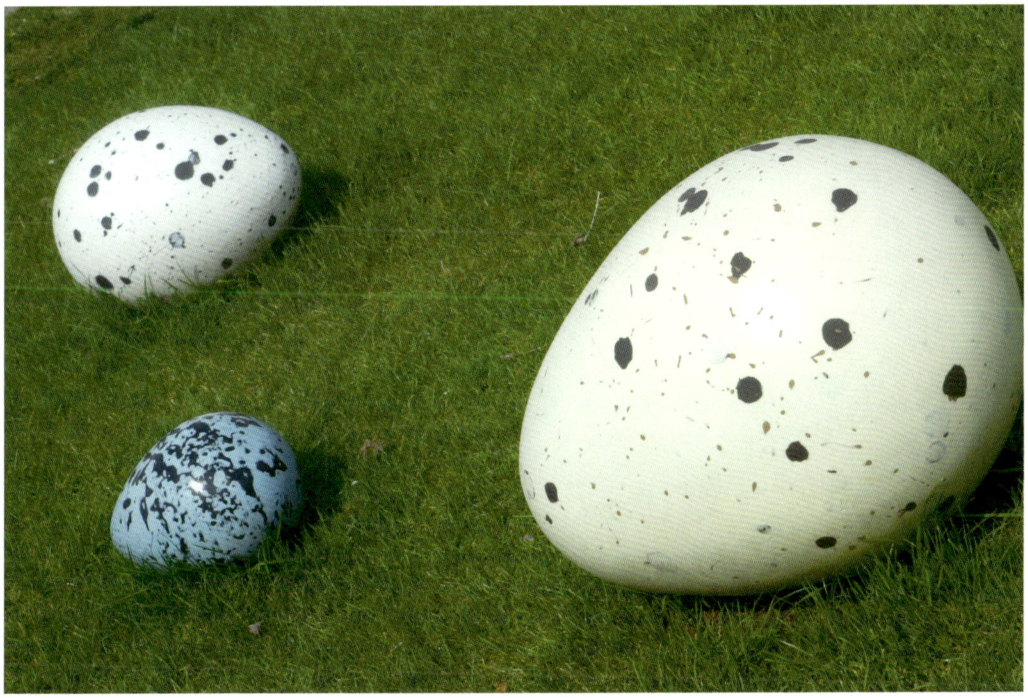

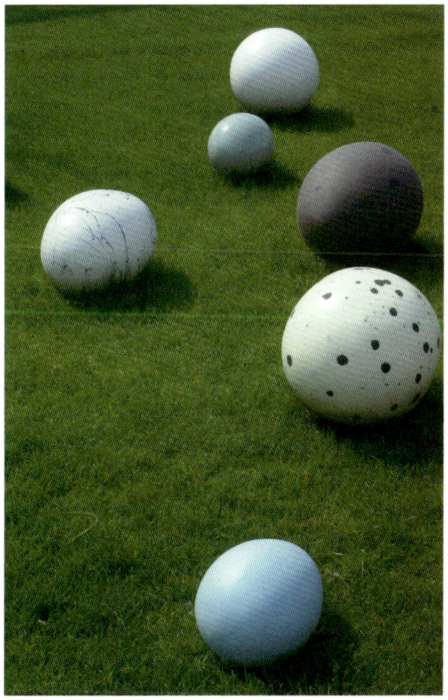

the herring gull, is twenty-two and one-half inches long. The work has seen two stages of presentation: the eggs were initially grouped close together in a temporary location and are now dispersed in a larger configuration in the Sculpture Park. The unexpected scale of the eggs draws attention to the natural beauty that impressed Ottmers and emphasizes an appreciation for the significant, yet often unnoticed, role that wildlife plays in our everyday world. In the broadest sense, *Full Circle* is a gently provoking commentary on the continuity of life as well as its transience. The porcelain medium is an ironic reinforcement of this fragile yet constant cycle. The work's fifteen recognizable shapes, with their particular colors and markings, also speak to the ecological identity of the region and the pride of place that such an association inspires. Ultimately, these grand birds' eggs are charged with the beauty and wonder of both nature and art, as their installation in a garden and sculpture park poignantly asserts.

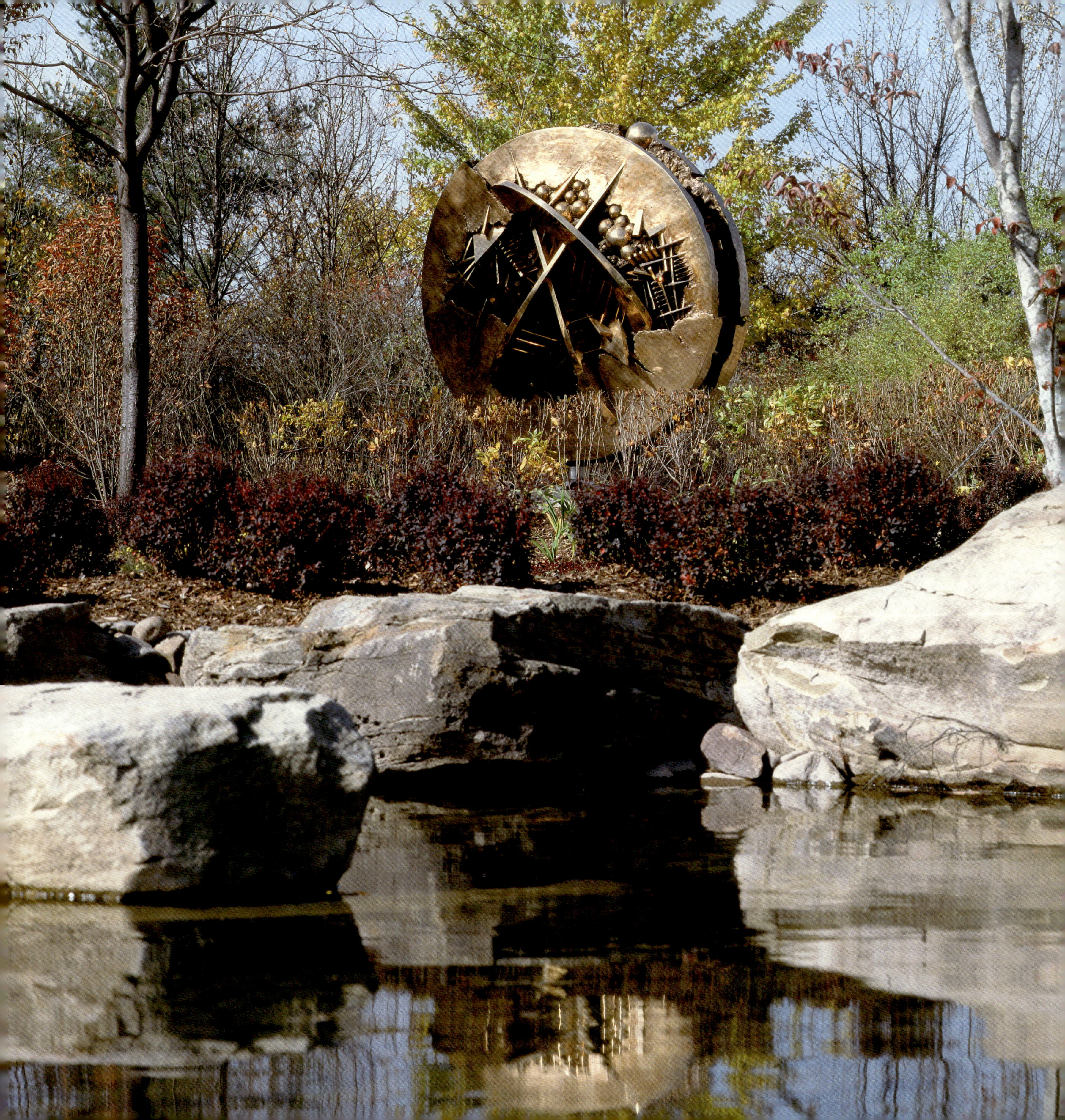

Italian, born 1926

ARNALDO POMODORO :: DISK IN THE FORM OF A DESERT ROSE

1993–1994; Frederik Meijer Gardens cast, 1999–2000

Bronze, 2/2 (second in an edition of two), diam. 9 feet, 11 inches (302.3 cm)

Gift of the Meijer Foundation, 2000.09

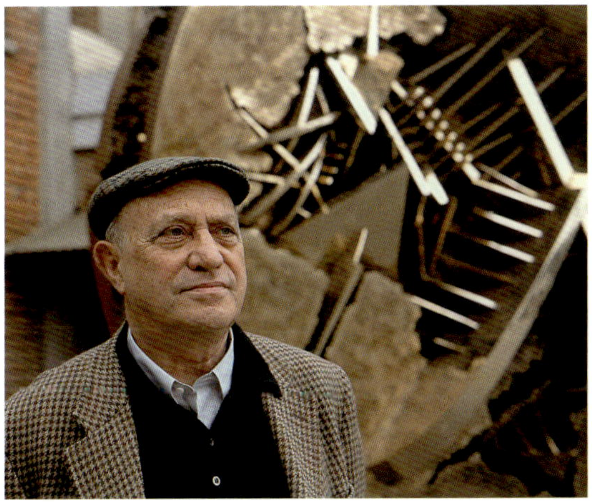

Arnaldo Pomodoro at his Milan studio, 2000

THE MONUMENTAL bronze sculptures of Arnaldo Pomodoro are heralded among the most profound works of contemporary art. Displayed prominently in collections ranging from the Vatican to the United Nations, his works are highly prized by museums and are sited in a multitude of urban centers in both Europe and America. Pomodoro was born in Morciano di Romagna, and came of age in Italy's culturally rich Marches region. He studied engineering at the University of Bologna and worked briefly as an engineer, but his interest in design eventually led him to create theater sets and costumes. In 1952, he began to work as a goldsmith in collaboration with his brother, Gio. By the end of the decade, he had exhibited his jewelry and bas-relief sculptures extensively and made his first trips to Paris and New York. Fine craftsmanship and attention to detail became the hallmark of his repertoire; these qualities are related to his mastery of and preference for the lost-wax casting method.

In the 1960s, Pomodoro began to show large-scale work, including massive bronze spheres, columns, and disks, which captured the imagination of the international art community. Early in his career, Pomodoro developed a vocabulary of imagery based on pure geometric forms whose smooth surfaces are broken by a related array of lines, shapes, and textures. Although the general forms and polished surfaces reflect the influence of modern masters such as Constantin Brancusi and Umberto Boccioni, the unique, eruptive elements can also be seen as references to archaic and futuristic designs. The year 1964 was of great critical

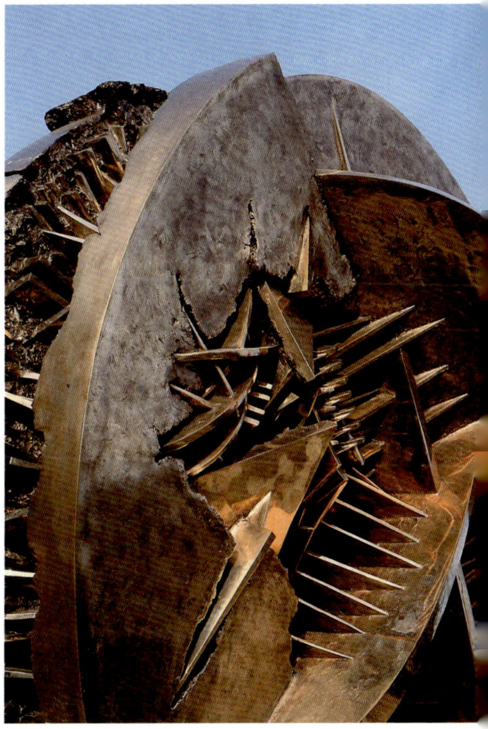

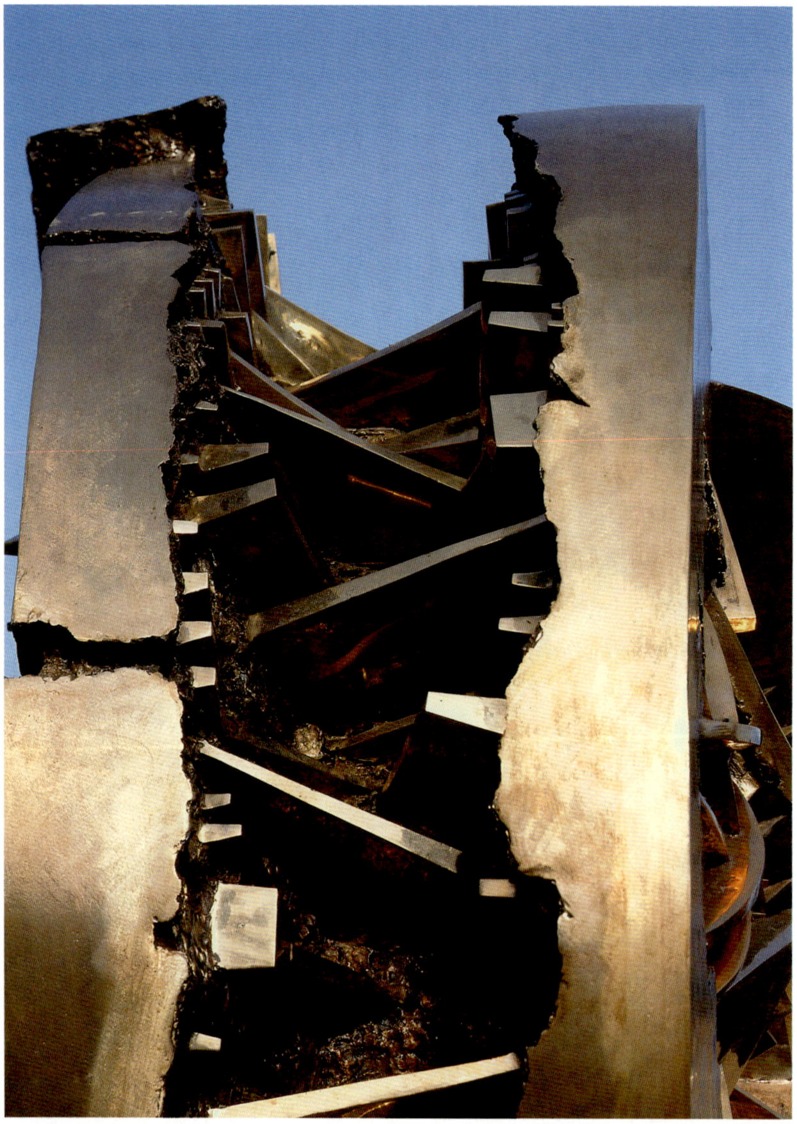

significance to the artist; he earned the International Prize for Sculpture at the São Paulo Bienal and was given a one-person show at the famed Venice Biennale. Ten years later, only two decades after the first public showing of his work, Pomodoro was the subject of a major retrospective. In addition to his burgeoning career as a sculptor, he also found time to teach and serve as an artist-in-residence at Mills College in Oakland, California, and at the University of California, Berkeley.

From the mid-1970s, Pomodoro's oeuvre is marked by an increasing number of important commissions and exhibitions. *Triad,* commissioned by the shah of Iran but later installed at the PepsiCo Sculpture Garden in Purchase, New York, and *Pillars for the Amaliehaven,* installed in front of the Royal Palace in Copenhagen, are among numerous prominent examples of his commissioned works. Considering his facility for monumental bronze sculpture and his sensitivity to its context, Pomodoro is the undisputed and most prodigious heir to centuries of tradition in Italian art reaching from the Roman to the Renaissance and Baroque eras. In 1981, he was awarded the Henry Moore Prize at the Hakone Open-Air Museum in Japan. Three years later, he was the subject of a prestigious installation of more than sixty works at the Forte Belvedere above the city of Florence. Pomodoro has remained actively involved in theater and set design and in printmaking. In 1996, he established a foundation outside Milan for the preservation and permanent public display of his work.

Disk in the Form of a Desert Rose is an important and representative example of Pomodoro's sculpture on a monumental scale. It was created in an edition of two. The first casting, from 1993–1994, was installed in Turin, Italy; the Frederik Meijer Gardens' cast dates from 1999–2000. The eruptive core emerging from both sides of the disk's platelike surfaces captures the very essence of Pomodoro's style. Viewing the work in profile not only reveals the tension between the two planes, which seem to be pulling apart from one another, it also exposes the articulated inner core of the disk, where the roiling expansion and compression of the piece apparently originates. Unlike many of his other works, the planar surfaces in this sculpture are not altogether smooth and highly polished. Instead, those areas closest to the fissures resemble the parched texture of the desert floor. The complexity of details, sensitivity to texture, and deep shadows cast through undercut forms can be directly linked to the sculptor's highly developed design sense, as well as his experience with lost-wax casting.

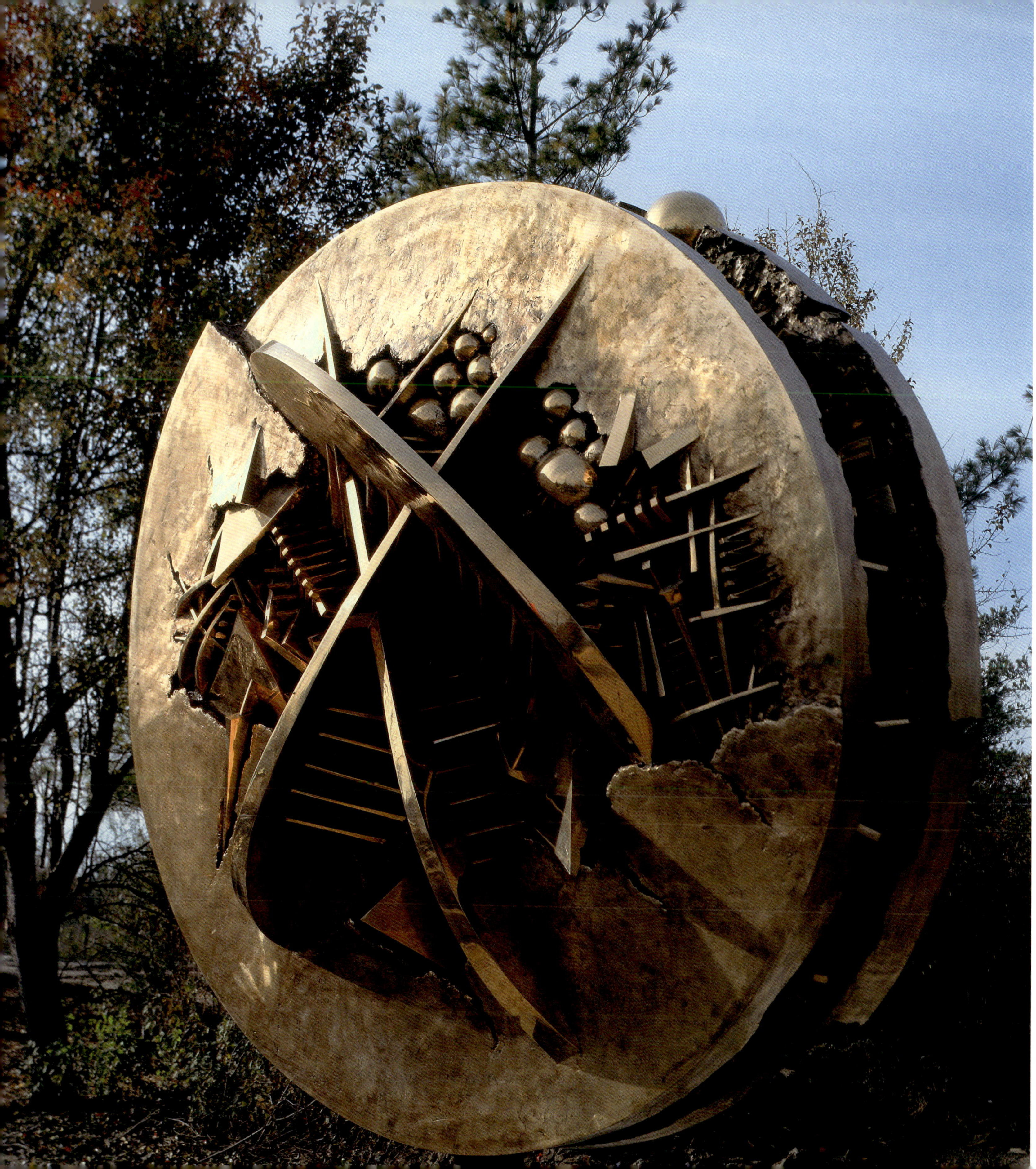

American, born 1907

GEORGE RICKEY :: FOUR OPEN SQUARES HORIZONTAL GYRATORY—TAPERED

1984

Stainless steel, 2/3 (second in an edition of three),
h. 16½ inches (41.9 cm) above water

Gift of the Meijer Foundation, 2001.07

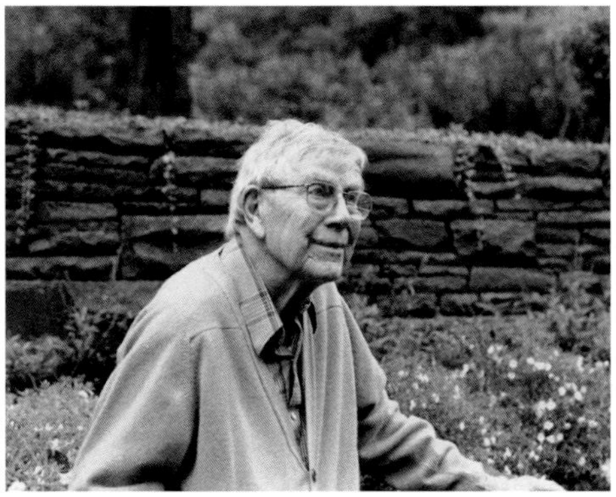

George Rickey at his studio in East Chatham, New York, 1999

THE CAREER of American artist George Rickey is synonymous with kinetic sculpture. Born in South Bend, Indiana, in 1907, Rickey grew up near Glasgow, Scotland. He studied drawing in 1928 and 1929 before moving to Paris, where he studied with several of the leading design modernists, including André Lhote, Fernand Léger, and Amédée Ozenfant. Rickey returned to the United States in 1930, and began his teaching career as a painting instructor. However, it was during his military service in World War II that Rickey began to experiment with sculpture. As a gunnery instructor, he had access to a well-equipped machine shop that led to his production of a series of small mobiles. Following the war, he became familiar with the concepts of Russian Constructivism and the work of Naum Gabo and Antoine Pevsner, which in largely nonrepresentational terms placed great emphasis on the formal elements of sculpture. By 1950, Rickey had abandoned painting in favor of three-dimensional form.

In sculpture, Rickey explored movement, searching for equilibrium among elements rather than dramatic motion. His pursuits would help define kinetic sculpture—one of the most important developments in the history of twentieth-century art. The period from the late 1950s through the mid-1960s was critical for him: he utilized a vocabulary of simple geometric shapes and lines and worked on an increasingly large scale. Moreover, he eliminated color by focusing almost exclusively on the use of stainless steel, which allowed him to place greater emphasis on issues of form and movement. Unlike many artists who explored the potential

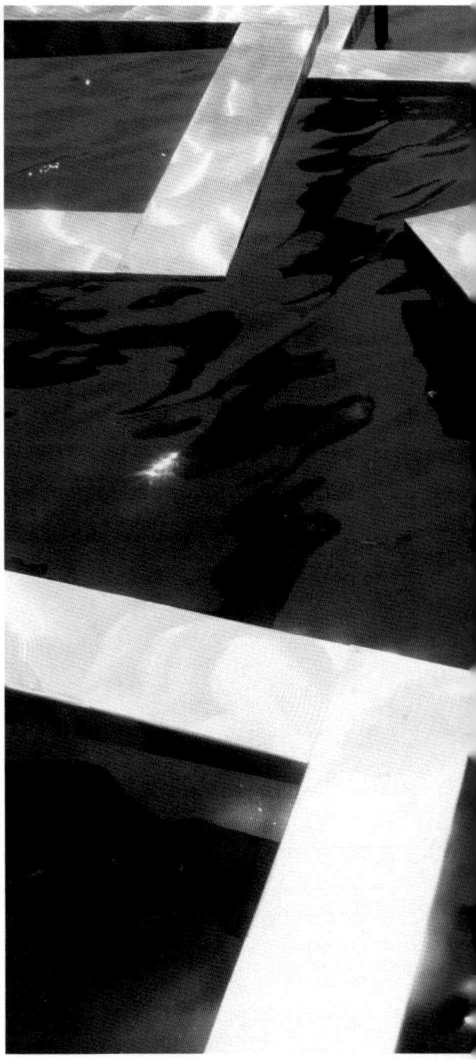

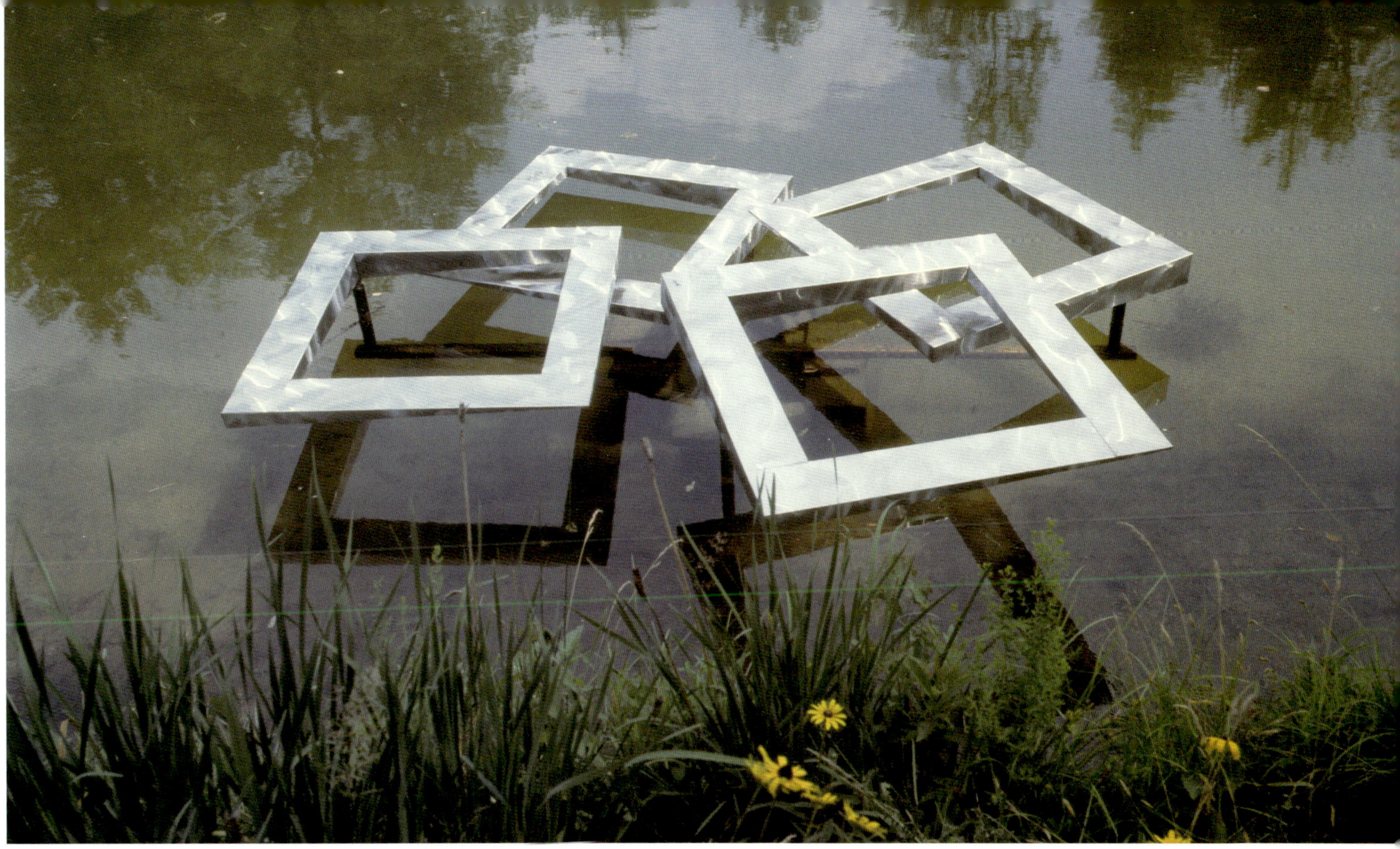

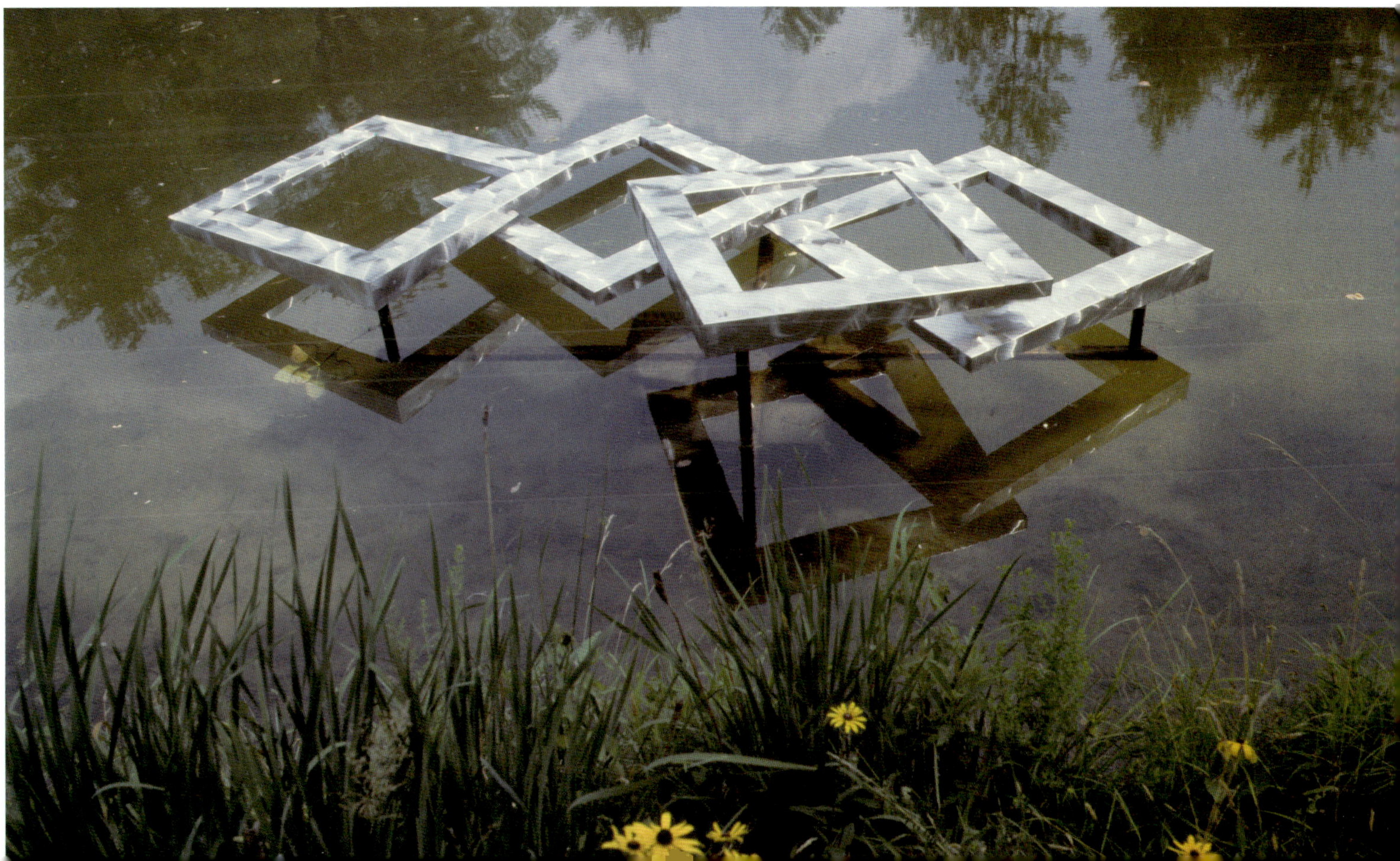

of Kinetic Art, Rickey never turned to motorized movement. The very essence of sculpture as a three-dimensional form engaged with the concepts of volume, space, and light had, thanks to Rickey, been expanded to include the direction, speed, and nuances of air and the continually changing relationships of forms that air currents put into motion. His sculpture is precisely engineered to achieve harmonious, ever-evolving compositions whose individual components move gracefully and securely, even under strong winds.

George Rickey's close association with Indiana, the state of his birth, and southwestern Michigan, where he taught and worked as a museum director in the late 1930s, has led to the placement of many examples of his sculpture in a relatively concentrated geographic area. In general, most works are either wall installations in which elements move parallel to a vertical surface or freestanding compositions whose armatures operate from a vertical pole. The Sculpture Park's *Four Open Squares Horizontal Gyratory—Tapered* is a unique piece in this region, as well as nationally, because it is a horizontal composition that functions in a water setting.

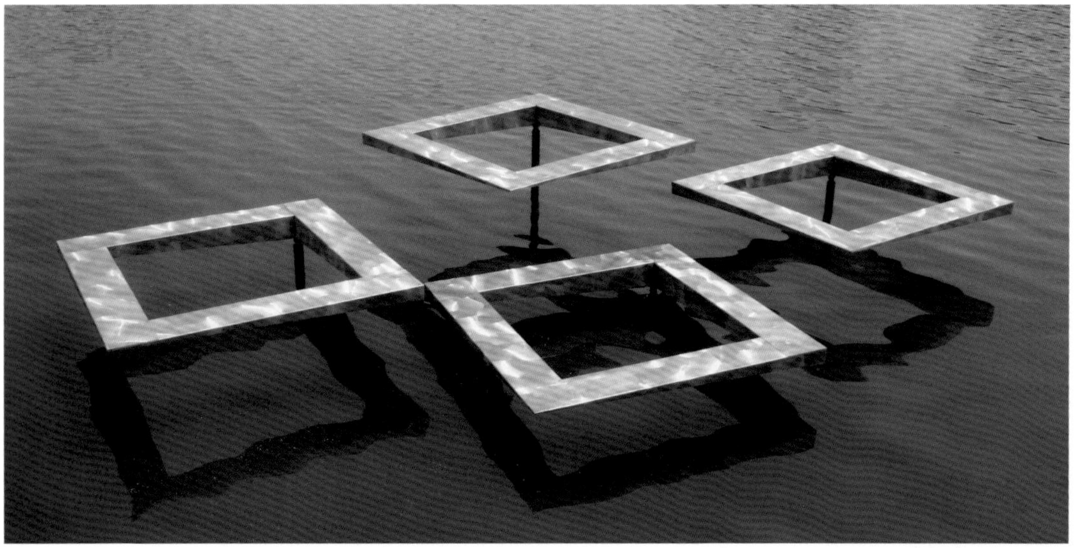

Each of the squares is fastened to a vertical pin that, in turn, is attached to an underwater brace placed securely on the pond floor. Because of the sculptor's carefully engineered design, the pins, topped with their square forms, emerge subtly, nearly invisibly, from the water, creating the illusion that the sculpture is floating above the surface of the pond. Water becomes an integral part of the kinetic composition. Because of its inherent fluid and reflective qualities and its shimmering, vibrating surface, water heightens the illusion that the squares hover freely above or glide effortlessly across a liquid "base."

As with all of Rickey's kinetic sculptures, the movement of *Four Open Squares Horizontal Gyratory—Tapered* is driven by air. Each square revolves independently around a ball bearing on the tip of its own pin, so the speed and uniformity of their respective revolutions vary. The height of the pins above the water differs slightly, while beneath the surface, the pins have been laid out along the underwater brace so that the squares will overlap without touching one another. The parameters of space between the squares have been carefully calculated by the sculptor, but ultimately the compositional choreography is controlled by nature. Such an interesting duality is more understandable when considering the sleek rectilinear forms and the swirling, flickering texture of polished stainless steel in relation to the fluid elements of water and the transient effects of light across its surface. Rickey has created a set of mechanical water lilies that, while not formed of the natural world, comes to life because of it.

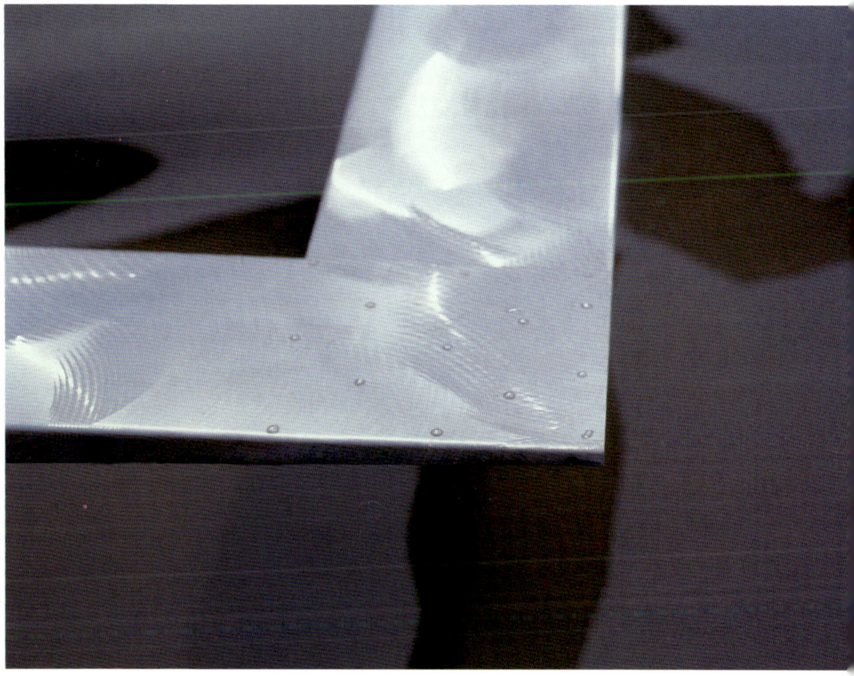

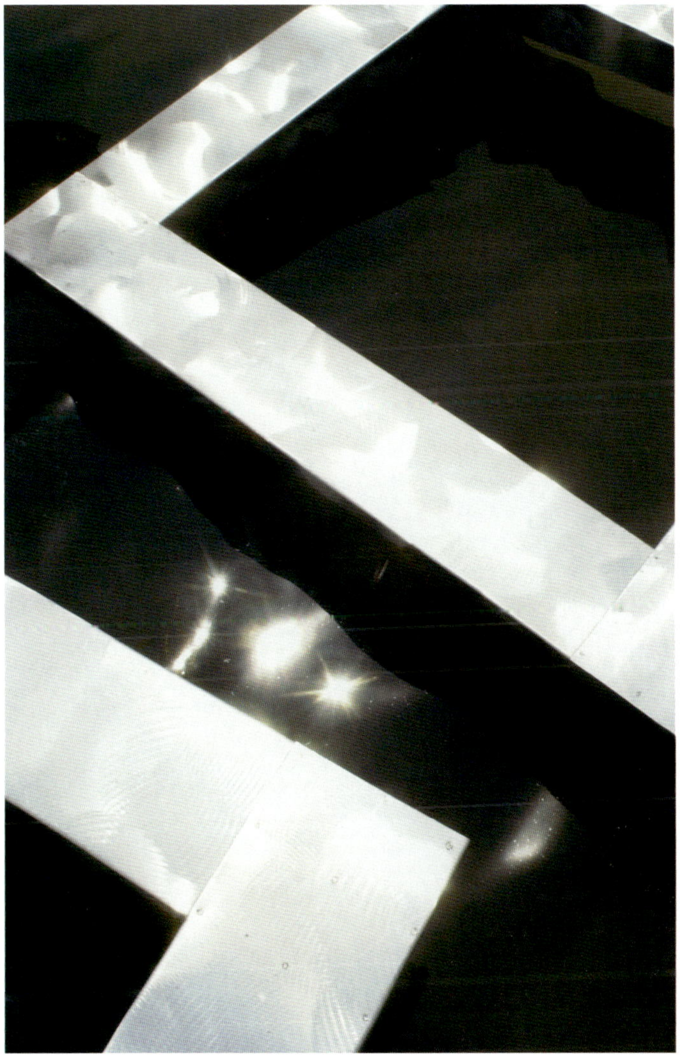

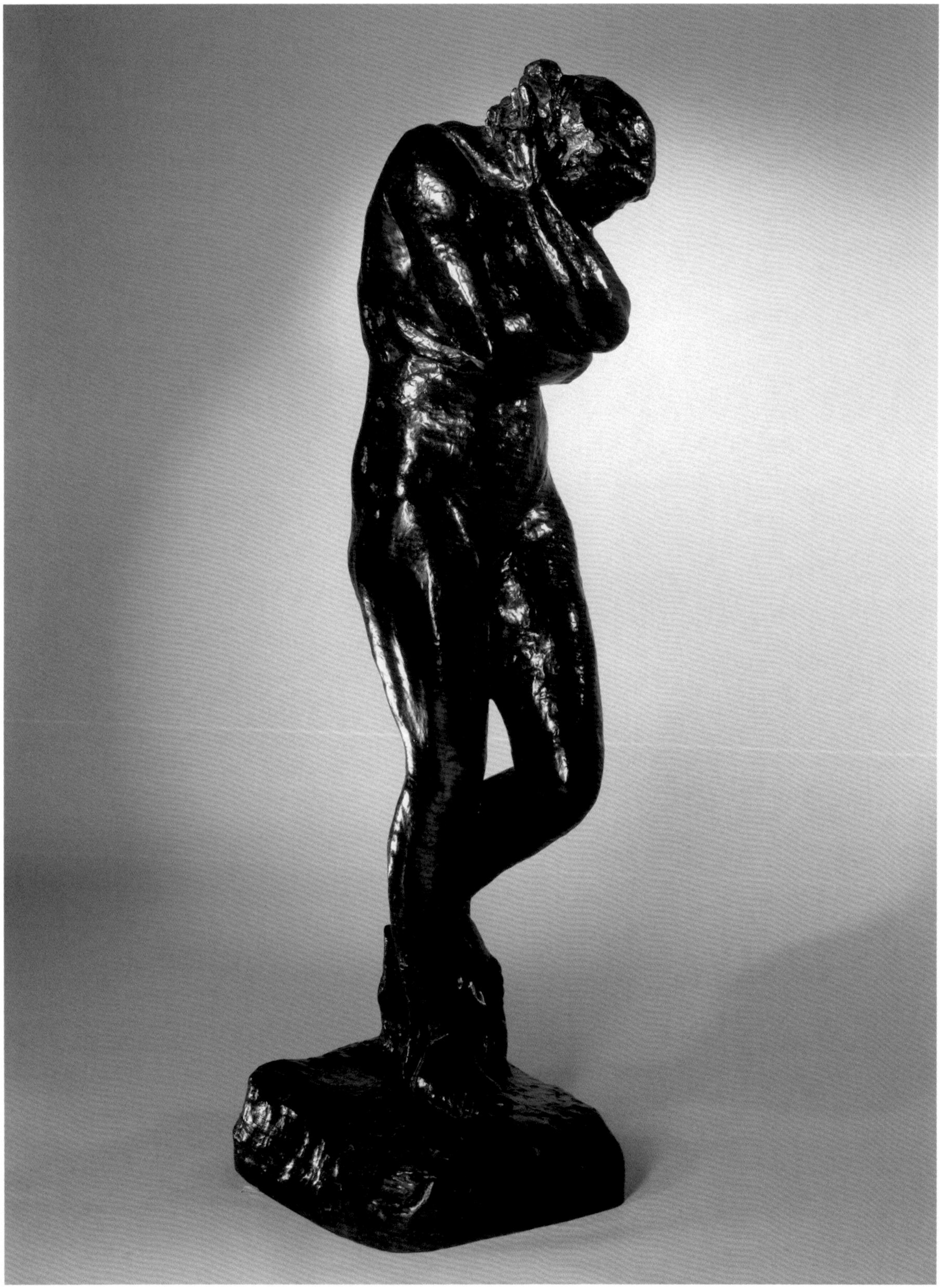

AUGUSTE RODIN :: EVE

1881 (model); Frederik Meijer Gardens cast, before 1920
Bronze, h. 68½ inches (174 cm)
Gift of the Meijer Foundation, 2000.11

TOGETHER WITH Michelangelo and Bernini, Auguste Rodin is among the best known sculptors in the history of art. He was born in 1840 to a working-class family in Paris. During his childhood, he showed an interest in and talent for drawing; at the age of thirteen, he entered the Petite École—the French art academy for the decorative arts. The young Rodin showed great promise, winning first and second prizes for sculpture in 1857, but he failed to gain admission to the École des Beaux Arts, the renowned fine arts institution. Over the course of the next two decades, he was forced to make his living as a craftsman in ornamental sculpture and as a professional assistant to highly regarded masters of the age like Albert-Ernest Carrier-Belleuse. Simultaneously, Rodin worked on his own sculpture in private. In 1875, he made his first trip to Italy. There he encountered the work of Michelangelo, which was to have a profound impact on his entire career.

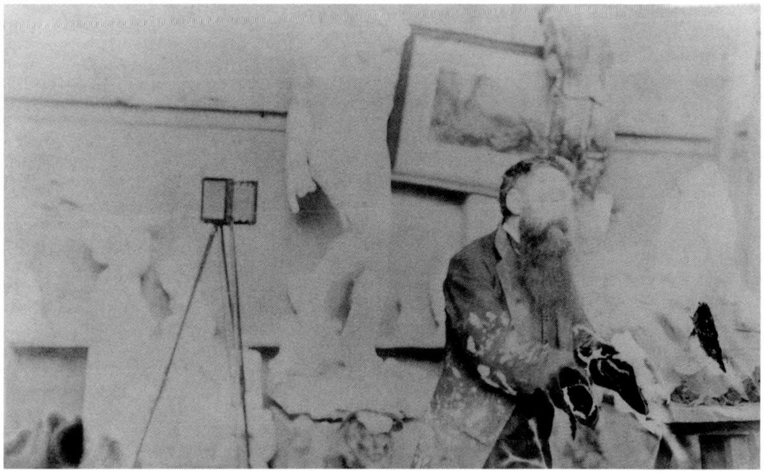

Auguste Rodin in his studio, ca. 1887

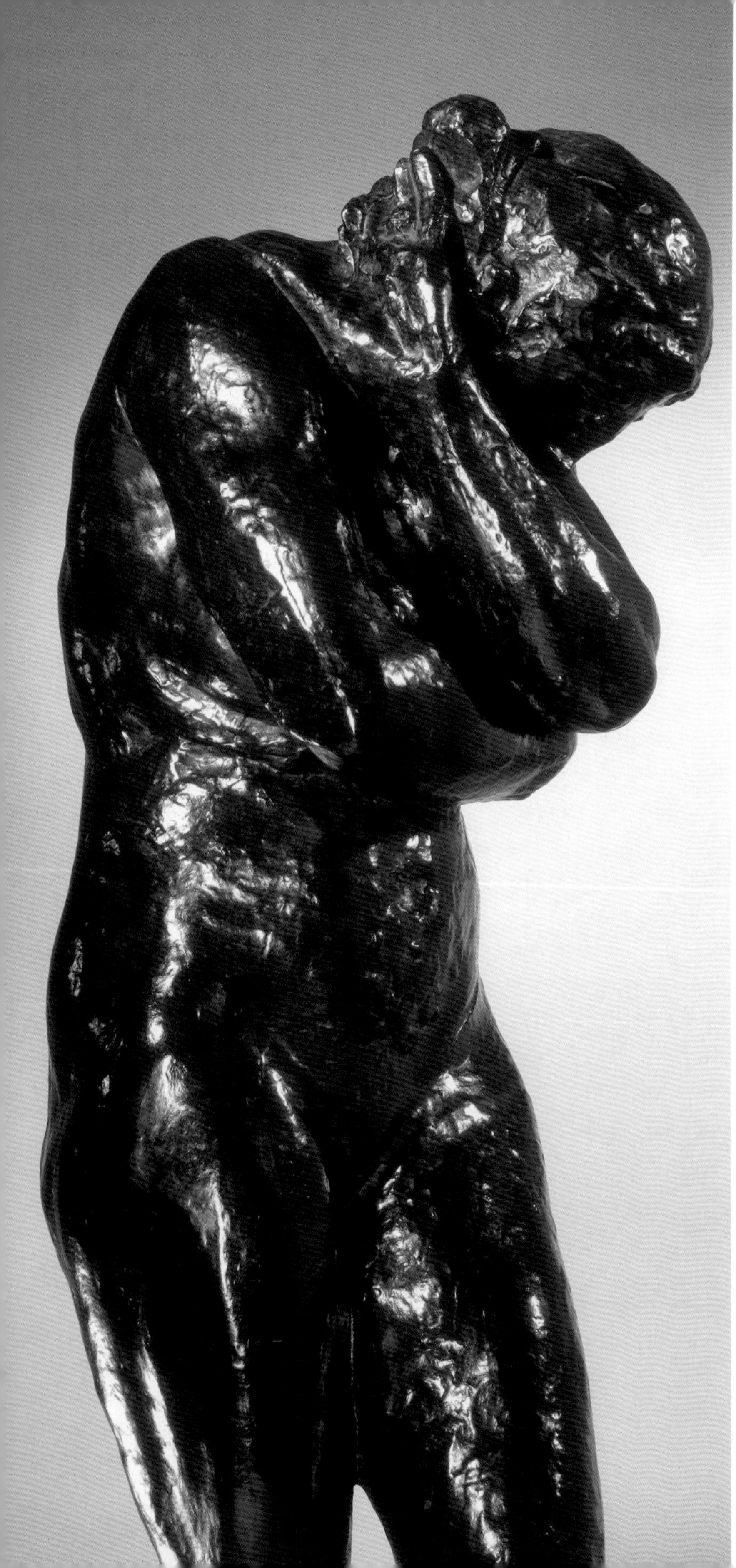

Recognition came to the sculptor in 1877, when he exhibited his first major work, traditionally known as *The Age of Bronze,* causing a critical uproar. The work was attacked on the grounds that the lifelike figure of an athletic male striding forward—radically different from the idealized conventions of the time—must have resulted from body casts, and consequently that the form was not freely modeled. The controversy continued until 1880, when, with the assistance of fellow artists and a few government allies, the work was declared entirely original and a cast was acquired by the state. It was also in 1880, with his reputation established, that Rodin received an important commission for a set of monumental bronze doors intended for a new museum of decorative arts in Paris. The doors, whose content was drawn loosely from literary sources such as Dante's *Inferno,* eventually became known as *The Gates of Hell.* Although the museum was never built, the sculptor's eighteen-foot scale model for the doors became a critical resource for a variety of subjects that would eventually be realized as independent works, most notably *The Thinker, The Three Shades, The Kiss, Adam,* and the Frederik Meijer Gardens' sculpture, *Eve.*

Adam and *Eve* were produced as life-size models in 1880 and 1881, respectively. These Old Testament figures were initially conceived as free-standing works to flank the doors of *The Gates of Hell.* This tragic couple from Judeo-Christian tradition was seen in association with their fall from grace and their expulsion from paradise, and they would have served as a poignant introduction to the scenes of anxiety, anguish, and mortality described in the relief imagery of the *Gates.* It is known that Rodin's model for *Eve* was an Italian woman who also posed for several later projects. The sculptor greatly admired her statuesque and muscular form. Furthermore, as with many of his models, Rodin appreciated her ability to hold an unorthodox or non-academic pose through which he could manifest dramatic narrative and emotional power. Thus, in the *Eve,* the weight of the figure is borne by the right leg, while the left leg is lifted in an awkward manner. The pose rejects the refined, tranquil proportions of the classical contrapposto, or weight-shift position, prevalent in Western art since antiquity, to achieve a highly emotional bearing in the figure. The head is bent down and the upper back is hunched, while the arms are raised in a protective manner that suggests fear, shame, or despair. In the cowering, inward turn of the body, the figure seems confined within her own physical and psychological space.

The surfaces of the sculpture, especially in the area of the face, are rough. Such uneven texture would become an important hallmark for much of Rodin's work. This characteristic of the master's aesthetic may have resulted, in part, from his admiration for Michelangelo's unfinished sculptures. (Another tradition claims that the model became pregnant, found the studio too cold, and failed to appear frequently enough for the master to finish the work.) Along with his use of exaggerated or simplified anatomical forms, Rodin's rough and seemingly unfinished modeling serves to increase the expressive potential of his figures.

Eve was first exhibited in 1889. Both marble and bronze commissions resulted from the original model. Casts were made at both full and half scale. The Frederik Meijer Gardens' cast is a full-scale version and was made before 1920, when it was known to be in a private collection in Paris. It remained with the family by descent until it was acquired for the Gardens' permanent collection in 2000. The *Eve* is an important example by the father of modern sculpture. Rodin's influence on the development of modern art is incalculable. He set sculpture free from the confines of traditional classical form, which in the hands of late-nineteenth-century artists had become stagnant, and once again—like Michelangelo and Bernini before him—made sculpture a vehicle for intense personal expression.

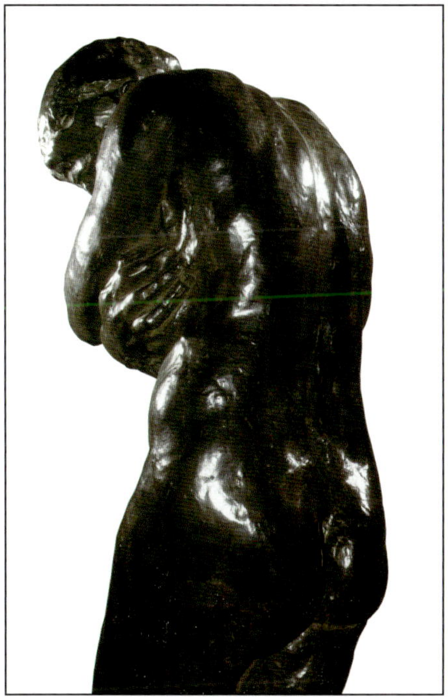

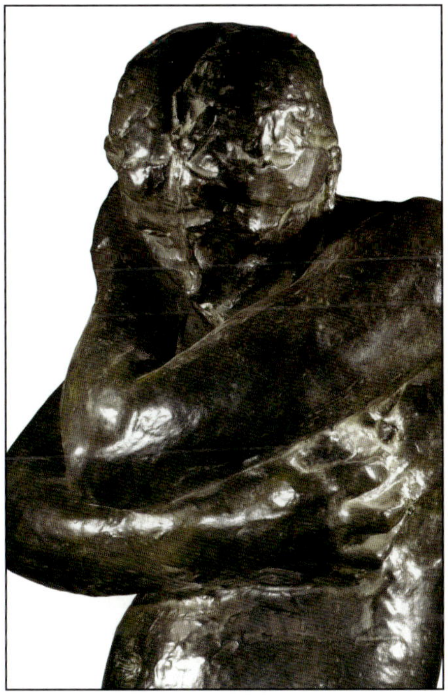

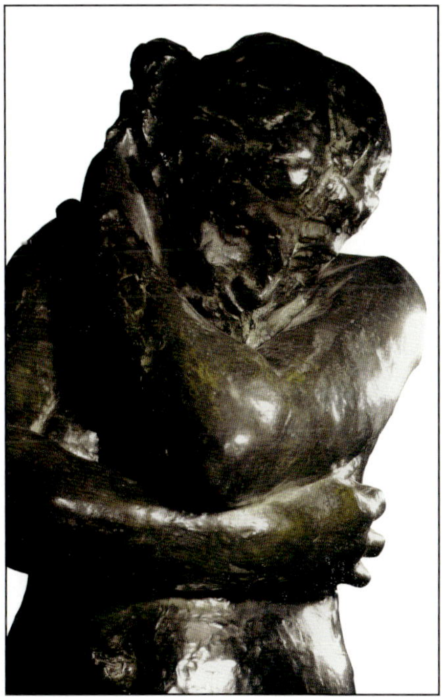

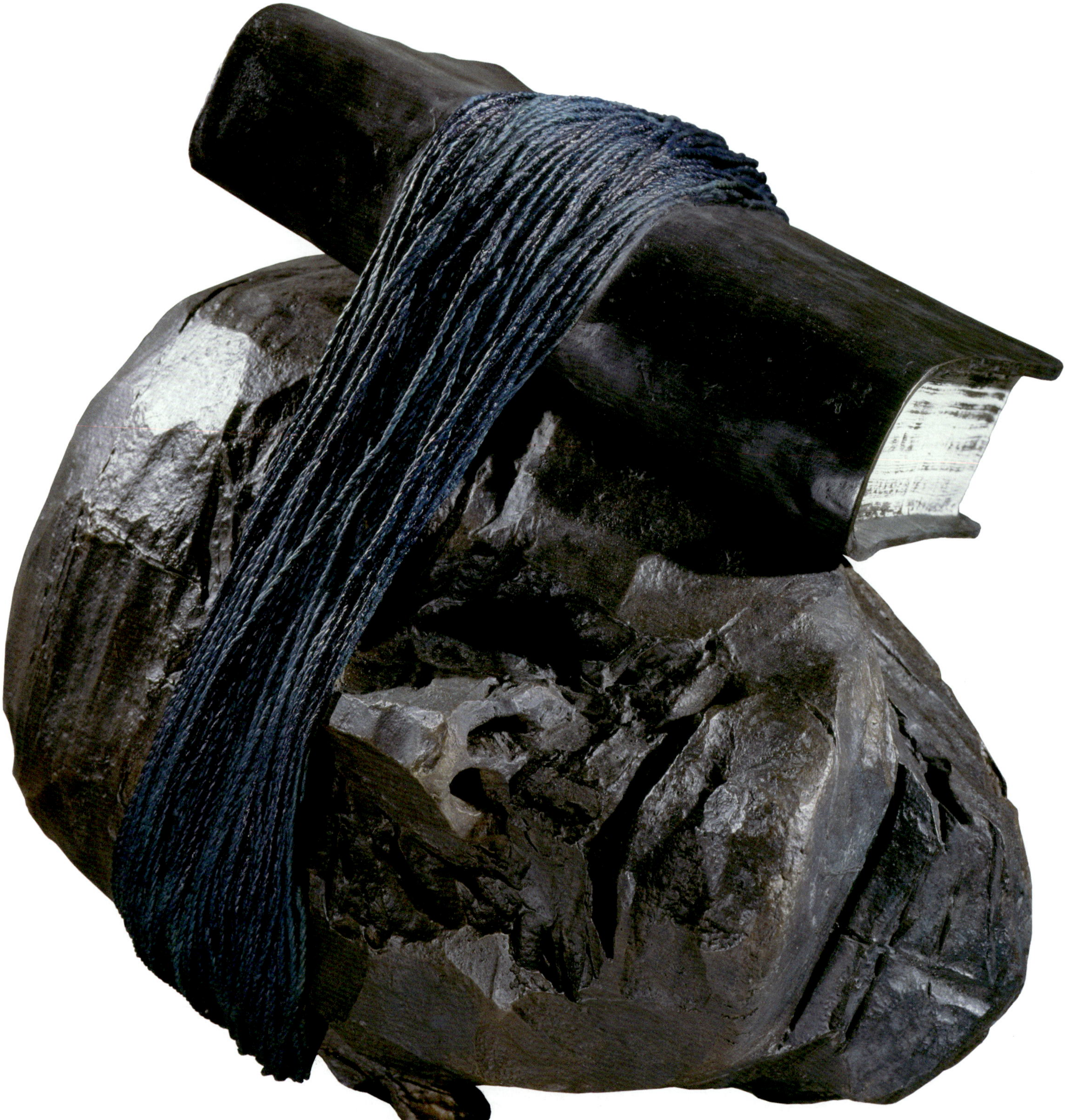

British, born 1948

BILL WOODROW :: LISTENING TO HISTORY

1995; Frederik Meijer Gardens cast, 2001
Bronze, A/P (artist's proof for an edition of three), h. 29½ inches (74.9 cm)
Gift of the Meijer Foundation, 2001.09

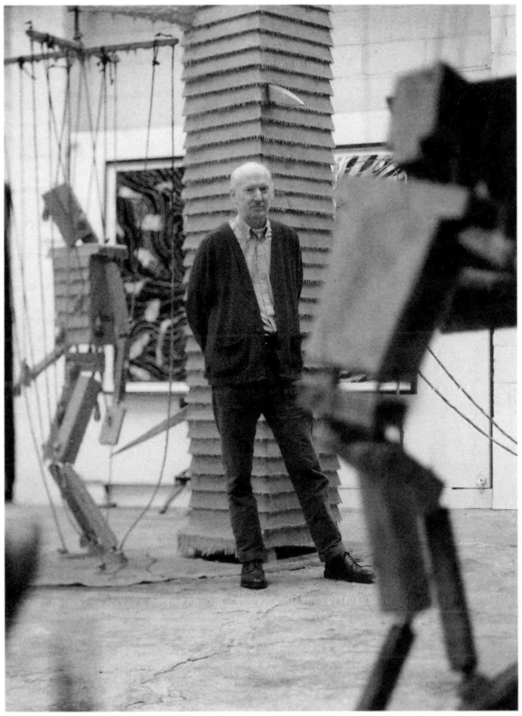

Bill Woodrow in his London studio, March 2001

IN CONTEMPORARY European art, Bill Woodrow is a leading figure of the British school of sculptors who, with Antony Gormley and Anish Kapoor, came of age in the 1970s. Woodrow was born in Oxfordshire, England, and educated in Winchester and London. He attended St. Martin's School of Art and the Chelsea School of Art, earning a diploma from the latter in 1972. Following his first one-person exhibition in 1971, at London's celebrated Whitechapel Art Gallery, and his first international exhibition in 1979, Woodrow exhibited widely in Europe. His sculpture first appeared in the United States in 1985. Three years later, he was given a solo exhibition at the Seattle Art Museum and received the prestigious Anne Gerber Award. Undoubtedly, two of the artist's most important exhibitions have been at the São Paulo Bienal in 1991 and at the Tate Gallery in London in 1996. Woodrow's work has been enthusiastically collected by major public institutions in both Europe and the United States.

Woodrow has become increasingly well known for his bronze sculpture, but the materials of his early work were quite different. Discarded items collected from scrap yards, refuse sites, and dumps were frequently used. Metal panels were cut out of large abandoned appliances such as refrigerators, washing machines, and automobiles. These were reconfigured with other forms to create new objects that were unrelated to their former context. The original object remained identifiable, however.

Audiences soon came to realize the importance of narrative and the role of irony that these recycled familiar forms elicited. Critics championed Woodrow's powerful transformation of mundane castaways from contemporary culture. Even when the artist began his transition away from the use of found objects in the 1980s, the eclectic nature of his earlier imagery and his concern for keen narrative remained.

Listening to History, from 1995, portrays a monumental human head with a large book bound to its left ear. The book presses the right side of the head toward the earth, and indeed this bronze sculpture is intended to be displayed at ground level. The work's powerful intrigue comes, in part, from the viewer's standpoint above it—the seeming weight of the book is intensified and the layer upon layer of intricately described cording cannot be ignored. The head is based on an existing stylized portrait of the artist; the book, with its well-worn cover, and the cording recall Woodrow's early interest in everyday objects. *Listening to History* is one of a series of related works in which a head or a book have been employed. Perhaps the best known of these is the colossal *Regardless of History,* from 1999, created for display in London's Trafalgar Square. The objects used in these sculptures are poignant symbols, and the intended metaphorical narratives vary as the combination of objects changes.

An interpretation of *Listening to History* is intentionally broad. The head may refer to an individual or symbolize a civilization at large, while the book is a recognizable icon for knowledge in numerous cultures. The cording connects the two forms, but it also serves as a blindfold. As a result, traditional notions of acquiring knowledge through reading have, ironically, been prohibited. The book and the head, with one ear to the ground, not only call into question the transmission of information, but raise issues of comprehension and discernment as well. Although the sculpture's intended meaning is far from direct, an appreciation of its physical qualities is immediate. Head, book, and cording are combined in a compact, monumental form. Three distinct textures—the roughly described visage, the smooth planes of the book's cover, and the highly detailed cording—are further distinguished by their respective patinas. The viewer, drawn to these tangible effects, is equally absorbed in contemplating the sculpture's meaning. The book is closed and the eyes cannot see, but the whole is fully open to interpretation.

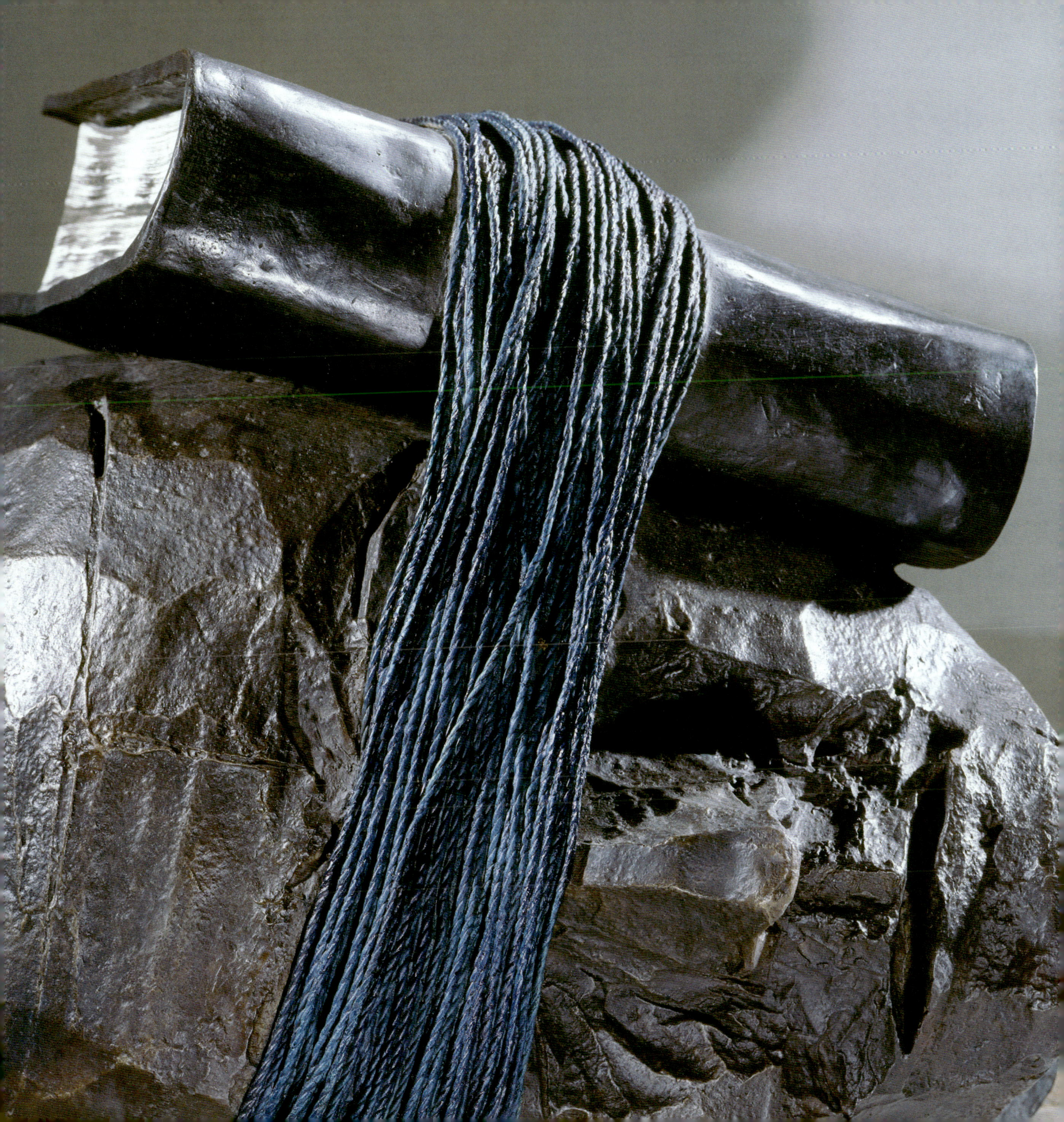

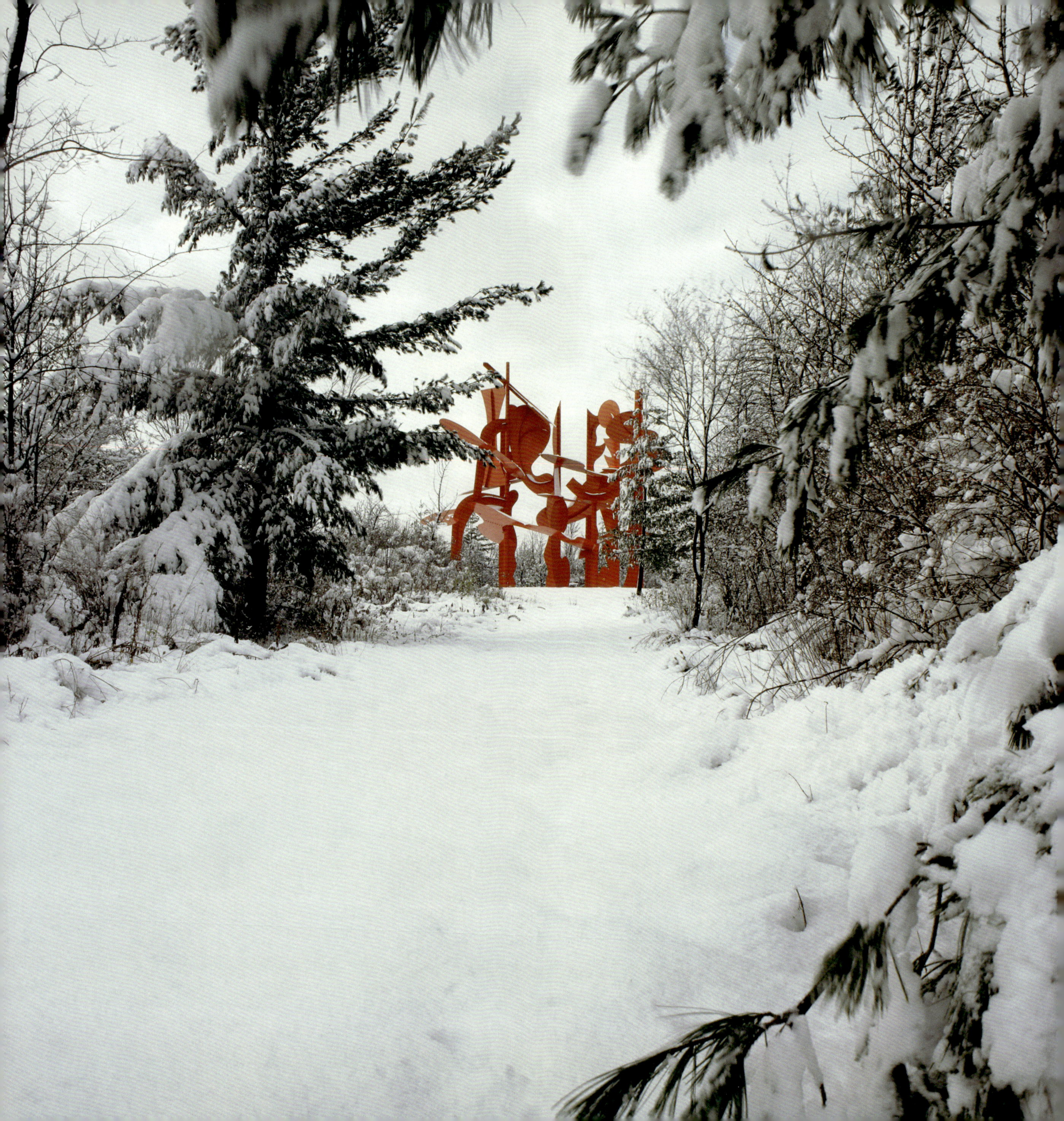

Photography Credits

The publishers have made every effort to trace all the relevant copyright holders and apologize for any omissions that may have been made.

Principal photography by Chuck Heiney Photography, except as indicated in the following additional credits.

© Magdalena Abakanowicz, courtesy Marlborough Gallery, New York; photo: Jan Kosmowski, 20

© Alan Bowness, Barbara Hepworth Estate, 49

Caleb Brennan, 16, 17 (top)

Photography: M. Lee Fatherree, 84, 85, 86, 87

Courtesy Frederik Meijer Gardens, 25

© The Estate of Keith Haring; photo: Jansen, 45

William Hebert, 24

This photograph has been reproduced by permission of the Henry Moore Foundation; photography: Bo Boustedt, 81

This photograph has been reproduced by permission of the Henry Moore Foundation; photography: Errol Jackson, 76

© 2000 Indianapolis Museum of Art; photography by Holliday T. Day, 104

Gerd Kittel, frontispiece, 94

© Anne Leigniel, 37

© Jacques Lipchitz, courtesy Marlborough Gallery, New York, 65

Sally Littlefair, 7

Photo by Robert Mapplethorpe, 92

Attilio Maranzano, 93, 95

Meijer, Inc., 12

Edward Mindock, 96

Courtesy Musée Rodin; photo: William Elbourne, 109

Rob Outlaw, 29

The Pace Gallery; photograph by Nancy Dine, 33

Photograph courtesy PaceWildenstein, 89

Photographique Ostier, 69

Photo: Jacek Poremba, 73

Christina Roederer, 57

© Mario Ruiz, 60

TGL, Williamstown, Masssachusetts, 105

Courtesy Yorkshire Sculpture Park, 72, 75

Copyright Credits